THE ELIMINATION OF
CORRUPT PRACTICES IN
BRITISH ELECTIONS
1868–1911

Oxford University Press, Amen House, London E.C.4

GLASGOW NEW YORK TORONTO MELBOURNE WELLINGTON
BOMBAY CALCUTTA MADRAS KARACHI LAHORE DACCA
CAPE TOWN SALISBURY NAIROBI IBADAN ACCRA
KUALA LUMPUR HONG KONG

THE ELIMINATION OF CORRUPT PRACTICES IN BRITISH ELECTIONS

1868–1911

BY

CORNELIUS O'LEARY

LECTURER IN POLITICAL SCIENCE
THE QUEEN'S UNIVERSITY, BELFAST

OXFORD
AT THE CLARENDON PRESS
1962

© *Oxford University Press 1962*

PRINTED IN GREAT BRITAIN

IN MEMORY OF
JOHN HENRY WARDELL
(1878–1957)

CONTENTS

ACKNOWLEDGEMENTS

I MUST express my gratitude to the Warden and Fellows of Nuffield College who enabled me, through a Nuffield studentship, to made this study.

Among all those who helped in the preparation of the book I must record a special debt to Mr. David Butler for constant guidance and criticism during the entire period of research. It is literally true to say that the book would never have appeared without his help. I am grateful to the Gladstone Library at the National Liberal Club, the National Trust, the National Union of Conservative and Unionist Associations, and the Record Office at the House of Lords for permission to use manuscript material, and to all the other libraries and record offices that have assisted me. For reading the book in typescript or proof and for much valuable advice and criticism I am indebted to Mr. R. B. McCallum, Master of Pembroke College, Oxford, Mr. M. G. Brock, of Corpus Christi College, Oxford, and to my colleagues at Queen's University, Professor Howard Warrender, Professor J. C. Beckett, Mr. A. S. Skinner, and my old friend Dr. K. H. Connell.

For any errors of fact or judgement I alone am responsible.

C. O'L.

The Queen's University, Belfast
October 1961

INTRODUCTION

AT the beginning of the nineteenth century the British House of Commons was the preserve of the aristocracy and landed gentry. Those who were entitled to elect members to Parliament were but a small fraction of the total adult male population, although they comprised a rough cross-section of the occupations and classes in the country. Through long custom unchecked by any attempt to rationalize the electoral system the voters were scattered haphazardly throughout the kingdom; they were a rarity in the growing industrial towns while very numerous in the ancient decaying boroughs of the south of England. The oft-vaunted freedom of the electorate—an essential principle of the Constitution—was in practice inhibited by three major influences: the political ignorance and indifference of the vast majority of those living in a stratified society where only the upper classes could legislate and rule; the traditional right of certain members of these classes—the great landowners in the counties and the patrons in most boroughs—to dictate the elector's choice;[1] and the traditional relationship between member and constituents based on the theory that since the vote was a marketable commodity the member must look after his supporters. From the point of view of the electorate as a whole the privilege of the franchise was conceived in terms of personal advantage in the narrowest sense.

One hundred years later, however, the electoral system in Britain was but one step removed from universal suffrage. The composition of the House of Commons was slowly coming to resemble the pattern of the electorate. The voters had developed an interest in politics and both the control of votes by 'influence' and their disposal for a consideration had become an ugly memory. As Trollope had predicted, the popular constitution had obtained true sovereignty, and the characteristic purity of British elections was held up as a model for other countries.

Democratic theory played only a marginal part in this great change. The efficient cause is rather to be found in the closely

---

[1] These points are elaborated in Chap. I.

linked chain of statutes passed between 1832 and 1895. The
whole taken together might in retrospect be conceived of as a
grand democratic design, but only in the last stages was the
final result apparent to the politicians who were bringing it
about.

These statutes fall under two headings—those dealing with
the structure of the electoral system and those dealing with its
operation. Up to now the former have had the lion's share of
publicity and scholarly attention. The genesis and development
of the movement for broadening the franchise have been carefully charted and studied, but the transformation of the electoral geography of the United Kingdom by successive Reform
Acts has been surprisingly neglected. So too has the special
subject of this study—the elimination of corrupt electoral
practices.

The student of electoral morality in nineteenth-century
Britain finds himself more or less in virgin country. Only one
large-scale study exists, and that appeared nearly fifty years ago
—*Electoral Reform in England and Wales* (1912) by Professor (later
President) Charles Seymour of Yale. Seymour's work covered
all aspects of the reform movement—franchise extension, electoral geography, and electoral morality, but his treatment, while
very accurate and painstaking, sacrificed depth, colour, and in
places lucidity. Professor Norman Gash's *Politics in the Age of
Peel* is extremely useful for the 1830's and 1840's and Mr. H. J.
Hanham has a very interesting chapter on electoral corruption in his *Elections and Party Management*. Apart from these
there are only technical manuals on election law.

The history of the elimination of corrupt practices is essentially the story of the interrelation of three factors—the standards
laid down by Parliament for the conduct of elections, the
machinery set up to inquire into that conduct, and the response
of the electorate to both.

Corrupt practices at elections long preceded the statutes that
designated them corrupt. Bribery, the most serious, was also the
oldest and always ranked as an offence at common law. It was
first employed, not to get into Parliament but to keep out of it.
When, however, seats in the Commons became attractive, as
they did in the sixteenth century, it was inevitable that the
small electorates would come to realize their bargaining power.

INTRODUCTION 3

Between the end of the seventeenth century, when the first
statute was passed against bribery, and the passing of the first
Reform Act in 1832 a number of efforts were made by the House
of Commons to check the ever-growing trend, but these never
went very far. The penalties imposed by the laws were far too
strict to be regularly enforced and the machinery for enforcing
them was more cumbersome than efficient.

Undue influence has much the same history as bribery.
Violence or physical intimidation at elections, although common law offences, tended to be accepted as part of the normal
behaviour of a rude and inhumane age. There was never any
clear distinction between the 'legitimate' influence of landlord
and factory-owner over tenant and employee and the 'undue'
influence of a manipulator of electoral power over the un-
tutored minds of the 'free and independent'. So too, indeed,
was the distinction between the 'consideration for the borough'
and the open bribe.

The works of Seymour and Gash have shown that there was
no continuous improvement in electoral morality after 1832.
On the contrary, bribery and treating[1] were never more prevalent than in the decades immediately after the passing of the
Great Reform Act. The first real attempt to cope with them was
made in 1854, when an Act was passed which provided for the
first time a working definition of the three chief corrupt practices, practicable penalties for venal candidates and voters, and
additional machinery to deal with controverted elections.

Fourteen years later, however, there had been little improvement. The new inquisitorial machinery (the Royal Commissions)[2] brought to light many electioneering scandals that would
otherwise have remained hidden, but the penalties imposed
were not an effective deterrent. The two great political parties
were already assuming their characteristic form, and through
their rivalry more seats were being contested and more money
spent on elections. Possibly the greatest weakness of the election
law was the absence of any limit to election expenses. Provided
that he did not do it so openly as to risk a petition, there was

[1] Treating, the third main corrupt practice, grew out of the social fabric of the
eighteenth and nineteenth centuries. It was never a common law offence. See
Chap. I.
[2] These were set up in 1852 (15 & 16 Vict., c. 57).

every inducement to a candidate to open his purse. The persistence of open voting gave plenty of scope for new and subtle forms of undue influence and intimidation. Lastly, the Commons' privilege of jurisdiction over controverted elections—which they had held for some two and a half centuries—was productive of much expense, inefficiency, and partisanship.

Up to 1868, with the exception mentioned above, no serious attempt had been made to eradicate corrupt practices. Within fifty years, however, the situation had so changed that the fourth great measure for extending the franchise could pass through both Houses without a voice being raised about electoral corruption.

This work covers the period between the Parliamentary Elections Act of 1868, which took authority over contested elections from the House of Commons and gave it back to the judges of the High Court, and the Representation of the People Act of 1918, which virtually established universal adult suffrage. Developments before 1868 are briefly sketched in Chapter I. Our purpose is to find the answers to two questions:

1. What caused the change in the attitude of Parliament to these practices?
2. How did the politicians manage to get their reformed ideas across to the public?

Even within these limits the scope of the work is such as to preclude a uniform treatment in depth. The absence of general works on the electoral system—and especially of detailed studies of the general elections—has necessitated a broad survey of ten out of the eleven general elections in the period; the pivotal election of 1880 is given more elaborate treatment. The legislative side of the subject has been thoroughly covered, but at the level of the constituencies it is well to remember that it is impossible in a work of this kind to make good the lack of a general electoral history and *a fortiori* of those monographs on individual constituencies without which generalizations must be tentative. Nineteenth-century Britain as a whole stands in need of a Namier; its boroughs and counties require an Albery.[1]

That the constituencies figuring in these pages are mainly corrupt constituencies is determined by the nature of the subject and its limitations. This is essentially an essay in political pathology.

[1] See below, p. 56.

CHAPTER I

Before 1868

I

THE British code of electoral morality is almost as old as Parliament itself. From the earliest centuries statutes were passed governing electoral procedure and prescribing qualifications for members and voters, implying that the setting of these standards was the business of Parliament. The Acts requiring residence for burgesses, regulating wage-rates for knights and burgesses, and commanding that elections be carried out with due publicity and freedom were the first beginnings of the process that led eventually to resumed payment of members and the Corrupt and Illegal Practices Acts.

The earliest examples of electoral bribery were of a negative type—agreements between burgesses and their constituents to serve for less than the statutory rate of wages,[1] or to accept less than their statutory travelling expense allowance.[2] The fourteenth- and fifteenth-century cases of members staying the minimal time with the King in Parliament and stealing away before the end of the session could happen only in an age when both electors and members regarded their functions as an irksome duty rather than a privilege.

Gradually, as the two Houses developed their distinctive character, seats in the Lower House came to be valued by the merchants, lawyers, and country squires—to whom the restrictive laws of the fifteenth century[3] had virtually confined Parliamentary representation. The number of counties and the character of their electorate remained more or less fixed, but

---

[1] Two shillings a day for burgesses and 4s. for knights of the shire. Cf. *History of Parliament, 1439–1509* (London, 1938), p. lxxxviii.

[2] See E. Porritt, *The Unreformed House of Commons* (Cambridge, 1903), i. 155–7, for a number of examples of negative bribery in the fifteenth century.

[3] The Forty-shilling Freeholder Act of 1429 (8 Hen. VI) being the best-known example.

royal prerogative increased the number of boroughs. Their electorates were almost as diverse in the sixteenth century as in the early nineteenth, and were already tending to become smaller, and thus more manageable.[1]

The conditions were soon present for the effective exercise of positive bribery, treating, and intimidation or undue influence —the three great impediments to electoral freedom. In the reign of Elizabeth I great noblemen (such as the Earl of Essex) could dictate their choice to the small corporations. This dealing in what was euphemistically called 'parliamentary interest' soon extended to monetary interest. In the same reign occurred the first authenticated case of positive electoral bribery, that of Thomas Long, who having been returned for the borough of Westbury and 'being found to be a very simple man and not fit to serve in that place',[2] was asked how he had come to be elected and immediately admitted before the House that he had bribed the Mayor and another corporator with £4. The House ordered the corporation of Westbury to repay Long and fined them £20 'for their scandalous attempt'.

Long in his simplicity had bribed openly, but borough members in the reign of James I, and to a greater extent in the succeeding reign, bribed under the guise of contributions to municipal debts or undertakings, insignia for the town, or gifts to the poor.[3] By now even the borough officials were accepting bribes: the practice of paying wages to burgesses had in most cases lapsed by the end of the sixteenth century.

Bribery was from the beginning the characteristic vice of borough elections. Treating, intimidation, and undue influence arose in the counties, where the electorates were much larger. The preamble to the Forty-shilling Freeholder Act and the Huntingdon petition of 1450[4] (the first example of a contro-

---

[1] Even in the fifteenth century patronage existed in the boroughs. Bishops and nobles could determine the return in several ways—by ordering the tenants or appointing the borough officials or finding amenable sheriffs. Cf. *History of Parliament, 1439–1509*, p. cxvi.

[2] The Commons summoned the Mayor and the other corporators to appear before them, but the *Parliamentary History* notes that nothing further was heard of the matter. Cf. *Parliamentary History*, i. 765–6.

[3] Porritt, *The Unreformed House of Commons*, i. 157–9. Porritt does not mention the Long episode.

[4] Cf. *History of Parliament, 1439–1509*, pp. ci–civ. One of the grounds for this petition was that the sheriff refused a poll of the freeholders. The right of a

verted election) both refer to the 'tumults' that occurred at
county elections; and the earliest reference to treating is found
in 1467. These grew out of the increasing publicity given to
elections: the more subtle forms of landlord influence over
tenants are less well-documented but they too grew out of the
current social conditions.

Fraudulent returns by sheriffs were also among the earliest
corrupt practices mentioned in statutes. The Act of 1429 imposed a fine of £100 and one year's imprisonment on any
sheriff[1] found guilty of electoral misconduct and an Act of 1445
allowed suits against sheriffs. As actions against the sheriffs in
the Common Law courts were slow and uncertain, the tech-
nique of an election petition was resorted to as early as 1450.
Petitions were dealt with by the Chancery, which issued the
writs and had arrogated to itself the right to amend the returns.
Yet all these penalties and procedures did not prevent sheriffs
from altering the returns and devising various expedients to get
favoured candidates elected—and their own fines paid too. To
cope with the deficiency in the Act of 1445 (which allowed suits
against the sheriff but not against anyone else) Elizabeth I's
Attorney-General found it convenient to have election petitions tried by the Star Chamber where there could be an unlimited number of defendants and penalties could be imposed
at discretion.[2]

Hitherto the House of Commons had not concerned itself
with the administration of the electoral law or the settling of
disputed elections.[3] In Elizabeth's reign, however, a precedent
was set, 'which, though not sustained in later Elizabethan
Parliaments, ultimately filched from the Crown power essential
to the evolution of parliamentary government'.[4] This precedent

candidate to demand a poll was not finally established until the early seventeenth
century. See below, p. 8.

[1] The role of the sheriff in elections during the fourteenth, fifteenth, and sixteenth centuries cannot be overstressed. One of the earliest statutes forbade sheriffs
to return themselves as members, and the complicated indenture system as well as
the Acts cited below seem to have been intended as checks on the sheriff rather than
the electors (*History of Parliament*, p. civ). The sheriff was the returning officer in
both counties and boroughs until the fifteenth century.

[2] One sheriff who altered a return was fined £200 by the Star Chamber and
imprisoned. Cf. Neale, *The Elizabethan House of Commons*, pp. 255–9.

[3] The case of Thomas Long seems to have been quite exceptional and (unlike the
Norfolk case) was not appealed to as a precedent for over a century.

[4] J. E. Neale, *Elizabeth I and Her Parliaments, 1584–1601* (London, 1957), p. 186.

arose out of an election petition from Norfolk which the House
of Commons, despite a message from the Queen, heard independently of the Chancery judges.[1]

The Parliament of 1604 went a stage further by overruling
the Chancery judges' decision in a disputed return and by
remaining firm (in spite of the protests of the King that the
judges had the right to decide) in their contention that they
alone were the proper judges of their own returns.[2] The King
eventually gave way and from that time until 1770 petitions
were decided by a vote of the whole House of Commons—
sometimes after a preliminary investigation by a Committee of
Privileges.[3]

In 1625 the House decided that sheriffs were bound to grant
a poll if demanded.[4]

Throughout the seventeenth century money bribes and treating increased with competition for seats. There were also
occasional instances of rioting and intimidation. However, no
attempt to remedy these practices was made by Parliament
until 1696.

The aim of the Act of 1696 was to counter not only treating
but all kinds of 'excessive and exorbitant Expences' and by it
any candidate offering 'Money, Meat, Drink, Entertainment
or Provision', or any promise of the same would be disqualified.

The preamble to the Act said that it was intended that all
elections 'may be hereafter freely and indifferently made without Charge or Expence'.[5] Its lack of success may be indicated by

Cf. by the same author, 'Three Elizabethan Elections', *English Historical Review*,
xlvi (Apr. 1931), 209–38.

[1] For the details see Neale, *Elizabeth I and Her Parliaments*, pp. 184–7.

[2] The House ordered one Goodwin (although an outlaw) to take his seat as
member for Buckinghamshire. Cf. G. Davies, *The Early Stuarts, 1603–1660* (Oxford,
1937), pp. 3–5.

[3] Cf. *Journals of the House of Commons* (1623), i. 729.

[4] Ibid. (1625), i. 801. A manual called *The Office of a Sheriff* published in 1682
said that the contemporary mode of election was 'by voices or holding up of
hands, or by any other like way whereby it may be discovered who hath the
greater number'. Cf. Porritt, *The Unreformed House of Commons*, i. 185. The
sheriff would first take the 'view', and decide who had the greater support. A
poll would be demanded if a candidate believed that some of those present were
not entitled to vote. The 1625 case cited above was a late example of a sheriff
refusing a poll. When taking the poll became obligatory, and, still more, when
sheriffs were forced to employ poll clerks (by the Act of 1696) the power of the
sheriff to influence the return was dealt a death-blow.

[5] 7 & 8 Will. III, c. 4.

the facts that while Pepys paid £8 to the thirty-two electors of Harwich in 1689, Lord Egmont spent £1,000 on the same number of voters in 1727, and one candidate who contested Weobley in 1690 and 1717 spent in the latter year over ten times the amount spent in the former.[1]

Borough corporations were by now openly selling the seats[2] to wealthy candidates and charging fees for admission to the freedom where that was a condition of membership.

All the practices mentioned above were becoming diversified: candidates were expected to support local industries, build roads and bridges, provide a water supply, and generally to 'do something for the Corporation'. At the county contests (which were rare) the freeholders would be lavishly entertained as a compensation for their journey to the county capital where, as a matter of course, they would vote for the candidate sponsored by their landlord. Other factors, tending to drive all but the very wealthy out of borough electioneering, were the Act of 1710[3] setting up a property qualification, although it was often ignored, and the growing custom of returning officers charging sometimes exorbitant fees for erecting the hustings and paying poll clerks. Three other statutes made the position of the borough patrons more secure—the Act of 1705 compelling the re-election of office holders, the Septennial Act of 1716, and the Last Determinations Act of 1729, which gave the force of law to the most recent judgement of the House on the borough franchises.[4] These were inextricably confused with the issue of disputed elections which were generally, if not always, regarded not as judicial questions to be settled impartially, but as partisan struggles. A disputed election could have grave political repercussions as, for example, in 1742 when Walpole, defeated by one

---

[1] J. H. Plumb, *Sir Robert Walpole, the Making of a Statesman* (London, 1956), pp. 59–60.

[2] The first recorded purchase of a seat was in 1698 by the Marquis of Wharton 'the patriarch of the art of electioneering' who managed to control from twenty to thirty seats—at a cost of £80,000. Cf. Porritt, *The Unreformed House of Commons*, i. 354. By 1714 the purchase of seats was notorious. But until the end of the eighteenth century the transactions were generally between candidates and electorates (mainly small), not candidates and patrons.

[3] Ibid. 166–9, 181, 356.

[4] Many petitions heard by the Commons concerned not the behaviour of the candidates so much as the right of certain classes to the vote. Hence the 'last determinations', which meant that the decision on one petition might not prejudice a later one.

vote on the issue of the Chippenham petition, felt compelled to resign.

The growing cost of elections, resulting from the competition to get seats in the House of Commons, caused votes to be regarded as marketable commodities with a fluctuating, but generally appreciating, value and indirectly contributed to the narrowing of the franchise in most borough constituencies from which petitions were presented. It also tended to drive out of the Commons the small country squires and merchants, replacing them by plutocrats, 'Nabobs', and 'Carribbees', and encouraged place-hunting.[1] When elections were so costly, an alliance with the Government became attractive to many M.P.s, especially when the Government itself entered the market in the reign of George III.

By the middle of the eighteenth century the electoral system both in theory and practice had assumed the forms that it was to maintain until 1832. The boroughs had been fixed in number in the reign of Charles II and it was now unlikely that their electoral structure would be altered. Freemen, burgage holders, scot and lot voters, and capital burgesses were scattered through the kingdom in such confusion that even today no two authorities can agree on how the franchises of the 203 English boroughs ought to be classified. Patronage had made such strides that 205 members owed their seats to individuals and 30 to the Government—almost half the English membership.[2] At the same time a mere 44 boroughs (28 per cent. of the total English borough representation) had electorates of more than 500.[3] As the century wore on the boroughs in the south of England declined while the new northern and midland industrial cities, Birmingham, Manchester, Sheffield, and Leeds, were unrepresented. The price of seats was regulated by the demands of the market: a safe seat in 1761 for the lifetime of a Parliament,[4] would cost £2,000; by 1807 the ordinary rate was £5,000—

[1] See Plumb, *Sir Robert Walpole, the Making of a Statesman*, p. 60, for the adverse effect of elections on the fortunes of small county families in the early eighteenth century.

[2] Sir L. Namier, *The Structure of Politics at the Accession of George III* (London, 1957, 2nd ed.), pp. 139–50.

[3] Although the county electorates were larger, Namier calculates (op. cit., p. 73) that probably not more than one in twenty voters were free of the influence of the landed gentry.

[4] Namier, *The Structure of Politics at the Accession of George III*, p. 166.

£6,000. In some boroughs where there was no patron, and the
corporation were not in control, enterprising voters would form
themselves into a committee to bargain collectively with prospective candidates.[1]

The attitude of the politicians generally to the great increase
in bribery and treating in the eighteenth century was not consistent. On the one hand, bribery was an offence at common
law and both the 'Treating Act' of 1696 and the 'Bribery Act'
of 1729[2] passed into law accompanied by stern denunciations of
the scandal of purchasing votes. Both of these statutes came at
times when bribery was extremely prevalent at all levels of the
public service and the House seemed determined to stamp it out.[3]

The penalties in the Act of 1729[4] were severe but were
applied only occasionally. The two members for Petersfield
were fined and imprisoned for bribery in 1774, the same fate
befell the members for Ilchester in 1804, and in 1817 the proprietor of Grampound, Sir Manasseh Lopez, was fined £10,000
and sent to prison for two years.[5] Collective punishments were
occasionally applied. The boroughs of Shoreham (1771), Crick-
lade (1782), Aylesbury (1804), and East Retford (1830) had the
electors of the surrounding hundreds brought in to swamp the
venal elements. The same remedy would have been applied in
the case of Grampound but for its proximity to several other
boroughs. It was therefore disfranchised in 1821 and its two
seats given to Yorkshire.[6]

These measures, however, were merely scratching the surface
of electoral corruption. The reason why the House forbore to
go deeper was that in the late eighteenth and early nineteenth
centuries it was considered perfectly legitimate and honourable
for a member to show 'regard' to his constituents and to be

[1] Porritt, *The Unreformed House of Commons*, i. 356–8.
[2] Seymour's terminology is misleading (cf. *Electoral Reform in England and Wales*,
p. 165). The Act of 1696 covered bribery as well as treating. The Act of 1729 prescribed an oath which any voter at the request of a candidate could be obliged to
take; and imposed a fine of £500 and perpetual exclusion from the franchise on
voters found guilty of bribery.
[3] Cf. *Parliamentary History*, v. 433–5 (1689), 993 (1694–5); viii. 701–2 (1729);
Journals of the House of Commons, xi (1696); xxi (1728–9).
[4] 2 Geo. II, c. 24.
[5] By an Act of 1809 (49 Geo. III, c. 118) a penalty of £1,000 was inflicted on
anyone found guilty of buying or selling seats.
[6] The only example of a change in the state of the English representation between
1678 and 1832. See *Hansard*, N.S. v. 626–33, 854–7.

'indefatigable in serving his friends'.[1] Whether an offer of money
or some other advantage was to be held as corrupt was determined entirely by circumstances. Hence the severe penalties inflicted on a few for offences not materially different from those
to which many members owed their seats.

The one significant reform effected in the late eighteenth
century was in the mode of trying contested elections. In 1770
George Grenville[2] introduced a Bill to take away the determination of contested elections from the Commons as a whole and to
confine it to a committee. In his opening speech Grenville said
that it was well known that many members approached every
controverted election in a partisan spirit. In spite of the opposition of Lord North and his ministers the Bill was passed, and in
1774, after Grenville's death, it was made permanent—again in
spite of the administration.[3]

The contrast between the levels of electoral morality at the
end of the pre-Reform period and the later nineteenth century
was as great as that between the eighteenth-century parliamentary factions and the modern pledge-bound political party.
The purchase of electoral power went on at all levels of the
system: nomination boroughs were purchased outright from the
proprietors, or leased for a period; boroughs with electorates
that could not be controlled were won over by the 'annual dinner
and septennial bribe'[4] (where the quirks of the system allowed
the voters to be poor and ill-educated), or by more discerning
gifts and favours where the wealthy capital burgesses or burgage-
holders had the deciding voice.

In the fifty years preceding the first Reform Act contested
elections, though (except in Middlesex and Yorkshire) rare in
the counties, and almost unknown in the nomination boroughs,
were quite frequent in London and the cities and large towns
which had the franchise. These more than lively contests provided the raw material for Hogarth, Gillray, and other political

---

[1] Namier, *The Structure of Politics at the Accession of George III*, i. 199 (1st ed.).

[2] *Parliamentary History*, xvi (28 Feb.–5 Apr. 1770), 902–26. Grenville proposed
that a hundred M.P.'s names be placed in six urns, from which an official of the
House would draw out twenty-five. The petitioner and respondent might each
strike off six, and the remaining thirteen would try the petition.

[3] During the debates in 1774 one member stoutly contended that treats ought to
be given at elections, and that the Bill would suit the elected not the electors. Ibid.
xvii (25 Feb. 1774), 1072.

[4] Seymour, *Electoral Reform in England and Wales*, p. 166.

cartoonists.[1] They were the only opportunities for the working classes to participate freely in any stage of the electoral process, and their participation was determined by copious treating and bribery—even in the largest electorates. The popular heroes Burdett, Cochrane, and for a time Sheridan were all wealthy men. The Wilkes case and the election of Fox in 1784 did seem to infuse some genuine political interest into the London masses, but for the most part their lack of education and their almost complete divorce from the arts of governing and law-making made them regard the vote simply as a title to so much easy money or free beer.

Pre-reform elections can be summed up in Hogarth's march to Finchley, the procession of the 'Cripples' in Chippinge, or even the ceremonial polling by Mr. Christopher Corporate at Onevote.[2] Ironically enough even the radical candidates, who were most in favour of electoral purity and freedom from influence, found themselves obliged to pay this tribute to Demos.[3]

2

None of the various elements (aristocratic, middle class, or working class) in the movement for parliamentary reform after 1780 attempted to work out a plan to eliminate electoral bribery and treating. They concentrated rather on the extension of the franchise and the abolition of nomination boroughs—the principal means in their view towards purifying the electoral system.[4]

This does not mean that the reformers condoned these practices or considered them ineradicable. In the 1820's several attempts were made to disfranchise corrupt boroughs and transfer their seats to the large unenfranchised cities, yet all but one fell foul of the House of Lords. Nevertheless, the precedent was

[1] Especially the contests at Westminster and Southwark after 1780. J. Grego, *A History of Parliamentary Elections* (London, 1890), pp. 125–55, 257–88, gives an entertaining account of the hazards undergone by candidates seeking to represent 'popular' constituencies.

[2] Cf. Stanley Weyman, *Chippinge*, and Thomas Love Peacock, *Melincourt*.

[3] For example, T. S. Duncombe was forced to bribe to secure election in 1826 for Hertford.

[4] Cf. G. Veitch, *The Genesis of Parliamentary Reform* (London, 1925), and H. W. C. Davis, *The Age of Grey and Peel* (Oxford, 1929), for a study of the various reform movements. The ballot question is considered below, pp. 25 ff.

then established that a constituency with an incorrigibly corrupt electorate could lose the privilege of the franchise.

When the Whigs drew up their Reform Bill in 1830–1 they hoped that one of the consequences of enfranchising the £10 householders, and at the same time abolishing the rotten boroughs and widening the area of the smaller ones, would be to get rid of the old venal electors. At an early stage in the debates Palmerston[1] openly said that by introducing 'a respectable and honest body of voters' it was hoped to remove 'the great expenses attending elections, arising from gross and disgusting bribery'. These ministerial intentions were to some extent frustrated by the clause in the third Bill preserving the freeman franchise,[2] although the other ancient rights were to die with their holders. Other efforts by the Government in the direction of electoral purity were to increase the time allowed for petitioning and to reduce the period of polling to two days.[3]

The most unexpected consequence of the 'not very murderous instrument of 2 Will. IV, § 45'[4] was that most of the features of the unreformed system continued—pocket boroughs, royal influence, and corrupt practices. Professor Gash sums this up well, 'between the vanished Sarums and Gattons, and the new Manchesters and Marylebones, lay a wide and almost untouched field where the eccentricities and contrasts of the old system still found room to flourish'.[5] In the counties the power of the landed gentry was strengthened by the Chandos clause, which had enfranchised the most dependent class of tenants (the £50 tenants-at-will), and by an increase in county representation.[6] The boroughs showed the same diversity as before: there were

---

[1] Palmerston went on: 'The present mode of election was the most offensive and disgusting that could be imagined and any one who had been engaged in a general election . . . would bear him out.' *3 Hans.* ii. (3 Mar. 1831), 1328.

[2] The freemen, the most venal of the 'ancient righters', were generally, though not always, found in the larger boroughs.

[3] By 5 & 6 Will. IV, c. 36 (1835), borough elections were reduced to one day's duration.

[4] N. Gash, *Politics in the Age of Peel*, p. x.

[5] Peacock said the same thing more succinctly in a preface to the 1856 edition of *Melincourt*: 'The boroughs of *Onevote* and *Threevotes* have been extinguished: but there remain boroughs of *Fewvotes*. . . .' Cf. H. G. Nicholas, *To the Hustings: Election Scenes from English Fiction* (London, 1956), p. 1.

[6] Although the English (and Welsh) county electorate had been increased from 247,000 to 345,000 by the Act of 1832 the average number of electors per county constituency was 2,000. In 1761 it was 4,000. See above, p. 10.

small nomination boroughs (like Newark, Calne, or Totnes), there were larger boroughs where 'a liberal scattering of gold', to quote Seymour, would ensure the result, there were still larger boroughs where it would be impossible to bribe or treat more than a fraction of the electorate, but skilful management might capture the floating voters—even in Liverpool, with an electorate of more than 10,000, bribery was extensive after 1832.

Although the £10 qualification had given the vote to most of the middle classes living in boroughs, in some places it enfranchised the working classes as well, and in these boroughs the new electors showed themselves no less susceptible than the old. In the elections immediately after Reform the 'normal' price of votes ranged from £1 to £10 in most boroughs.[1] Indeed, the abolition of many close boroughs gave an impetus to bribery since the new electors had to be won over individually, not by-passed in favour of a patron. Loans, payment of rent, and contracts (especially in the government boroughs) all supplemented the open hand-out.

Treating too increased in the decades after Reform. When the inns and public-houses were the organizing centres for campaigns it was quite natural that the landlords should soak the candidates by giving plenty of free drink and charging it up to them afterwards. Often treating was indistinguishable from the hospitality that electors, especially in the counties, had come to expect as their due, and opposing candidates would agree to share the cost between them. Sometimes an extra inducement would be added, e.g. the 'buttered ale' of Coventry or the 'dinner money' at Newcastle-under-Lyme.

Apart from the cost of winning votes candidates were liable to the increasing 'legal' expenses of the returning officers and the polling clerks and the payment for registration, which is discussed below. In Gash's estimate an expenditure on each side of £2,000 to £5,000 on a borough election 'could not be regarded as abnormal' in the thirties and forties.[2]

Violence or intimidation at elections was also common at this period. In most of the large urban constituencies the more

[1] Gash, *Politics in the Age of Peel*, p. 127. He goes on: 'there can be no doubt that in most borough elections bribery was practised, even if it was not always the deciding factor'. See also pp. 70–77.

[2] Ibid., p. 131. Even an uncontested pocket borough (the cheapest of all) would cost between £200 and £300.

genteel electors were sometimes terrorized on polling day by
gangs of hired bullies and deterred from voting. Sometimes the
candidates encouraged this 'radical intimidation'. The more
serious cases of protracted riots at Coventry in 1832 and Wolverhampton in 1834, which were the subject of parliamentary inquiries, served to highlight a general trend.[1] Other forms of
undue influence were exclusive dealing and cooping, which
occurred sporadically at borough elections.[2] On the whole
county landlords still managed to control their tenants without
having to resort to threats or even formal directions.

The continuance on an increasing scale of all the pre-Reform
corrupt practices in the 1830's and 1840's was partly due to two
new factors (one of which was a direct result of the Reform Act),
registration societies, and the political clubs.

The Reform Act introduced to Britain a system of registering
voters.[3] The system was based on the parochial Overseers of the
Poor, who were expected to draw up the lists of voters. Shortly
after the Act was passed 'registration societies' sprang up in the
constituencies where contests usually occurred to encourage
people to register their claims, as otherwise they would not be
entitled to vote.[4] The societies were avowedly partisan and were
the prototypes of the later Conservative and Liberal Associations: sometimes they had salaried secretaries, the precursors of
the modern party agents. They soon discovered ways of utilizing
the system to the best advantage of their party—making claims
for apathetic voters, paying their fees, objecting to hostile ap-
plicants, and even securing admissions to the register on fraudu-

---

[1] Gash, *Politics in the Age of Peel*, pp. 137–53. The Coventry mob had been
hired in the interest of 'Bear' Ellice, paid three times the usual wage of rural
labourers, and given plenty of gin. They were then instructed to stop Tories from
voting, which they did.

[2] 'Exclusive dealing' meant that tradesmen and shopkeepers would lose custom
unless they supported a particular candidate: 'cooping' was large-scale abduction
of voters. It was more common in Ireland than in England, though it sometimes
occurred in English boroughs. See below, p. 56, also *P.P. 1835*, viii, esp. 105–6.

[3] There had been a system of registration for Irish elections since the eighteenth
century.

[4] In counties qualified voters had to send in *once* a formal claim to be registered
(with a small fee) to the Overseer of the Poor. Borough freemen had to lodge their
claims with the Town Clerk; occupiers were automatically listed by the Overseer.
Revising barristers sat once every year in open court to alter the register and deal
with disputed claims. For a discussion of this little-known by-product of the Reform
Act see J. A. Thomas, 'The System of Registration and the Development of Party
Organization 1832–1870', *History*, xxxv. 81–98. (1950)

lent grounds. As early as 1838 Peel was able to write about 'a perfectly new element of political power, the registration of voters . . . a more powerful one than either the sovereign or the House of Commons. That party is strongest, in point of fact, which has the existing registration in its favour.'[1] Although the registration societies were unknown to the law, the revising barristers regarded them as an integral part of the electoral system, and came to rely on them more than on the inefficient Overseers of the Poor.[2]

The first permanent local party associations were registration societies, but although there were many other purposes that they might serve besides 'keeping up the register', they lacked the necessary co-ordination. The need for a co-ordinating link was met by the London political clubs—the Carlton, founded in 1832, and the Reform in 1835. From the start they were not only social centres but points of contact for the party following throughout the country. They supplied two new functionaries— the party whip[3] who recommended suitable candidates to local associations that wished to recruit them from London, and the national agent with a staff of officials housed in the London Club and providing the leaders with up-to-date information on the state of party fortunes in the constituencies. Gash has re- vived interest in the careers of the first national party agents, F. R. Bonham at the Carlton and Joseph Parkes and James Coppock at the Reform.[4]

The exact role of the national agents in the elections and the

[1] Seymour, *Electoral Reform in England and Wales*, p. 125.

[2] Later improvements to the system were made by Graham's Act (1843) which imposed checks on the overseers, awarded costs against frivolous objectors, and allowed an appeal from the revising barristers to the Court of Common Pleas; Clay's Act (1851) permitting compounders to pay rates; and an Act of 1865 increasing the costs against frivolous objections from £1 to £5.

[3] The party whip, as such, dates from the early 1800's, but until this time they were not concerned with candidature. Francis Place was the prototype of the Party agent.

[4] It is an interesting fact that three men coming from widely different social levels were equally competent in this novel profession. Bonham, once a junior minister and a friend of Peel, waş of Irish landowning stock; Parkes, a radical solicitor, was a founder of the Reform Club and had been secretary to the Commis- sion on Municipal Corporations; Coppock was a struggling lawyer of humble origin whose voluntary efforts for the Liberals at Finsbury in 1835 attracted the notice of Parkes who brought him into the Club organization. It is noteworthy that Bonham's ministerial career came to an end as a result of a charge of partiality to a railway company. See N. Gash, 'F. R. Bonham: Conservative "Political Secretary", 1832–1847', *English Historical Review*, lxiii (Oct. 1948), 502–22.

degree to which they were able to co-ordinate the party efforts
is not easy to assess through lack of evidence,[1] but some light is
thrown by the investigations into corrupt practices in certain
boroughs. The Special Commission on the Sudbury election of
1841[2] found all three[3] involved in the unsavoury affairs of that
borough. Bonham had introduced two Conservative candidates
to the local supporters, though he was 'no party to any pecuniary arrangement'. Parkes had received £500 from the Liberal
Whip (Ellice) which he gave to Coppock, who then went down
to Sudbury and spent it (with £3,000 more which the candidate
gave him) presumably in bribes, since he refused to answer
questions on the ground that he might incriminate himself—he
had vainly tried to claim professional privilege as the candidate's solicitor. Two years before Coppock was proved to have
bribed a voter at Ludlow with £30.[4]

In his evidence before the Select Committee of 1835 Parkes[5]
admitted that the agent for a candidate in a corrupt borough 'is
affected with a complete knowledge' of the circumstances of the
election. Solicitors in many cases, 'he was ashamed to say', took
the oath that they were not paid agents, when appearing before
House Committees. As a remedy the first national agent for the
Liberals surprisingly recommended the complete abolition of
'all pecuniary agency of any sort or kind', and suggested that the
work of managing elections and registration devolve on voluntary local committees. Twenty-five years later, when he had
already been ten years out of the Reform Club, in the dignified
non-political office of Taxing Master to the Court of Chancery,

[1] R. H. Hill, *Toryism and the People, 1832–1846* (London, 1929), p. 57, points out
that in the provinces the work of the Carlton Club was restricted to the *management*
of elections and that any systematic payment by the club would have been regarded as an unwarrantable arrogation of the authority enjoyed by the local Tory
gentry.

[2] See below, p. 21.

[3] Though Bonham was the sole national agent for the Conservatives the duties
on the Liberal side seem to have been shared by Parkes and Coppock. The title
'national agent' is anachronistic. Whenever any of them appeared at an election
trial (before a House of Commons Committee or a Royal Commission) they were
referred to as 'parliamentary attorneys' or 'parliamentary agents'. Theoretically
every lawyer was entitled to practise before a House Committee and the three
maintained the pretence that they were hired in their professional capacity by the
individual candidates concerned.

[4] *P.P. 1840*, ix. 27–241.

[5] *P.P. 1835*, viii. 100, 114. See below, pp. 19 ff.

Parkes gave the same advice to another Select Committee. At the same time Philip Rose, who with his partner, Markham Spofforth, had been appointed by Disraeli to succeed Bonham in 1853, admitted the frequency of corrupt expenditure by agents, and suggested improvements in the law.[1]

Thus the gradual evolution of the two-party system and the rivalry it engendered helped to keep up the cost of electioneering—and especially of corrupt electioneering. The heads of the embryonic national organizations used these methods not because they approved of them, but because they were deemed an unfortunate necessity in the constituencies where contests took place, which ranged from over two-thirds of the total in 1832 to two-fifths in 1847.[2]

In the interests of the party they could only be dispensed with when the electoral law was tightened up.

3

During these decades the attention of the House of Commons was frequently directed to the prevalence of corrupt practices and the inadequacy of the existing law. Three years after the passing of the Reform Act the House set up a Select Committee 'to consider the most effectual means of preventing Bribery, Corruption and Intimidation'.[3] It was a high-powered committee with Lord John Russell and Spring Rice for the ministry, Grote and Molesworth for the radicals, Graham for the Stanleyites, and Goulburn for the Conservatives. The witnesses they summoned were of the same type as were to appear before similar committees during the next forty years—mainly election agents, lawyers, and, in this case, one distinguished foreign expert, Alexis de Tocqueville.[4] The committee were astute enough

[1] *P.P. 1860*, x. 98–133. Rose had previously been personal lawyer and agent to Disraeli.

[2] It must be remembered that at this time the mass parties were in their infancy. Until 1867 local interests still predominated at general elections and in many of the smaller boroughs the candidates' relatives attended to registration as well as the other duties of electioneering. But the trend was there, even in the thirties, as Peel saw.

[3] Cf. *P.P. 1835*, viii. 3 (Report); 5–717 (Minutes of Evidence).

[4] De Tocqueville described the French *scrutin de liste* and expressed his belief in its secrecy. *P.P. 1835*, viii. 234–45. Another witness, Alexander Cockburn, a young lawyer practising before House Committees, said that since the main difficulty lay in pinning down responsibility on the members the law of evidence ought to be

to summon the election agents from several reputedly corrupt boroughs and the evidence confirmed their worst suspicions. The printed evidence provides the first inventory of corrupt practices at British elections.[1]

In the same year Russell introduced a Bill to set up a Special Committee to carry out preliminary local inquiries in boroughs where corruption was indicated. The Lords' amendment required a joint address to the Crown upon which a Commission consisting of a judge and members of Parliament would make a local investigation. Russell, however, objected to the judge and the Bill was dropped.[2]

The first attempt to remove the jurisdiction over election petitions from the House came in an unsuccessful private member's Bill of 1837 which would have replaced the Grenville Committees by a tribunal of assessors (with a certain standing at the bar) holding office for life. A similar proposal was made in 1839.[3] The mover of the 1839 motion, Lord Mahon, spoke of 'the enormous and intolerable abuses' still connected with the trial of petitions, especially the way in which the issue was still determined by party preferences. Peel defended the principle that the jurisdiction belonged to the House, but admitted the justice of the objections,[4] and on the same day introduced a Bill which was supported by the Liberal Government and quickly passed into law. It abolished the Grenville Committees and provided that at the beginning of every session the Speaker would appoint a 'General Committee of Elections' consisting of six of the more experienced members, and that these would try

made more severe (ibid. 214–25). Thirty-three years later, Cockburn again appears in this story in a different connexion. See below, p. 36.

[1] The report said: 'In the present state of the inquiry . . . they abstain from making any observations upon the result of the Evidence.' *P.P. 1835*, viii. 3. Since this was the first inquiry of its kind it is not surprising that the Select Committee found themselves at a loss to evaluate the evidence. Many of the facts referred to in preceding pages are derived from the Minutes of Evidence.

[2] Between 1832 and 1840 the Lords threw out several Bills designed to punish guilty constituencies or prevent corrupt practices. Cf. Seymour, *Electoral Reform in England and Wales*, pp. 201–3.

[3] *3 Hans.* xxxix (27 Nov. 1837), 284–321; ibid. xlv (14 Feb. 1839), 379–434.

[4] The main objections to the House Election Committees in the 1830's were that they decided most petitions on partisan grounds; that it ought not to be necessary to prove agency before offering evidence of bribery; and that the costs were too high—respondents had to summon witnesses (and keep them in London) and hire counsel without recovering costs, even if successful.

all election petitions.[1] Just before the election of 1841 Peel introduced a similar bill (with some minor improvements)[2] and Russell brought in a Bill to compel candidates to testify on oath before the Election Committee (this clause was struck out by the Lords) and to enable evidence of bribery to be given before proof of agency[3] at petition hearings. Both of these Bills became law.

When the first petitions came up for trial after the 1841 election and it was seen that the new Election Committee was more strict and impartial and had greater power than its predecessors, several petitions were suddenly withdrawn. There was nothing new about this; petitions were frequently compromised or 'swopped'.[4] But this time it was too blatant. On 6 May 1842 the radical Roebuck moved for a Select Committee to inquire into the withdrawal of the petitions from six boroughs,[5] and Peel, now Prime Minister, agreed.

The Select Committee, with Roebuck as chairman, proved conclusively that all six petitions had been withdrawn through corrupt motives and that both parties were implicated.[6] Peel felt impelled to introduce further legislation. His Act of 1842[7] provided that if a petition were abandoned under suspicious circumstances the House Election Committee might inquire further, and that treating before the test of the writ, during the campaign, or after the return would rank as a corrupt practice.

The effect of Peel's Act of 1842 could not be seen until after the next election. Meanwhile, however, one notorious borough not investigated by the Roebuck Committee was attracting the attention of the House. The Election Committee investigating a petition from Sudbury[8] discovered that in the electorate, which numbered less than 600 (mostly poor handloom weavers), about 400 not only expected to be bribed but regularly took the bribery oath with perfect indifference, so that the local clergyman had come to an arrangement with the election agents that

---

[1] 2 & 3 Vict., c. 38.   [2] 4 & 5 Vict., c. 58.
[3] 4 & 5 Vict., c. 57.
[4] Gash, *Politics in the Age of Peel*, pp. 241, 264. A petition against Disraeli at Shrewsbury in 1841 was swopped for one against the Liberals at Gloucester.
[5] Reading, Penryn and Falmouth, Bridport, Nottingham, Lewes, and Harwich.
[6] *P.P. 1842*, v. 77–88 (Report); 97 ff. (Minutes of Evidence).
[7] 5 & 6 Vict., c. 102.
[8] See above, p. 18. H. G. Nicholas makes a convincing case for identifying Eatanswill with Sudbury. Cf. *To the Hustings*, p. 21.

the oath would not be demanded by either side.[1] The committee
found that 'gross, systematic and extensive Bribery' characterized the borough and recommended that it be disfranchised.[2]
A Special Commission was sent to investigate on the spot. The
findings of this Commission confirmed those of the committee,[3]
whereupon the Government introduced a Bill to disfranchise
the borough which passed the Commons but was thrown out by
the Lords. The Commons, however, in two succeeding sessions
sent it up again, and in 1844 the Lords gave way.

The elections of 1847 and 1852, especially the former, showed
that bribery and treating still continued, and that the Acts of
1841–2 were unable to eliminate compromises since the agents
merely altered the time of the compromise. Nevertheless, the
number of petitions rose steeply, as did the number of elections
annulled for bribery, although fewer constituencies were being
contested.[4]

During these years public opinion was roused to 'a lukewarm
degree of disgust',[5] and a pressure group, the Anti-Bribery
Society, was founded, which though very obscure and apparently short-lived,[6] at least showed the first stirrings of public
conscience on the subject.

Again, however, it was the affairs of a particular borough
that sparked off further legislation. In 1848[7] the Lords threw
out a Bill empowering the Commons to appoint a Select Committee to see whether the affairs of a suspect borough merited
further investigation, and, if satisfied that they did, to recommend the appointment of a Royal Commission, with full inquisitorial powers, to go down to the constituency.[8] Nevertheless,

---

[1] *P.P. 1842*, vii. 855–941. The Governor of the Sudbury Court of Guardians said
that the effect of chronic bribery on the character of the weavers was more than
'all the precepts or preaching of all the Ministers of the Gospel could rectify'. Ibid.
943–5.
[2] Ibid. 941.   [3] *P.P. 1844*, xviii. 247–561.
[4] See below, App. II.
[5] Seymour, *Electoral Reform in England and Wales*, p. 223. The *Westminster Review*
since the late 1830's had been inveighing against electoral corruption. Cf. especially
xxxix (Feb.–May 1843), 113–46.
[6] Its prospectus has not been preserved in the British Museum.
[7] And in 1849 a Bill to force candidates to take a bribery oath met the same fate.
[8] All this time the House Election Committees were hampered by their inability
to force witnesses to testify under oath and by the custom that the petitioner proved
just as much corruption as would convict the respondent, and (because of the
expense) generally went no further. A Royal Commission (this term is used in

in 1852, after a petition from St. Albans, the Government proposed a special Bill to set up a Commission for the borough, as in the case of Sudbury, which was successful in the Lords. The Royal Commission reported that since 1832 the proportion of the electoral expenses that went on bribery had increased from one-third to two-thirds, and that approximately £24,000 had been spent in that period on 500 electors.

A Bill consigning St. Albans to the same fate as Sudbury was rushed through both Houses, but as the two Commissions had been so successful the question was again raised whether the procedure ought to be standardized. After some haggling with the Lords an Act was passed providing for a joint address to the Crown (not an address by the House of Commons, as was first proposed) requesting a Royal Commission to go down to any constituency in which the House Election Committee suspected that corrupt practices extensively prevailed. The Act was passed just before the election of 1852.[1]

After the election a record number of petitions (49) was heard, and the number that succeeded on the ground of bribery (25) was far higher than at any previous election.[2] The Act of 1852 was invoked in the case of six[3] boroughs all of which were revealed as having large corruptible elements (from one-third of the electorate upwards) while some, in addition, regularly perjured themselves—the freemen electorates being the worst.

When the Reports of the Royal Commissions were made available the short-lived Derby–Disraeli Government of 1852 was in power. The ex-Home Secretary, Spencer Walpole, introduced a Bill in August 1853 to consolidate and rationalize the anti-corruption laws. He proposed a definition of bribery, a reduction of the fine for guilty candidates from £1,000[4] to £50 as more practicable, and a declaration by candidates that they had not indulged in bribery.[5]

Walpole's Bill was introduced too late in the session, but in the following year Russell (as Leader of the House of Commons)

---

preference to 'Special Commission', since it was appointed in the same manner under the royal sign manual) would have full powers to force witnesses to testify.

[1] 15 & 16 Vict., c. 57.
[2] P.P. 1866, lvi. 519–26. See below, App. II.
[3] See below, p. 28, n. 3.
[4] See above, p. 11, n. 5.
[5] 3 Hans. cxxix (12 Aug. 1853), 1699–1705.

introduced a Bill[1] on similar lines, which contained comprehensive definitions of bribery, treating, and (for the first time) of undue influence or intimidation. The penalties for candidates guilty of bribery were expulsion from the House during the lifetime of the existing Parliament and a fine of £50; for candidates guilty of treating and undue influence a fine of £50 and risk of prosecution for misdemeanour, but not loss of the seat; for voters guilty of bribery a fine of £10 and prosecution for a misdemeanour, for voters guilty of the other offences the striking off of the vote. Russell's Bill also contained another innovation—the election accounts.[2]

There was a note of urgency in Russell's speeches[3] on the Bill with which most of the members who spoke on both sides of the House agreed. The only opposition came from back-benchers such as Colonel Sibthorp, who openly professed their devotion to the existing practices.[4]

The 1854 Bill passed into law. After the next two elections the number of petitions dropped and over the next fourteen years parliamentary interest in corrupt practices and the allied subject of franchise extension declined. Nevertheless, the defects of the system were reported on by a Select Committee set up in 1860 to investigate the working of the 1854 Act.[5] They found that while the evidence afforded 'no sufficient grounds for believing that corrupt practices at elections have in recent years increased', yet the system of election auditors was quite useless—many candidates ignored them and those that did not invariably had their accounts passed. The Select Committee recommended that the other provisions of the Act of 1854 be continued, but

[1] For the debates on the Bill of 1854 see especially *3 Hans.* cxxx (10 Feb. 1854), 412–40; cxxxii (3 Apr. 1854), 336–58, 911–42; cxxxiv (10 July 1854), 1443–78. In Apr. 1854 the Attorney-General introduced a Bill to disfranchise the guilty voters reported by the Commissions in the six boroughs, but it was withdrawn on 29 May.

[2] In future every candidate was to publish itemized accounts of his expenditure which an election auditor might inspect.

[3] Russell said in his opening speech: 'It must be admitted on all sides that the corrupt practices which have prevailed of late at elections, have involved all parties concerned in them in disgrace and have also tended materially to compromise the character of this House.' *3 Hans.* cxxx (10 Feb. 1854), 412.

[4] Sibthorp said that the Bill was 'an attempt to prevent a humble individual like himself from doing that which it was his duty to do in the station in life in which he was placed, and which he owed to those who sent him there'. Ibid. cxxxii (3 Apr. 1854), 343–4. Sibthorp's family had represented Lincolnshire since 1714.

[5] *P.P. 1860*, x. 1–7 (Report); 23–293 (Minutes of Evidence).

that the system of auditors be repealed, and that the Election
Committees be obliged to report to the House the names of
people found guilty of bribery or treating.[1] An Act of 1863
implemented the last two recommendations; otherwise the subject of corrupt practices was left in abeyance until 1867.

During this period, while the various governments of Peel,
Russell, and Derby tried by piecemeal reforms to eradicate, or
at least reduce, the incidence of electoral corruption, the
radicals were advocating one panacea for electoral ills—the
ballot. It had first been proposed as a practical suggestion in
1776 by the middle-class reformer, Major Cartwright. It won
numerous adherents in the next two decades, but like all radical
proposals it passed out of favour during the Napoleonic wars,
until it appeared again in Bentham's 'Radical Reform Bill' of
1819. In the Reform debates of 1830–2 the ballot had a powerful advocate in the Cabinet, Lord Durham, and he won over
two orthodox Whig ministers, Lord Althorp and Sir James
Graham.[2] However, the opposition of Grey, Lansdowne, and
Brougham (not to speak of William IV) was too strong and the
ballot was dropped, but it had nearly become part of the ministerial scheme and the London radicals pressed the Cabinet to
reintroduce it.

After Reform the 'philosophical' radicals, some of whom
were successful at the election of 1832, organized a campaign
for secret voting.[3] Grote, the historian, who had been returned
by an enormous majority for the City of London, made a point
of introducing every year a resolution for the ballot, and up to
1839 won an increasing number of parliamentary supporters.[4]
But the solid phalanx of orthodox Whigs and Tories was too

[1] They also recommended a reduction in the penalty for bribery. There were
altogether thirty-nine recommendations, mostly of a procedural nature. The consensus of opinion among the witnesses was given by Sir Frederick Slade, Q.C. (who
had been one of the Commissioners at St. Albans and Canterbury): 'I do not think
that you will ever prevent bribery. You might as well try to prevent the sexes
coming together as try to prevent bribery' (ibid. 191).

[2] It has been suggested that Graham at least was advocating the ballot for
tactical reasons—to force the old Whigs to concede a low franchise. But Althorp (as
well as Durham) was prepared to accept a £15 or £20 franchise, if accompanied by
the ballot. It is not certain how the Cabinet went ultimately. Cf. Sir D. Le Marchant,
Memoir of John Charles Viscount Althorp, Third Earl Spencer (London, 1876), p. 293.

[3] Cf. S. J. Reid, *Life and Letters of Lord Durham* (London, 1906), ii. 145–6.

[4] Macaulay, George Grey, Ellice, and Disraeli (when looking for a seat) all
spoke in favour of the ballot.

strong for him. Grote did not stand again in 1841, the other
radicals of note disappeared from the House, and for the next
twenty-five years the cause of the ballot was promoted by
second-rate figures like Henry Berkeley in the face of increasing
parliamentary indifference. The inclusion of the ballot among
the Six Points of the People's Charter also tended to discredit it
in the eyes of the middle classes.

The arguments against the introduction of the ballot were
that the franchise was a trust[1] held on behalf of the whole
community and so the duties ought to be publicly performed;
that secrecy would lead to hypocrisy and dishonesty; that it
would be more difficult to detect corrupt practices, and that the
French and American systems were not free of corruption. The
most important argument (which was, however, not often expressed openly) was that the 'legitimate' influence of the governing classes, which the Reform Bill was intended to preserve,
would be jeopardized under secret voting.

The arguments for the ballot were more logical. The trustee
argument was rebutted by the proposition that the voter was not
accountable to others for the performance of his duty, and that
the law, while theoretically making the voter responsible to the
public, in fact placed him under the control of private people—
chiefly landlords. Against 'legitimate influence' the radicals[2]
argued that if the influence coincided with the opinion of the
voters it would be superfluous, if it were contrary it would force
them to betray their own conscience. They argued that secret
voting would be the only real remedy against bribery[3] as well
as against undue influence.

In the 1850's and 1860's these subjects had merely an
academic interest. The Great Exhibition, the Crimean War, the
fluctuations of trade, the income tax, the University and Civil
Service reforms all tended to turn the minds of legislators and
public away from constitutional law and practice. But their
interest could be quickly revived.

[1] The 'trustee' argument. Cf. *The Times*, 1 July 1857; see also below, p. 76.
[2] Not all radicals supported the ballot during these years. John Stuart Mill had
first supported it but changed his mind about 1859. Grote in his old age also believed it was no longer necessary. Cf. M. St. J. Packe, *Life of Mill* (London, 1954),
pp. 370, 415.
[3] Because would-be bribers could not be sure of success. This view had the
authority of Coppock, *P.P. 1860*, x. 299.

CHAPTER II

The Parliamentary Elections Act and the General Election of 1868

I

IT was obvious in the early 1860's that the electoral reforms of the previous decade, especially the system of election auditors, were proving ineffective. But in spite of all the discussion the only change in the law was the relatively minor Act of 1863.[1] The whole question was brought abruptly to the fore after the general election of 1865.

The election of 1865 took place under circumstances 'of as little excitement as can perhaps ever be expected to attend the choosing by a great nation of its representative body'.[2] The Parliament elected in 1859 had died a natural death; there was no important issue; the Whig–Liberal Government dominated by the father-figure, the octogenarian Lord Palmerston, appealed to its record of maintaining peace abroad and a successful fiscal policy at home.

The election addresses and speeches concerned such pedestrian subjects as church rates, the malt tax, and the finer points of Gladstonian finance.[3] Electoral reform—and a fortiori the ballot—appeared in the addresses only of the faithful followers of Bright and Berkeley; out of deference to Palmerston the rest ignored it.[4]

There was never much doubt about the result during the campaign. In fact, the Government increased their majority—a feat unequalled in the thirty-three years since the first Reform Act.[5]

---

[1] See above, p. 25. [2] *Annual Register 1865*, p. 153.
[3] Cf. *The Times*, 4, 25 July 1865.
[4] Bright stated on 19 Sept. 1865 that reform must be postponed until the end of Palmerston's official life. Palmerston died on 18 Oct. Cf. J. H. Park, *The English Reform Bill of 1867* (New York, 1920), pp. 91–92.
[5] The Liberals secured 367 seats, the Conservatives 290. The Liberals increased their 1859 lead by 15 seats.

Beneath the placid surface, however, the election was the most keenly contested of any since 1841. There were 204 English contests[1]—double the number in 1859—and the official expense returns were the highest yet—£752,000 were accounted for in the official returns but the actual expenditure was much higher.[2] *The Times* was able to say (13 Feb. 1868): 'The testimony is unanimous that in the General Election of 1865 there was more profuse and corrupt expenditure than was ever known before.'

The evidence for this statement was not available until the petition trials were under way before the House of Commons Election Committees. Fifty petitions were lodged and thirty-five came up for trial, one-fifth of the entire total since 1832. The member was unseated in thirteen cases—a not unduly high proportion. Four of the successful cases led to Royal Commissions[3] (Great Yarmouth, Lancaster, Totnes, and Reigate) following reports that the Election Committee believed that corrupt practices were generally prevalent.

The Commissioners, like their predecessors in the 1850's, unearthed a good deal of evidence that the Election Committees had either neglected or failed to discover.[4] In the two medium-sized boroughs of Yarmouth and Lancaster[5] the Commissioners found that all the elections since the Act of 1854 had been corrupt, that the electors were debased by long-standing habits of venality, and that the requirements of the Act regarding election expenses were cynically evaded. In Yarmouth a mere 10 per cent. of the total expenditure of the Liberal candidates[6]

---

[1] One cause of the increase in the number of contests was the retirement of many older members.

[2] Cf. *P.P. 1866*, lvi. In proposing the motion for a Select Committee in 1869, the then Home Secretary, Bruce, said that the actual expenditure in 1865 was close on a million. *3 Hans.* cxciv (4 Mar. 1869), 649. See below, p. 59.

[3] Since 1852 there had been appointed ten Royal Commissions following a joint address from both Houses of Parliament: 1853—Canterbury, Kingston-upon-Hull, Cambridge, Maldon, Barnstaple, Tynemouth; 1857—Galway Town; 1859—Gloucester, Wakefield, Berwick-on-Tweed. In one case (Clitheroe in 1853) the House of Lords refused to join in the address.

[4] For the Reports and Minutes of Evidence of the Royal Commissions see *P.P. 1867*, xxvii (Lancaster); xxviii (Reigate); xxix (Totnes); xxx (Yarmouth).

[5] Lancaster had 1,400 electors approximately, Yarmouth 1,500.

[6] Alexander Brogden, one of the Liberal candidates, had entered into an agreement with his fellow candidate, Philip Vanderbyl, to pay £6,000 for bribery—half of which Vanderbyl would return if elected. Neither was elected and Brogden lodged the petition. The successful Conservative candidates paid £890 to their agents (accounted for), augmented by £4,000 contributed by their friends.

was accounted for in the official return; since the remaining 90 per cent. was devoted solely to bribery that was not surprising. One-third of the electorate were proved to have given or received bribes. In Lancaster competition between the parties was so keen that the Liberals spent £7,459, mainly in open bribes, and the Conservatives £7,070. The official returns of the parties were £1,404 and £1,129 respectively and the Liberal agent indignantly repudiated any suggestion that money spent over and above what he had accounted for was of any concern to him.[1] In the words of the Commissioners, 'the deluge of corruption [in 1865] has been more universal and has reached a higher level of society than ever before'.[2] It had involved two-thirds of the Lancaster electorate.

Reigate was a borough roughly half the size of Lancaster and Great Yarmouth, and was unusual among boroughs of its size in that there had been for many years no tradition of landlord influence and intimidation.[3] Here again there was the keenest rivalry between the parties, chiefly manifested in large-scale colourable employment—labourers, for example, being paid from three to six times their daily wage for loss of time on nomination and polling days, and large numbers of committee men with non-existent duties earning from £2 to £10.[4] Hotels and public houses were kept open for weeks on end before the election—at the expense of the parties. These practices had prevailed since 1858 when there had been two by-elections. In 1865 the proportion of the electorate affected by bribes of one kind or another was nearly one-half, and the candidates' published expenses amounted in both cases to much less than their actual outlay.[5] As late as 1855 Totnes[6] with a mere 395 voters had been a semi-proprietary borough of the Whig Duke of Somerset,

---

[1] *P.P. 1867*, xxvii. 92.   [2] Ibid. 19.

[3] The building of a railway station greatly increased Reigate's prosperity; its population increased from 10,000 to 12,000 between 1861 and 1865.

[4] One canvasser said before the Commissioners: 'I asked persons for their votes but you might as well have asked them for their lives unless you had money to give them.' *P.P. 1867*, xxviii. 10.

[5] Ibid. 11–12.

[6] When the serge trade stopped (in the 1830's), Totnes, in common with most of South Devon, suffered and its importance, never very great, declined further. Its electorate was 217 in 1832 and 395 in 1865: Reigate, which lost a seat in 1832 because it had less than 200 voters (152), had increased by 1865 to 912. For the history of the Somerset influence in Totnes after 1832 see N. Gash, *Politics in the Age of Peel*, pp. 117, 154, 164–6.

who was lord of the manor, and being always sure of at least one seat did not have any reason to bribe. The Conservatives, however, could never win a seat except by heavy bribery.[1] In 1863 the pre-Reform practice of creating fictitious qualifications was revived by the Liberals and from that time the influence of the Somersets (who had been sponsoring independent Liberals) was at an end—partly because the Duke was now Lord Lieutenant of the county and wished to have no part in the squalid affairs of the borough.

By 1865 two Liberals[2] were in the field, but the knowledge that they would be involved in heavy expenditure deterred many prospective Conservative candidates until Spofforth,[3] who had been charged by the local Conservatives to find a gentleman with 'a commercial spirit', recommended a Colonel Dawkins who was anxious for a seat and willing to spend £2,000. The Colonel was accepted, but before the contest was over he had spent more than £4,500. The fourth candidate (a Conservative) stood on purity principles and spent a mere £350, although he was willing to profit from the large illegal expenditure of his colleague. The Liberals, on hearing of opposition, furtively brought down £2,000 to the borough for direct bribery. The result showed that on the state of the register no Conservative had a chance of being returned and that the Conservatives had been persuaded to stand only to bring to the town the largesse associated with elections.

The Commissioners found that Totnes had in thirty years been transformed into another Sudbury. Less than one-third of the voters were unaffected by bribery and not only did the corrupt taint spread to every class from bankers and magistrates down to the poorest labourers, but witness after witness deliberately perjured themselves before the Commissioners and threw every obstacle they could in the way of the inquiry.

[1] Witnesses traced the corruption of the borough back to the election of 1837 when two candidates (Liberal and Conservative) polled an equal number of votes. The Conservatives used to bribe tenants on the Somerset estates with very large sums, varying from £60 to £150 a head, to vote against the Duke's nominee and then face the eviction notices they were certain to receive.

[2] John Pender and Alfred Seymour; the latter, a distant relative of the Duke, was originally the Somerset candidate, the former, a rich Manchester merchant. Both had been elected in by-elections at which they bribed heavily, Pender in 1862 and Seymour in 1863.

[3] See below, p. 44.

The investigations by the four Commissions proved what many had suspected, that the law regarding election expenses was a dead letter and had been so even before the election auditors were abolished. They also strikingly demonstrated the power of a tribunal with inquisitorial powers to get at facts that might be concealed from a House Election Committee. The committee on the Totnes petition unseated Pender for personally bribing a voter by the offer of employment: the Royal Commission discovered that that was almost the only charge that was unfounded.[1]

2

The Royal Commissions had been appointed on 14 June 1866 but their hearings were very protracted, and the reports were not presented to the House of Commons until 21 February 1867.[2] By then there was a new government, the last Derby–Disraeli Government, and its policy had already been formed.

An indication of the reaction of the House towards the revelations of electoral corruption in 1865 had been given during the debates on the Liberal Reform Bill of 1866—even before the Royal Commissions had been appointed. On 28 May 1866, when the Bill was in committee, the Conservative member for Northamptonshire, Sir Rainald Knightley, moved an instruction that the committee be empowered to provide for 'the better prevention of bribery and corruption at elections'.[3]

Gladstone immediately rose to object that there was no precedent for treating electioneering habits in the same Bill as extension of the franchise and redistribution; he said it would inevitably bring into the arena of party conflict a subject that ought to be treated on a non-partisan basis, and would, moreover, imperil the whole Bill by making it needlessly complicated. The Liberals who followed took the same line, the Attorney-General (Sir Roundell Palmer) and John Bright especially

---

[1] See *P.P. 1867*, xxix, for Minutes of Evidence and Report of the Totnes Commission. See also below, p. 37, n. 3.

[2] On that day Colonel Wilson Patten pointed out to the Home Secretary (Spencer Walpole) that part of the Lancaster Report was already in circulation and 'causing a good deal of uneasiness'. Walpole did not know of this and deeply regretted that it had occurred. *3 Hans.* clxxxv. (21 Feb. 1867), 726.

[3] Ibid. clxxxiii (28 May 1866), 1320. For the debate see ibid. 1320–47.

suggesting that this was another Conservative stratagem to wreck the Reform Bill. Among those who supported Knightley were Bernal Osborne, recently elected Liberal member for Nottingham, who claimed that the Government were fighting shy of a subject that was more urgent than franchise extension and challenged Gladstone as to when he proposed to deal with it, and the member for the litigious borough of Boston, M. Staniland, who said that in a borough on the east coast (from which no petition had been presented) out of 1,000 electors 700 had been bribed at an average cost of £35 per head.

Disraeli made the point that corruption was most rife in the boroughs created in 1832 and claimed that his own party had nothing to fear from an investigation. The instruction was passed by 10 votes; Gladstone promised to consider it dispassionately but warned that he was not 'sanguine' about its chances of influencing the Government.[1]

Within the month the Government had resigned, ousted by the Dunkellin amendment, and the Conservatives were in office once more. It might be thought that the Conservative support of the Knightley amendment was simply a party manœuvre, but Disraeli soon showed that they were willing to tackle corruption as well as reform of the franchise—and in the same Bill. On 25 February 1867, when introducing the main reform resolutions to the House,[2] he said that the Government also intended to bring in a clause providing for a new kind of election petition trial—an on-the-spot inquiry by two assessors with an appeal to the House.[3] If the House did not wish to encumber the Reform Bill unduly the Government would incorporate this clause in a separate Bill to be introduced on the same day. Disraeli admitted that they had given 'thoughtless and incautious' support in 1866 to the Knightley amendment, but subsequent events had forced them to the conclusion that 'any Ministry would not be doing its duty if it did not attempt

[1] Lowe and the Cave voted with the Conservatives and the result was greeted with great cheering. Cf. Park, *The English Reform Bill of 1867*, pp. 155-6.

[2] The first stage of the Reform Bill of 1867 was the presentation of resolutions by the Government on 11 Feb.; on 25 Feb. the House resolved itself into a Committee to discuss the resolutions. For Disraeli's speech see *3 Hans.* clxxxv (25 Feb. (1867), 943 ff.

[3] If the House wished it might then appoint a Select Committee, subject to the petitioner entering into recognizances to bear the expenses, if necessary. Disraeli insisted that all this was a mere outline of the Cabinet proposals.

vigorously to grapple with this question'. He also promised to
disfranchise the four corrupt boroughs and transfer the seven
seats to towns with a considerable increase in population since
1832.[1]

Since the Reform Bill took precedence the introduction of
the Corrupt Practices at Elections Bill was delayed until 9 April
1867—the day before the former went to committee. During the
intervening weeks several attempts were made in the Commons,
notably by Sir Laurence Palk and Serjeant Gaselee, to expel
the members for the four boroughs, or at least to remove them
with other magistrates found guilty of corrupt practices, from
the Commission of the Peace.[2] Disraeli fobbed off these demands, and when one member moved an address to the Queen
asking that a magistrate from Dover, who he had ascertained
had been twice found guilty of sharp practice by Election Committees of the House, be struck off the magistracy, the government spokesman (Bentinck) moved an amendment to substitute
the names of all magistrates found guilty of corrupt practices by
Election Committees or Commissions. The address was accepted
but no immediate action was taken by the Lord Chancellor.

When introducing the Bill on 9 April for Disraeli, Northcote
omitted the proviso (promised in February) that when one
candidate was convicted of bribery his opponent, if his own
conduct were irreproachable, should get the seat. Otherwise
there was no change. The new election tribunal would consist of
a panel of eminent lawyers, and the petitioners might withdraw
the petition at any stage of the inquiry, provided they paid the
full costs. An unsuccessful M.P. might appeal to the House
which would then set up a Select Committee.

Leave to introduce was granted almost without discussion,
and on 2 May at a very late hour the Bill came up for a second
reading, Disraeli promising a general debate on the motion for
a committee. This occurred on 6 May, but here again the debate

[1] There was no debate on Disraeli's speech, but later the Cabinet decided to
follow the second course and introduce a separate Bill.

[2] See 3 Hans. clxxxvi (19 Mar. 1867), 123–8, 167–203; (28 Mar.), 730; (9 Apr.),
1382. It is interesting to note that the objects of these strenuous efforts included not
only the members for the corrupt boroughs who were also J.P.s (Vanderbyl of Great
Yarmouth and Seymour of Totnes), but also W. H. Leatham, M.P. for Wakefield,
who had been found personally guilty of bribery by an Election Committee in
1859, and Churchward, the Dover J.P. and mail contractor, who had first been
censured as far back as 1853.

was very brief.[1] Sir Stafford Northcote being the only Conservative and Sir George Grey the only Liberal front-benchers taking part. Northcote pointed to the inadequacy of the existing machinery—the greatest uncertainty as to the result on account of compromises, the long delays in getting before the House, and the obvious danger that petitions be treated as matters of party. The Government were trying, Northcote said, not to find the measure which was theoretically perfect but one that they might hope to carry—in a House where their followers were in a decided minority—and if the clause for a review by the House, to which the Liberal lawyer, Sir Robert Collier, objected[2] were not acceptable, they would withdraw it. In fact, they had put it in merely to carry the Bill.

Sir George Grey expressed the general Whig reaction—it was 'most objectionable' to transfer the jurisdiction which the House had possessed for so long, but if it had to be done then let it be to the judges, whose decisions would command authority. He also noted the incompatibility of combining an inquiry into the disposition of a seat with a general inquiry into the state of a constituency; the efficiency of the general inquiry must be sacrificed for the sake of the local issue. Beresford Hope,[3] an independent Conservative, claimed that the real cause of corruption was the 'category of doubtful and slippery expenses' which in moderation might be necessary but when used to excess became, in fact, mere bribery. Bernal Osborne treated the members to a new tirade on the insincerity and venality without which he was convinced half of them would never have entered Parliament.[4] Bribery would continue as long as it was fashionable and gentlemanly—loyal adherents would continue to be made peers and obsequious followers, baronets. But he admitted that the Government were going as far as they dared and that their proposal could scarcely have been made a few years before.

On the motion of Sir Robert Collier the Bill was referred to a Select Committee of the House under Northcote's chairman-

[1] 3 *Hans.* clxxxvi (2 May 1867), 1912; clxxxvii (6 May), 56–66.
[2] On the ground that this provision would lead to protracted litigation and be an advantage to wealthy candidates.
[3] Beresford Hope was the proprietor of the *Saturday Review*, which throughout these years concentrated its fire on the high cost of elections. See below, pp. 38–39.
[4] 3 *Hans.* clxxxvii (6 May 1867), 64–66.

ship, the Government raising no objection.[1] The committee was
appointed on 16–17 May, deliberated from 21 May till 11 July,
and reported back to the House on 12 July 1867.

The most important amendments proposed by the Select
Committee[2] were that the jurisdiction over controverted elections be transferred not to the panel of 'eminent lawyers', but to
the Court of Queen's Bench; that the right of appeal to the
House be abolished, but that a judge might reserve points of law
to a three-member Court of Election Appeals; that the penalties for bribery be made more severe—on a second conviction the
candidate would be disqualified for life from sitting in the House.
The trial was still to take place in the constituency concerned.

The amendments were mainly the work of Sir Robert Collier
and Russell Gurney. The most important, which transferred
the jurisdiction to the Queen's Bench, was carried by thirteen
votes to one,[3] but an amendment by Collier to make conveyance
of voters illegal was heavily defeated.

The Government raised no objection to the amendments and
at first intended to proceed with the Bill, but when Sir George
Grey asked if it could be deferred until the next session, since the
amendments were extensive and would require full consideration, Disraeli replied that he was under the impression that 'no
considerable, or, indeed, any opposition, would be offered to
this Bill' by the other side,[4] though if there were likely to be
opposition it would affect his decision on whether to proceed or
not. On 29 July the Bill was withdrawn, and on 16 August
Disraeli replied to a Conservative back-bencher[5] that although
he could not predict the course of business for the next session
he would be 'very sorry' if the Bill did not pass then and was in
favour of introducing it as early as possible.[6]

[1] The committee consisted of a well-balanced combination of politicians and
jurists: Sir George Grey, Sir Stafford Northcote, Sir Robert Collier, Q.C., Russell
Gurney (Recorder of London), Sir Rainald Knightley, Lord Elcho, Lord Edwin
Hill-Trevor, Messrs. Lowe, Whitbread, Mowbray, Baxter, Brett, Clive, Beach,
Hunt, Otway, Scourfield, and Knatchbull-Hugessen.
[2] For the Minutes of Proceedings of the Select Committee see *P.P. 1867–8*, viii.
1–12.
[3] E. H. Knatchbull-Hugessen, who made several unavailing attempts to restore
the jurisdiction of the House. Knatchbull-Hugessen was member for Sandwich and
was to figure in a celebrated petition trial thirteen years later. See below, pp. 152 ff.
[4] *3 Hans.* clxxxix (25 July 1867), 84.
[5] Darby Griffith. See below, p. 40, n. 3.
[6] Ibid. (16 Aug. 1867), 1606.

Thus the principle of transferring jurisdiction over controverted elections from the House of Commons to the judges of the High Court was first embodied not in the Election Petitions and Corrupt Practices at Elections Bill, 1868, but in the abortive Corrupt Practices at Elections Bill, 1867—not admittedly in its original form but in the form to which the Select Committee, led by the Liberal lawyers, had changed it, and which the Conservative leader of the House had accepted. The importance of this change passed almost unnoticed owing to the absorbing interest of the Second Reform Bill.[1]

One can only speculate as to the motives that induced Disraeli to adopt a policy that ran counter to one of the oldest traditions of the House of Commons. It is probable, however, that he became convinced that, as in the current matter of the franchise, only a radical reform would prove effective, and so he was willing to take another 'leap in the dark'.[2]

On 13 February 1868 the Chancellor of the Exchequer introduced the new Bill. Having briefly recounted the history of legislation governing election petitions and indicated that recent experience had tended 'to form the opinion of the House gradually but surely, that there is something in the existing principle, which is essentially vicious',[3] Disraeli said that the Cabinet after 'their deepest consideration' had unanimously decided to adhere strictly to the recommendations of the Select Committee and had drafted a Bill accordingly, but had just encountered an unexpected difficulty. They had taken for granted that the judges would acquiesce and had been astonished a fortnight earlier when the Lord Chief Justice, Sir Alexander Cockburn, had written to the Lord Chancellor (Lord Chelmsford) conveying the judiciary's 'strong and unanimous feeling of insuperable repugnance'[4] to their proposed new duties.

The judges' objections fell under three headings: firstly, they

[1] See *The Times*, 10 Apr. 1867. One alteration made to the election law during 1867 was the clause in the Reform Bill prohibiting payment for conveyances in boroughs, excepting the four large rural boroughs. See below, p. 47, n. 2.

[2] It is hard to resist the conclusion that in spite of all his exertions Disraeli did not consider the Bill of very much importance. It is referred to only once in his official life (cf. Monypenny and Buckle, iv. 581), and a search in the Disraeli Papers unearthed only one letter on the subject, which is referred to below, p. 40, n. 3.   [3] For the debate see *3 Hans.* cxc (13 Feb. 1868), 700–27.

[4] *P.P. 1867–8*, lvi. 491–3. On 31 Jan. the Lord Chancellor had written to the Chief Justice asking him to consult the judges as to 'the best mode of providing

firmly believed that to make them try election petitions would be to subject their decisions to public debate and partisan acrimony and their prestige must inevitably suffer; secondly, since these duties were 'altogether beyond' the scope of those they undertook they could not 'with justice or propriety' be forced upon them; lastly, they pleaded overwork, and asked the Chancellor, as head of the profession, 'to protect us, if possible, against this, in every respect, most objectionable measure'.[1]

Faced with this formidable opposition, Disraeli admitted his disappointment, but did not wish to exert pressure on the judicial body. As a *faute de mieux* he proposed a 'Parliamentary Elections Court' of somewhat higher status than the 'panel of eminent lawyers' proposed in the previous year, but still with less prestige than the judges of the High Court. The court would consist of three members who would each be paid £2,000 a year —in order to attract such men 'as would command the confidence of the House and country'. They would try petitions locally and there would be no appeal from their decisions, but the proviso in the Act of 1854 for appointing a Royal Commission on a joint address would still be preserved, to meet cases where the court believed that they had not got to the root of the corruption.

For the Opposition Gladstone refused to pronounce on the principle of the Bill, but pointed out that all those in favour of transferring jurisdiction agreed that it should only be to the highest tribunal possible, and that to establish a tribunal without any parallel in the history of the British courts would create new difficulties without solving old ones. He added, however, that it was much easier to find fault with the ministerial proposal than to suggest an alternative course.

This was by way of rebuke to the two Liberals who were afterwards to prove the most indefatigable opponents of the Bill—Ayrton[2] and Bouverie.[3] Both were strong supporters of

assistance for the event of a General Election'. Cockburn's reply (afterwards printed as a parliamentary paper) was dated 6 Feb. and began by saying that he had procured a copy of the Bill and found—apparently for the first time—that the Government intended to transfer jurisdiction to the courts. This is another indication that the Bill of 1867 had made little or no impact outside the House of Commons.

[1] Ibid.   [2] Liberal M.P. for Tower Hamlets.
[3] Liberal M.P. for Kilmarnock, Bouverie had been chairman of the ineffectual Totnes Election Committee. See above, p. 31.

the existing system and made speeches declaiming any public lack of confidence in the House Election Committees. Bright pointed out that no petition ever came from large cities such as Birmingham, Manchester, or Glasgow. He inferred from this that larger constituencies—and of course the ballot—would obviate the necessity of transferring jurisdiction. Berkeley also spoke for the ballot.

With the exception of Knatchbull-Hugessen, all the members of the Select Committee of the previous year who spoke expressed bitter disappointment at the judges' reaction, and felt that the proposed court would be worse than useless. Why, asked Lowe, should the judges refuse a duty imposed on them by Parliament? 'They are like the meanest public servants, only a body of public servants.' Sir Robert Collier and Russell Gurney said the same thing more diplomatically. Sir Roundell Palmer reminded the House that the whole of the judicial arrangements were then under review and that this might dispose of the overwork argument.

Since the Bill was supported by the leaders of both parties the press welcomed it with varying degrees of enthusiasm. *The Times*, still in the middle of the Delane era, had several outspoken leading articles deriding the existing system, asserting that there was an 'overwhelming' public opinion in favour of a transfer and censuring the judges for their recalcitrance. Unless the Commons were to insist on their original plan their sincerity (which had been suspect for a long time) would be everywhere called in question. *The Times* hinted that the judges were refusing a great honour for insubstantial reasons and was quite sure that any other tribunal would be an alteration for the worse. The subject was especially urgent since 'the great increase in the number of the moneyed class is as threatening a spring of danger as the adoption of Household Suffrage'.[1]

The opinions of the most influential daily newspaper were not shared by the most influential weekly.[2] In a style as pungent as *The Times*, the *Saturday Review* stated what it considered to be

---

[1] *The Times*, 13 Feb. 1868. See also issues of 14–15 Feb. It is hard to see where the evidence of that 'overwhelming public opinion' can be found, since the issue had not been canvassed before, and *The Times* itself had ignored the Bill of 1867.

[2] The *Saturday Review* reached the peak of its influence in this year, the last of John Douglas Cook's editorship. See M. M. Bevington, *The Saturday Review 1855–1858* (New York, 1941), p. 319, also *Saturday Review*, 22 Feb. 1868.

the defects of the Bill: the Government were allowing petitions still to be tried as actions between two parties instead of having a general investigation into the state of a constituency; for this purpose judges would be no better than members of the House —what was needed was Commissioners with inquisitorial powers; no step was being taken to curb expenditure, especially the 'endless customary tolls' which were inflicted on members, or paid agency which was indefensible on any political theory and 'productive of illimitable corruption'. Nor would extra penalties help: it would be much better for the House to agree on efficient methods of inquiry rather than to banish or crush culprits whom the present difficulty was to catch.

Press reaction and the feeling in both parties that the dignity of the House demanded that their ancient privilege, if it had to be transferred, should go only to the highest judicial tribunal, and not to a new makeshift court, made Disraeli modify his plan. On the second reading[1] (on 5 March) he admitted that the objections were well founded and offered a compromise: that two judges of the Common Pleas, Exchequer, or Queen's Bench be detailed solely for the trial of election petitions and otherwise have the rank of 'Honorary Justices'—but with full salaries. If the House were willing to pass the second reading *pro forma* a new clause would be drafted as soon as possible embodying the changes. This, Disraeli added, should meet the Lord Chief Justice's objection about derangement of business. Gladstone agreed to this course.

Commenting on the change in the Government's plan *The Times* noted that there was more earnestness now than there had been before in Parliament's attitude to corruption: the leaders of both parties were glad to play the role of moral reformers.[2] The new proposal was far more worthy of consideration than the old. Even the *Saturday Review*, while reiterating its preference for Commissioners ('Well-trained barristers might do well what country gentlemen have up to now done badly'), admitted that the Bill was better than nothing.[3] A speedy passage through both Houses seemed assured.

[1] *3 Hans.* cxc (5 Mar. 1868), 1141–3. Disraeli pleaded haste as an explanation of the previous plan. His speech on 5 Mar. was the first on the Bill that he made as Prime Minister.

[2] *The Times*, 7 Mar. 1868.

[3] *Saturday Review*, 4 Apr. 1868. 'The truth is that the Government Bill is only a

When the committee debate opened, however, on 16 March Disraeli found himself faced with a back-bench revolt of modest proportions—old Tories, such as Henley and Wykeham-Martin, joined with Ayrton, Bouverie, and the few Liberal back-benchers who objected in principle to the Commons' abdicating their rights and allowing an outside body to 'brand with infamy' their members.[1] These were followed by the members of boroughs that had been, or were to be, proved incurably corrupt, e.g. Vanderbyl of Yarmouth, Kinglake of Bridgwater, and Knatchbull-Hugessen of Sandwich. Lastly, there were some few Irish Liberals who feared—although the Bill did not yet apply to Ireland—that the Irish judges, who were markedly more partisan than the British, would have the same powers conferred on them.[2]

As the Opposition did not amount to more than fifty they could only harass and delay once it became clear that Gladstone, who played a very minor role in these debates, was not going to oppose the Bill. The Government was also reinforced by the Liberal members of the Select Committee, Sir Robert Collier and Whitbread, as well as Serjeant Gaselee and John Stuart Mill. The strength of the pro-Government forces was shown on the opening night when an amendment to retain jurisdiction in the hands of the House was defeated by a large majority. The principle was then clearly acceptable to the House—and the Government could scarcely have been certain of this before, owing to the lack of a second reading debate.

The committee debate proceeded with long intervals—16 March, 21 May, 25 June, 6 July. The Government were now convinced that it would pass before the end of the session and did not trouble to alter the course of business to give it precedence.[3] Nevertheless, as the debates proceeded, the Govern-

---

half-measure. The whole of our election system requires overhauling. It is better to do what is proposed than to do nothing, but far more will yet have to be done before we have exhausted all reasonable legal efforts to put down or to detect bribery.'

[1] For this debate see *3 Hans.* cxci (16 Mar. 1868), 296–321.

[2] The Bill was afterwards extended to Ireland and Scotland.

[3] This delay caused a remonstrance from a Conservative back-bencher, Darby Griffith, to Disraeli in the form of a question in the House challenging his sincerity in trying to get the Bill passed. Disraeli replied that there was no need for undue haste. Cf. *3 Hans.* cxciii (2 July 1868), 520–1. The same back-bencher was very indignant that the Prime Minister went back on his resolution to award a contested

ment had to take into account not only the obstructive tactics of Ayrton and Bouverie, but also the attempts of their own followers to broaden the scope of the Bill. On 6 July Mill succeeded in carrying an amendment to make the Bill operative only until 1870. On the same day[1] Lowe objected to the clause creating two new judges: how could two judges, he asked, try one-tenth of the petitions to be expected? Lowe proposed an amendment leaving out the word 'two' from the clause—his own suggestion was three. Serjeant Gaselee concurred and suggested that the judges would be willing enough to do an election circuit if they were paid an extra £500 a year. Others objected that the 'Honorary Justices' would have nothing to do between elections. Despite Disraeli's warning that the Lowe amendment would bring the Bill back to the Government's original proposal, which had proved unacceptable to the judges, it passed by a majority of 136 votes to 71.

Disraeli grumbled about the 'great difficulties he had to contend with' and promised a fresh statement. Three days later he said that the 'unequivocal' decision of the committee had been accepted by the Government and they had abandoned the 'Honorary Justices' clause. Instead he offered the following:[2] at the beginning of each Michaelmas term, each of the three superior Courts of Common Law would by majority decision elect one of their number to try election petitions;[3] each judge so elected would receive an extra £500 a year;[4] to relieve pressure of work in the courts three extra judges would be appointed; since the measure was experimental no vacancy in the courts would be filled without the consent of Parliament.[5]

The third proposal proved far more acceptable to the House than the others. An amendment by Ayrton requiring the election judges to accept resolutions of the House was defeated by a majority of more than three to one, and to Bouverie's question

seat to a 'pure' runner-up and wrote him a letter (7 July 1868) broadly hinting that he was deserting his own convictions. No reply has been preserved. Cf. *Disraeli Papers*, xxiii. 16.

[1] *3 Hans.* cxciii (6 July 1868), 722–58.

[2] See ibid. (9 July 1868), 915–17.

[3] The three chiefs—the Lord Chief Justice (Queen's Bench), the Lord Chief Baron (Exchequer), and the Chief Justice of the Common Pleas were exempted.

[4] Not, however, to be considered for pension purposes.

[5] If the three judges on the rota considered their number insufficient another judge (from the Exchequer) would be elected to join them.

whether the Government had received any communication from the judges, Disraeli made the fatuous reply that the Cockburn letter had been sent 'at a harsh period of the year, when people are not sanguine in their temperament', but now he was confident that the judges would 'take a larger and more expansive view of the circumstances of the case and of their duties'.[1] That pressure was applied discreetly behind the scenes seems probable. At any rate no further public statement was made by the Lord Chief Justice (or any other judge) and when the Bill passed into law the judiciary carried out its provisions with reluctance, as they admitted in the earliest petition trials, but without protest. The increase in their number and the extra £500 a year for the petition rota may also have helped to overbear in July the fears they had entertained in January.[2]

Disraeli had got what he wanted, but he was careful to see that the radicals did not transform his Bill into a much more thorough-going measure. Henry Fawcett, one of Bright's and Berkeley's friends, firmly believed that the returning officers' expenses should be borne by the county and borough rates (i.e. the voters) rather than the candidates, and he managed to carry an amendment to that effect on 18 July when the Government Whips were caught unprepared.

On the third reading, however, the amendment was left out and a motion by Fawcett for recommittal was defeated by a narrow majority.[3] The country squires who formed the backbone of both parties did not desire any increase in the rates, even though it would directly ease the financial burden on themselves as candidates.

[1] *3 Hans.* cxciii (10 July 1868), 1007–8.

[2] The *Morning Post* (11 July 1868) noted 'a very curious fact' in that the judge's protest had very little effect on the public. 'The majority thought the judges too sensitive, whilst not a few attributed to them the selfish motive of desiring to shirk additional and exceptional work.' Concerning Disraeli's motives in returning to the first proposal the *Saturday Review* (18 July 1868) wrote that the new judges were as 'foxes with firebrands at their tails set by a sagacious Cabinet among the Liberal standing corn'.

[3] In the words of the *Saturday Review* (25 July 1868) Disraeli had managed successfully to appeal from 'the free opinion of a Committee of one night to the prepared judgment of a carefully packed Committee upon another'. The amendment was first carried on 18 July by 84 votes to 76. The third reading amendment was defeated by 102 votes to 91. Fawcett also proposed a deposit of £100—to be sacrificed if the candidate did not poll one-tenth of the votes secured by the successful candidate. He withdrew this proviso on 18 July in order to carry the amendment, with the intention of bringing it up again on the report stage.

Other defeated amendments included Schreiber's proposal to postpone the municipal elections until the parliamentary election had been held; one by Beresford Hope to prohibit the use of public houses as committee rooms, and yet another by Mill to abolish paid canvassers. Newspapers of both political colours expressed regret that these amendments failed. The Bill passed through the Lords in five days and received the royal assent on 31 July 1868.[1]

The passing of the Election Petitions and Corrupt Practices at Elections Act, 1868[2] was greeted by the press with universal approval. Conservative papers, though critical of the original proposal, found the final settlement quite acceptable.[3] The Liberal papers for once found no reason to doubt Disraeli's sincerity and gave him due credit for his persistence in the face of obstruction from eccentric Liberals.[4] Of the independent papers, *The Times*, which had approved all along of the principles of the Bill while criticizing details—especially the composition of the election court—gave unstinted praise: 'The Bill, as it stands, marks an immense stride, which may be made hereafter the starting point of further progress, but sufficient for the present has been accomplished.' The *Saturday Review* modified its original tone to the extent of admitting that the Bill was a 'cumbrous but honest measure' and although all the most valuable reformist clauses—those of Beresford Hope, Mill, Fawcett, and Schreiber—had been struck out, at least their ideas had been discussed within the walls of Parliament; that was something new, and made the prospect of a better Bribery Bill 'neither very distant nor very hopeless'.[5]

[1] The Bill received its first reading in the Lords on 24 July and its third on 29 July.

[2] 31 & 32 Vict., c. 125; hereafter referred to as the Parliamentary Elections Act.

[3] The *Morning Post* (11 July 1868) called the Bill a measure 'eminently calculated to repress corrupt practices'.

[4] The *Daily News*, which in February had predicted the failure of the Bill, now warned Liberal obstructionists that the constituencies cared for the measure and not for mere details (11 July). The *Economist* (11 July 1868) said the Bill 'will administer a severe check to the more open and therefore more demoralising forms of bribery'.

[5] 'A step, therefore, and a great step has been gained; for in England, as elsewhere, the progress of ideas is a work of time; and one can scarcely expect Parliament to adopt at once and on a sudden, novel measures which in themselves may be intelligent and sound.' *Saturday Review*, 25 July 1868.

3

The election followed hard on the heels of the new Act. Parliament was prorogued on 31 July and although it was clearly understood that it would not reassemble, the dissolution was not announced until 11 November. Thus the campaign may be considered to have lasted over three months: most of the results were announced by 28 November.

It was an intensive campaign. Both parties made great efforts to capture the new working-class voters[1] and the future was foreshadowed by the appearance of two new party institutions, one national, the other local—the Conservative National Union and the Liberal Hundreds.[2] The former had been founded in December 1867, largely at the behest of the London and Westminster Working Men's Constitutional Association, to help to rally the working classes to the Conservative cause. For the first year of its existence the National Union did very little work and during the election practically its only task was to publish an inexpensive propagandist weekly, *The British Lion*. The minds of the leaders (especially Disraeli's) were groping after a new party machine, but it was not until after the election that Disraeli turned to Gorst and the National Union. There was a Conservative 'national committee' with Lord Abergavenny as chairman, but it proved quite ineffectual, and most of Disraeli's contacts with the candidates and associations in the country were maintained through Spofforth, who, since his partner Rose retired in 1859, had carried on the duties of principal agent, helping in the selection of candidates and providing money and information for the local associations. Disraeli expected that a large subscription would win the election for his party and pressed his wealthy supporters hard.[3] It seemed more important to find numerous candidates and provoke as many contests as possible rather than to improve the party organization.[4]

The Liberals, on the other hand, developed just in time for

---

[1] The total electorate of England and Wales had been increased by 88 per cent. by the Representation of the People Act, 1867.

[2] See below, Chap. IV, for the early history of the National Union.

[3] *Disraeli Papers*, xxiii, contain a number of letters from correspondents who had been asked for money. Disraeli expected his appeal to bring in £100,000.

[4] Only 211 seats were uncontested out of 658.

the election a new, highly efficient organization[1] in the large boroughs which had been made three-seat constituencies by the Redistribution Act of 1867. The Lords had intended to provide representation for a minority by inserting an amendment allowing each elector two votes only in a three-seat constituency. The new Liberal organization[2] set out to ensure that where the Liberals were in a minority they would win one of the three seats and where they were in a majority they would have all three. Its structure was democratic—an association to which every voter professing himself a Liberal might belong free of charge, and which in turn would elect a 'great committee' to regulate the campaign at the war level and maintain the closest contact with the voters. The 'Caucus', adumbrated in Birmingham by Joseph Chamberlain and Frank Schnadhorst,[3] soon spread to the other large boroughs, and mobilized its voting strength by directing different groups of voters to the candidate for whom they were to cumulate their votes. The scientific method of disproportional representation worked so well that in Birmingham and Glasgow, the two largest British cities after London, the Liberals easily won all three seats. In Liverpool, moreover, the Liberals managed to wrest one seat from the Conservatives. In the five counties with three seats each the cumulative vote had the intended effect of giving the minority party some representation—but in all cases the minority was Liberal.

The long course of the campaign was marked by the usual number of addresses and speeches by candidates in their own constituencies: nation-wide campaigning was still two elections off. The disestablishment of the Irish Church and other problems created by the Fenian rising were the chief issues canvassed, and they were canvassed *ad nauseam*.[4] For the great constitutional changes of the last two years both parties claimed the

[1] The Liberal Central Association, founded in 1861, still played a very minor role in electioneering. It came under the Whip's control in the 1870's

[2] For the development of the Caucus see H. J. Hanham, *Elections and Party Management* (London, 1959), pp. 125-54.

[3] Chamberlain, though long active in municipal politics, did not ener Parliament until 1876 when he was returned at a by-election. Schnadhorst started his career as a party agent in 1867.

[4] The *Saturday Review* wrote (7 Nov. 1868) that the human mind, with its limited capacity, 'may well decline to receive any additional arguments for or against the Irish Church'.

credit: the Conservatives for initiating the reforms, the Liberals for amplifying and extending them. The Parliamentary Elections Act was not considered sufficiently important to merit a reference, but as many as 151 election addresses mentioned the ballot as the ultimate remedy for electioneering evils.[1]

Rioting and open intimidation, which had diminished during the sparsely contested elections of 1857, 1859, and 1865, came back to the fore of the campaign. In Bristol a solicitor was so elated by the Liberal success that he mounted a white horse and led a triumphant procession through the streets, while his followers broke several windows of the opposing party's houses.[2] There were also several other boroughs where the riots were instigated by respectable people—a clergyman at Pontypool, several tradesmen at Tredegar—and there was an 'orange and green' skirmish at Manchester.

The final results, which gave the Liberals an increase of 15 seats on their 1865 majority, though disappointing to the Conservatives, was not unexpected, for it had been clear since late October that the minority clause was working in favour of the Liberals[3] through their superior organization.[4]

Both parties, however, profited by the election as far as their internal discipline was concerned. Disraeli's party was now more unified than at any time since the Corn Law split and the Liberals punished unreliable members by putting up more docile candidates against them. Serjeant Gaselee, the strong advocate of the Parliamentary Elections Act and Bernal Osborne lost their seats in this way; at the end of the election the latter uttered a violent philippic against all the corrupt practices which he said had disgraced the contest, but he did not lodge a petition.

---

[1] Bright's was the most noteworthy: 'Whether I look to the excessive cost of elections, or to the tumult which so often attends them, or to the unjust and cruel pressure which is so frequently brought to bear upon the less independent class of voters, I am persuaded that the true interest of the public and of freedom will be served by the system of secret and free voting', quoted in Morley, *Life of Gladstone*, ii. 367.

[2] The members for Bristol were Henry Berkeley and Samuel Morley.

[3] Cf. Monypenny and Buckle, *Life of Beaconsfield*, v. 89.

[4] The *Saturday Review* (7 Nov. 1868) commented: 'There is no instance in which any candidate of remarkable eminence will find or seek an entrance to Parliament through the door which ingenious theorists have persuaded the House of Lords to open.'

4

The general election resulted in thirty-four petitions from boroughs of the most varied kind all over England and Wales,[1] and at once provided a test of the efficiency of the new tribunal. The election law, intricate as it had been before 1865, was now further complicated by the additional penalties for bribery and the limited right to pay for conveyances.[2] The doctrine of agency, which had never been properly defined, had to be stretched to cover the new party machinery, and, as often happens in the development of case-law, the facts existed for quite an appreciable time before the theory was adapted to them. Although the complexity of the election law was partly due to the imprecision of the statutes themselves, the conflicting decisions of the House Election Committees had also played their part; and while they in turn had been attributed to the inexperience and partisanship of the committees, the ingenuity of election lawyers in 'pelting each other with cases'[3] to find precedents to their taste, made for further confusion.

The structure of the new tribunal contained features which might well have caused the judiciary misgivings, had they considered them instead of the general arguments about diminished prestige and overwork, which they thought sufficient to make Disraeli drop his original scheme. The election judges were required to try as a private lawsuit between petitioner and respondent what was really a quasi-criminal proceeding in which the constituency in particular and the public generally were interested. They could not go beyond the charges made in the petition, and if the petitioners wished at any stage to withdraw their case they could do so on payment of costs. If the judges thought that they had not unearthed the full facts their only remedy was to report to the Speaker that corrupt practices prevailed extensively—and, by usage, this clause soon came to apply only to bribery and undue influence, not treating.

Again, the flood of petitions after the first general election meant that each of the three judges had to try separately, and

[1] There were two cases only, neither of them important, from counties in England and Wales—Norfolk North and Yorkshire, West Riding. See below, p. 57.
[2] Section 36 of the Reform Act, 1867, made conveyance of voters *in boroughs only*, an illegal practice.
[3] W. Ballantine, *Some Experiences of a Barrister's Life* (London, 1890), ii. 41.

without a jury, some ten cases which between them covered most aspects of the rather amorphous election law, with no better guide than a host of conflicting decisions of House Election Committees (which in any case did not bind them) and with little time for consultation. On a point of law they could state a special case, but not on a point of fact.[1]

Nor did the personnel of the first election rota, two elderly judges of the Exchequer and Queen's Bench, and a younger one from the Common Pleas who had built up a great reputation in mercantile cases,[2] seem destined for success, as only one of the three (Baron Martin) had any political experience. (He had been Liberal member for Pontefract from 1847 to 1850, but had not been involved in a petition.)

Nevertheless, the election judges immediately set to work on their new duties and not only succeeded in dealing with the cases in a more satisfactory manner than the House Committees, but their decisions provided the beginnings of a *corpus* of election law far more scientific than the old. That they were able to do this was due in part to the skill of the new genre of election lawyers. The politicians, finding they had now to face a trial in open court, turned from the old House of Commons practitioners to the best criminal lawyers of the day. Three serjeants, Ballantine, Parry, and Sargood, and a younger Queen's Counsel, Henry Hawkins, appeared in almost all the English cases.[3] The main credit, however, must go to the judges themselves and especially to the youngest, Mr. Justice Willes, who gave several leading judgements and was, where possible, consulted by his older colleagues.[4]

[1] A special case was one referred to the entire Court of Common Pleas—after 1875 the Court of Queen's Bench.

[2] The first three English judges were Baron Martin (Exchequer), Mr. Justice Blackburn (Queen's Bench), and Mr. Justice Willes (Common Pleas).

[3] Ballantine was largely overshadowed by Hawkins, who appeared as his leader in one petition (Westminster). They opposed each other in the first Tichborne trial. Ballantine was the original of Chaffanbrass in Trollope's *Orley Farm*. Hawkins was uniquely distinguished both as election lawyer and judge. See below, pp. 51, n. 1, 197.

[4] As the Irish judges come in for their share of censure in these pages it may be stated here that Mr. Justice Willes was a native of Cork and a graduate of Trinity College, Dublin. He played a prominent part in drafting the Common Law Procedure Act of 1852, was raised to the Bench in 1856 without ever taking silk and was especially authoritative in cases on mercantile law. In addition to the leading judgements Willes drafted the rules of procedure for the election courts (see *P.P. 1868–9*, l. 173). He was made a privy councillor with the intention of being

The English petitions may be classified as follows:

1. Five cases which were important for the development of election law.
2. Three cases where corrupt practices were extensive and where the judge recommended a Royal Commission.
3. The remaining twenty-six cases of which six were successful.

1. The first important 'legal' case, that of New Windsor,[1] was also the first English[2] petition trial under the 1868 Act. Charges of bribery, treating, and colourable employment were brought against the sitting member. The judge was Mr. Justice Willes.

The colourable employment charge was abandoned by the petitioners. Of two charges of bribery one was proved, and here Willes laid down that in order to defeat the election bribery had to be either general, or by a candidate, or by an agent, but for agency 'authority to canvass' was necessary, and in this case the briber (a card-messenger) did not have that authority. The undue influence charge failed through lack of proof—though here agency was not denied. The treating charges, alleged that the candidate and his chief agent had treated to the extent of £27 at a meeting of Oddfellows (mainly tradesmen) within three weeks of the passing of the 1868 Act and a fortnight of the beginning of the election campaign. Here Willes found the practice to be 'objectionable' but since he did not consider the Oddfellows a political society or association he could not infer an exclusively corrupt motive. The petition was dismissed.[3]

The other cases were from Bewdley, Coventry, Tamworth, and Westminster.

At the Bewdley election the Conservative member, Sir Richard Glass, gave two agents over £4,000 which was spent mainly in treating—over twenty public houses were kept open and everyone got free drinks. The defence was that the chief agent, who was secretary of the Conservative Working Men's

---

promoted to the Judicial Committee, at the age of 58; but being sent on assize as a criminal judge taxed even his versatility and in a fit of depression he shot himself (1872). See *D.N.B.* lxi. 286–7 (1900 edition).

[1] The electorate of New Windsor in 1871 was 1,751. Cf. *P.P. 1872*, xlvii. 403. It had been deprived of a seat by the Reform Act of 1867. The sitting member, Roger Eykyn (Liberal), had been elected after a petition in 1866 and in the general election defeated his Conservative rival by 803 votes to 795.

[2] The first petition trial of all was heard at Wexford, on 12 Jan 1869.

[3] For judgement see *P.P. 1868–9*, xlviii. 208–12.

Association at Bewdley, paid for the drinks in his capacity as secretary, not as agent to Glass.

Mr. Justice Blackburn[1] ruled that the plea of double function failed. Glass apparently intended the money to be spent honestly, but had exercised no control over it, and since the secretary was clearly Glass's agent he was guilty of corrupt treating within the meaning of the Act of 1854. Thus, at its first appearance the plea that corrupt treating could be carried out on behalf of a candidate under the guise of entertainment by a party association was ruled out.

In the Tamworth case the difference between evidence of bribery and evidence of treating was clearly set down by Mr. Justice Willes. The practice before the House Election Committees had been to require proof of agency before allowing evidence of treating, but to allow evidence of bribery independently. Willes extended that by saying that while bribery was by definition corrupt, treating had to be linked to corrupt motivation.[2] The further point at issue in Tamworth was whether an energetic labourer who emphasized his own importance by hiring 130 men to 'protect' Sir Henry Bulwer was guilty of bribery. Willes, having noted that the precedents of House Committees were inconclusive,[3] decided on the merits of the case—a mere £64 being distributed between 130 and the fact that only nineteen of the men were voters—that the suspicion on which the petitioners acted was unfounded. Moreover, the petitioners damaged their case by omitting to call some material witnesses.

The Westminster case was brought by the supporters of John Stuart Mill against W. H. Smith[4] who had defeated him by a considerable majority. Smith had spent over £9,000, much of it on cabs, while the Liberals spent barely £2,000. The London and Westminster Working Men's Constitutional Association also spent 'substantial sums' to induce votes for Smith.

---

[1] *P.P. 1868–9*, xlviii. 6–11. Cf. *The Times*, 27 Jan. 1869.

[2] 'Nothing, therefore, can make it more obvious than that the Legislature did not intend that every bit of bread or sup of drink given to a voter in the course of an election should have the effect of defeating that election.' *P.P. 1868–9*, xlviii. 174.

[3] In three cases (Leicester, Oxford, Hull) House Election Committees had decided that employment of voters constituted bribery; in three others (Cambridge, Lambeth, Preston) they decided to the contrary.

[4] Smith was the son in 'W. H. Smith and Son'.

Baron Martin who judged the petition considered the association an 'independent agency' and said that candidates could
only be held responsible for a small number of agents. This
judgement, in spirit at least, runs counter to the Bewdley
judgement and shows how imperfectly the new party institutions were understood. It was not until 1880 that candidates
were held responsible for the acts of party associations, no
matter how numerous, which directly adopted them and were
obviously working on their behalf.[1] Incidentally, the hearing
showed that most of the funds of the Constitutional Society
were subscribed to by Smith and his business partners.

The last technical case of importance was the Coventry case,
where Mr. Justice Willes ruled that a supper given to celebrate
the efforts of the Conservatives at registration in the city was not
treating.[2]

2. The three English petitions that resulted in the appointment of Royal Commissions were from Beverley, Bridgwater,
and Norwich.

Beverley[3] was an ancient borough of 12,000 people and 2,672
electors. The tradition of bribery in the borough at both municipal and parliamentary elections went back many years,
certainly as far as 1841, but it was accentuated after 1857 when
Sir Henry Edwards became the Conservative M.P. Edwards
was the chairman of the Beverley Waggon Company and set
about making himself the political boss of the town. He established a Conservative Working Men's Association—staffed
largely by officials of his company—and provided it with a
constant flow of money for bribery, not only at election times
but between elections. His nominees secured control of the

[1] *P.P. 1868–9*, xlviii. 198–203. In this case the Conservatives hired both Hawkins
and Ballantine with Hawkins as the leader. Ballantine advised against calling as a
witness 'that old fool', the Hon. Robert Grimstone, who was the very unbusinesslike
agent for Smith; but Hawkins insisted, and ever afterwards was quite sure that he
would have lost the case but for the transparently honest explanations Grimstone
gave for the high expenses he had incurred. Cf. R. Harris (ed.), *The Reminiscences of
Sir Henry Hawkins* (London, 1904), i. 286.

[2] 'The mere fact of eating and drinking, even with the connection which this
supper had with politics, is not sufficient to make out treating.' *P.P. 1868–9*,
xlviii. 53.

[3] Petitions were lodged by the Liberals in 1857 and 1859 but did not succeed.
See *P.P. 1857*, v. 159; *P.P. 1859*, iii. 107. For the 1868 petition see *P.P. 1868–9*, xlviii.
2–6. For the Royal Commission see *P.P. 1870*, xxix. 5–22 (Report); 41–804 (Minutes
of Evidence).

corporation and of the 'pasture-masters';[1] even the local charities
were manipulated to Edwards's advantage. Though Edwards's
supporters 'exercised an almost absolute control and mastery
in the public and municipal affairs'[2] of Beverley the brains of
his organization was one man, Wreghitt, who was in effect the
arch-briber.

After 1857 the Liberal chances diminished appreciably and
when Anthony Trollope went there in 1865 in his second attempt
to get into Parliament his agent left him under no illusions over
his prospects.[3] Nevertheless he did not spend more than £400
and (with his colleague) was found guiltless of 'irregular payments' by the Commissioners.[4]

The gradual extension of Edwards's rule did not mean that
the Liberals gave up trying. Out of 2,700-odd voters in 1868
nearly 1,000 were open to bribery and of these a good third were
known as 'rolling stock'—an adequate bribe would make them
roll to the other side. The rest looked upon the money payment
—generally given quite openly—as their right, and regarded it
as a bribe only if offered by a candidate of a different party. No
figures were issued, but it was believed that many were bribed
by one side and voted for the other.

The Commissioners unearthed all this information in spite of
a desperate last-minute effort by Edwards to impede them.[5]
They scheduled him as having offered bribes at all the elections
since 1857, and likewise his fellow candidate, Captain Kennard,
in 1868—although Baron Martin, who heard the petition and
found the election void at common law on account of general
bribery, had exonerated both candidates and merely blamed
the party zealots.

[1] The Beverley Corporation controlled the ancient grazing rights of the
borough and derived an income of £4,000 a year from them. The pasture-masters
were elected by the borough.
[2] *P.P. 1870*, xxix. 11.
[3] Cf. A. Trollope, *An Autobiography* (Oxford edn. 1950), pp. 298–300, 315.
[4] *P.P. 1870*, xxix. 20. Trollope immortalized Beverley as Percycross in *Ralph the
Heir*. Sir Henry Edwards may be identified as Mr. Griffenbottom and Wreghitt as
Trigger.
[5] Edwards's counsel, after the inquiry had lasted three weeks, tried to deny the
right of the Commissioners to the Town Hall. The Commissioners ordered the
borough police to expel him but they refused. There was an uproar and the Commissioners adjourned to the Sessions House of the East Riding where they summoned the witnesses to follow them. Two refused and were committed to York
Castle for contempt.

To Bridgwater[1] belongs the distinction of having been the most corrupt borough of the post-Reform period. With a population of 12,000 in 1861, mostly employed in the coasting trade or in local factories, its electorate was doubled by the Reform Act of 1867. The local magnates were largely Liberals but all elections were keenly contested. There had been a petition in 1866 when one Westropp, who had nursed the borough for ten years and spent £10,000, was unseated for gross bribery. Westropp stood again in 1868, and on polling day he and his Conservative colleague were leading by majorities of 129 and 148 respectively three hours before the close of poll. In that short time some 290 voted Liberal compared with only seventy Conservative, and the two Liberals, Alexander Kinglake[2] and Philip Vanderbyl, who had been unseated at Great Yarmouth in 1865, won the seats. The election judge found that a large number of the Liberal votes during these three hours had been openly bought by the Liberal agents, and therefore declared the election void at common law. A Royal Commission was shortly sent down to the borough.

The Bridgwater Commissioners[3] made the most exhaustive inquiry ever visited on a British constituency. They surveyed back as far as 1832 and were able to state with certainty that at every election since then 75 per cent. of the constituency were 'hopelessly addicted' to giving or receiving bribes, and a very large part of the remainder to giving them. Bribery was the chronic disease of the borough. Every candidate either bribed or afterwards paid the 'fixtures' left by his agents or his predecessor. The accounts were invariably fraudulent. The real bills through long practice were sent in months after the election and so circumvented a petition. Among the various candidates whom the Commissioners found 'privy and assenting to some of the corrupt practices' at the elections were George Patton,

---

[1] See *P.P. 1866*, x (Report of the Select Committee on 1866 petition); *P.P. 1868-9*, xlix (Minutes of Evidence and Judgement on 1868 petition); *P.P. 1870*, xxx (Minutes of Evidence and Report of Royal Commission).

[2] Kinglake was the author of *Eothen* and the *History of the Crimean War*.

[3] The Commissioners were Thomas Chisholm Anstey, Q.C. (Chairman), Charles Edward Coleridge, and Edwin Plumer Price. Their inquiry began on 23 Aug. and ended on 25 Nov. 1869—lasting 47 days in all. The Commissioners issued two reports; the first giving their general conclusions (*P.P. 1870*, xxx. 5-7) appeared on 4 Nov.; the second giving the detailed history of the inquiry (ibid. 13-46) on 20 Dec.

afterwards Lord Justice Clerk of Scotland, and Walter Bagehot[1] both at the same election in 1866. Bagehot's candidature merits a closer study in the light of his evidence before the Commission.[2] He had been looking for a seat since 1865 and had been beaten at Manchester in the general election. When Westropp was unseated on petition in 1866 Bagehot was approached by the local Liberals to stand at the by-election—he had some business connexions there. He admitted that he knew of the bad reputation of the borough but claimed he thought that the general election had been fairly fought. Lovibond, the chief Liberal personality (and briber) assured Bagehot that the by-election would be fought fairly; nevertheless he insisted on an advance contribution of £600 'just in case' of a petition. Bagehot came to the borough, and made a speech about electoral purity which was politely received and afterwards printed, but his canvass was not very successful. On election day he had an uncomfortable feeling that votes were not honestly coming his way, but he had no direct knowledge that they were being purchased. However, the Conservative supporters of the future Lord Justice Clerk spent £2,000 in direct bribes of £10 each in a few hours and so won the election. After a discreet interval Lovibond and his friends waited on Bagehot and told him that £800 had been spent on his behalf, in addition to the £200 legitimate expenses, and asked to be reimbursed.

The same situation had faced Sir John Shelley, nephew of the poet, at an earlier Bridgwater election. He had flatly refused to pay the 'fixtures' left by his predecessor and so threw away his hopes of being elected at a later date. The great authority on the British Constitution, however, after some initial embarrassment, paid Lovibond, knowing his action was morally impermissible though he afterwards pleaded that he did not know it was also illegal.[3]

---

[1] Bagehot had become editor of *The Economist* in 1860, but for eight years before that he had been in his family business—shipowning and banking at Langport in Somersetshire, not far from Bridgwater. Cf. W. Irvine, *Walter Bagehot* (London, 1939), pp. 44–47.

[2] Bagehot's biographers gloss over this episode. In the most recent study, *Walter Bagehot* (London, 1959), N. St. John-Stevas writes (p. 17): 'Like Trollope, Walter had failed to secure election because of his integrity,' but fails to make the important distinction that Trollope was exonerated by the Beverley Commission, while the Bridgwater Commissioners scheduled Bagehot for corrupt payments. A selection from Bagehot's evidence is given below, App. III.

[3] Bagehot did not stand at the by-election caused by Patton's elevation to the

The Norwich Commissioners discovered that a considerable portion of the electorate (which had been increased from 5,000 to 12,000 in 1868) were susceptible to small bribes, and this was particularly true of the artisans. One agent had openly distributed guineas in the market place. However, the Commission did not schedule the candidate, Sir Henry Stracey. The borough was considered less incorrigible than the other two, and it took a later Royal Commission to make a more precise estimate of its corruptibility.[1]

3. Three Royal Commissions were set up in Ireland as a result of the petition trials—in Cashel, Sligo, and Dublin.[2] Cashel, with an electorate of less than 300, was the smallest borough in the United Kingdom, but two candidates had spent nearly £4,000 in wholesale bribery. In Sligo (also very small) bribery and treating were mixed with 'horrible intimidation' which featured mobs and repression by the troops.[3] In Dublin the Conservative candidate, Sir Arthur Guinness, spent a total of £16,000, although the electorate did not exceed 5,000. He had a vast network of committees which from the variety of officials and the vagueness of their duties were plainly excuses for bribery and colourable employment.[4]

When the Government received the Commissioners' reports two Bills, to disfranchise the boroughs of Beverley, Bridgwater, Sligo, and Cashel were quickly passed through both Houses and became law on 4 July and 1 August 1870.

The remaining petitions in the three countries did not provide much interest. In Bradford the Liberals petitioned against Henry Ripley and the Conservatives against W. E. Forster. The charges against the latter were dismissed as 'perfectly contemptible', but Ripley and his agents were proved to have spent

Bench in 1867, but he still hoped that 'purity might possibly prevail' and that he might conscientiously fight Bridgwater at the next general election. By then, however, Lovibond had hooked a much larger fish, Vanderbyl, the briber of Great Yarmouth. Bagehot stood for London University but failed at his third and final attempt. The very extensive schedule of bribers drawn up by the Commissioners included the names of Bagehot, Kinglake, Brogden, Vanderbyl, and Patton.

[1] Cf. P.P. 1868–9, xlix; P.P. 1870, xxxi. 829–916.

[2] For the Minutes of Evidence and the Reports of the Royal Commissions see P.P. 1870, xxxii. 5–394 (Cashel); 625–1053 (Sligo); xxxiii (Dublin).

[3] The Conservative candidate in Sligo (Major Knox, proprietor of the Irish Times) spent £4,000 on bribery, his opponent £200—on mobs!

[4] His 'officials' included 'street agents', 'gutter agents', and 'clergymen to the ward'.

£7,000 in treating in about 100 public houses, and Ripley was unseated.[1]

The results at Blackburn and Drogheda were invalidated on the ground of general intimidation. In Bristol a 'test ballot' among the Liberal voters at which bribery was proved was judged to be the equivalent of bribery at the actual election.[2]

5

The results of the petition trials showed that the new tribunal was able to get at a good deal of evidence that might be concealed from House Committees. Nevertheless there were constituencies from which no petition was presented that were as corrupt as those that appeared in the courts—as the Select Committee of 1869–70 and the Royal Commissions of 1880 were to prove.[3] For example: the borough of Horsham appears only once in the petition lists in this period, but William Albery in his exhaustive history states categorically[4] that at every election between 1832 and its extinction in 1885 'it is certain that these forms of corruption (i.e. bribery, treating, intimidation, exclusive dealing and occasionally cooping or abduction) affected more or less the voting if not the result of the polling'. A major defect of the system was the absence of a legal limit to election expenditure. Although many thousands of pounds might be spent the candidate could not be unseated unless a positive act of corruption had been proved. The total election expenses officially accounted for were £752,000 in 1865; in 1868 they had risen to £1,382,252.[5] In both cases the actual figure must have been considerably higher.[6]

[1] P.P. 1868–9, xlviii. 35–45. The electors of Bradford numbered 20,600. The result of the petition aroused a lot of local indignation against the Conservatives. Cf. Bradford Review, 30 Jan. to 6 Feb. 1869.

[2] An early British counterpart of an American primary election. Test ballots occur occasionally during this period.   [3] See below, pp. 60–63, 136 ff.

[4] W. Albery, A Parliamentary History of the Ancient Borough of Horsham, 1295–1885 (London, 1927), pp. 490, 447–63. In 1875 Mr. Justice Quain unseated a Liberal because his agent had openly offered travelling expenses to the voters. Sir Hardinge Giffard (the new Attorney-General) then stood, but he found the influence of the corrupt payments too strong to overcome, and he was unsuccessful.

[5] The House of Lords had decided in 1854 (Cooper v. Slade) that a payment of travelling expenses by an agent was ipso facto corrupt under the Act of 1854. But the House of Commons Election Committees believed that corrupt motivation must be proved, and some judges were inclined to agree with them. Cf. P.P. 1860, x. 196; P.P. 1868–9, xlviii. 225–6.   [6] P.P. 1868–9, l. 37.

Another difficulty was that in spite of the judges the law regarding agency was still only loosely defined.[1] Again there was no statutory provision for reconciling conflicting judicial decisions. In 1872 occurred a grotesque judgement by Mr. Justice Keogh, that a successful Home Rule candidate in Galway County had by spiritual intimidation so disqualified himself that not only was he to be unseated but all his votes were to be considered as thrown away, and his opponent awarded the seat, although he had polled less than a quarter as many votes. The main charge was that the Home Rule candidate (Captain Nolan) had secured the support of the priests to such an extent that his landlord opponent (Captain Trench) was anathematized from the altars of the Catholic churches in the county. Trench's supporters on polling day widely circulated an advertisement that Nolan was disqualified on the ground of spiritual intimidation, but no effort was made to ascertain how many of the (mainly Irish-speaking) electors saw the notice, or how many of those who did could reasonably be expected to believe it. The Dublin Court of Common Pleas, to which the case was referred as a special case, backed the 'Keogh judgement' by a three to two majority and it was cited as a precedent until 1874, when the London Court of Common Pleas decided at Launceston that although his actions (or his agents') might disqualify a candidate during an election, the voters were not expected to know this until an election court had proved it.

As far as Scottish and Irish elections generally are concerned it can be said that at this time Scottish elections were remarkably free of bribery but there was some landlord intimidation, while treating and intimidation were widespread in Ireland and bribery to a lesser extent. These points will be elaborated later on.

Analysis of Petitions* (1868–72)

Country	Number presented	Number successful	Number of special cases	Number of Royal Commissions
England and Wales .	34	12	4	3
Scotland . .	1†	..	..	..
Ireland . . .	16	10	2	2

* Nine petitions were heard between 1869 and 1872.

† The solitary Scottish petition was from Greenock. It failed.

[1] The Act of 1868 allowed an election judge, when doubtful on a point of law, to state a special case for the full court.

CHAPTER III

The Ballot Act

I

THE Ballot Act of 1872 differed from the other stages in the improvement of electioneering morals in that it was not so much an *ad hoc* measure as the culmination of a long reformist struggle.

Enthusiasm for the ballot among members of Parliament reached its peak in the 1830's, and, as has been shown, there was subsequently a general decline of interest until by the mid-1860's only Henry Berkeley and a dedicated few among the radicals seriously advocated it.[1] In the reformist ferment after 1865 only the radicals raised the ballot-cry, the Conservatives were dead against it, and the official Liberal view was given by Gladstone on the first reading of the Reform Bill of 1866, when he explained that, although his Bill involved a major revision of the electoral system, yet: 'I do not . . . refer to such questions as the question of secret voting, or the question of shortening Parliaments, which we cannot undertake to view with favour either now or at a future time.'[2]

This view had not changed by 1868. The ballot was never seriously considered during the debates leading to the Parliamentary Elections Act. Most members of both parties expected that the transfer to the courts of jurisdiction over disputed elections would be enough to check corrupt practices. However, during the election campaign a larger number of addresses than usual (151 in all)[3] on the Liberal side invoked the principle of the ballot.

The peculiar features of the 1868 election, the long campaign leading to excessive canvassing and expenditure, the rowdiness and rioting, the flood of petitions, and the trials in open court,

---

[1] See above, p. 26. [2] *3 Hans.* clxxxii (12 Mar. 1866), 24.
[3] See above, p. 46.

caused the new Liberal Government a good deal of heart-searching between the final results in November and the opening of the new Parliament in January. The upshot was that the Speech from the Throne 'recommended' the setting-up of a Select Committee to inquire into the whole subject of parliamentary and municipal electioneering.

The Home Secretary, H. A. Bruce, proposed the motion for the committee on 4 March 1869. He gave three reasons—the high cost of recent elections, the high cost of petitioning, and the consequent exclusion from the Commons of able men of moderate means. At this preliminary stage there was no need for Bruce to mention his own views, but he added significantly that, although his constituents had been for sixteen years in favour of the ballot, he had always abstained from voting on the question, as he believed in the 'trustee' argument: since the election, however, he had changed his mind and thought the advantages outweighed the disadvantages.[1]

Gladstone followed immediately and said that: 'So far as the ballot goes, I think that in every Liberal Government which I can recollect . . . the Ballot has been an open question.' For the Conservatives, Gathorne Hardy, while supporting the motion, asked suspiciously whether the inquiry would be impartial, and not a cloak for people who had already changed their minds.[2] Gladstone assured him that it would, and repeated the assurance on a motion that the committee be instructed to consider the question of secret voting, which was moved on 16 March.

2

The Select Committee consisted of twenty-one members drawn, as usual, from all parties. Lord Hartington was Chairman, and he and Sir George Grey mainly represented the Whigs. The radicals had Bright (now President of the Board of Trade), Leatham, James, and Fawcett; the Conservatives, Gathorne Hardy, Cross, Raikes, Hicks-Beach, and W. H. Smith. The Committee sat for four months, and since it was then too late to present a report they published the evidence, deferring the

---

[1] *3 Hans.* cxciv (4 Mar. 1869), 648–59.
[2] For the debates see ibid. 659–63, 1470–1522.

report until the following session. On 11 February 1870 Hartington moved the formal reappointment of the committee for the
purpose of presenting the report.

As in the case of the 1860 Committee, the witnesses were of
very varied character, representative of every kind of electioneering activity—election judges, returning officers, party agents,
town councillors, members of Parliament with special interests,
and experts on voting systems.[1] The returning officers and party
officials were questioned on the whole range of parliamentary
and municipal elections in their constituencies, the others were
asked more restricted questions.

The evidence from the constituencies served first to confirm
the results of the petition trials. The secretary of the Reform
Club at Blackburn frankly admitted that the Liberals had
bribed just as much as the other side, and thought that 90 per
cent. of the municipal electorate was open to bribery.[2] The
Mayor of Bradford gave corroboratory evidence on the charges
which lost Ripley his seat.[3] The Mayor of Stalybridge said that
during the entire campaign from August to November the
borough lay 'under a perfect reign of terror'.[4]

Evidence came too from constituencies where no petition had
been presented. Bernal Osborne's denunciations of Nottingham's venality were borne out by a former town councillor, who
said that at least half the municipal electorate were corruptible
and that by giving them the vote the Act of 1867 had ensured
that the parliamentary elections would be equally corrupt. In
his opinion, the tradition of bribery at parliamentary elections
went back at least to 1837.[5] Several witnesses from Liverpool

---

[1] For the Minutes of Evidence see *P.P. 1868–9*, viii. The three English election
judges appeared before the committee—but not the Scottish or Irish judges. Sir
Charles Dilke, M.P., gave evidence regarding the ballot used in France and the
United States; Arthur Arnold (who had travelled in Greece) described the Greek
ballot; John Vesey Fitzgerald (former Colonial Secretary in Victoria) and Lt.-Col.
R. R. Torrens, M.P. (a former Treasurer in South Australia) described the ballot
techniques used in these States. The most important Irish witnesses were Dr. Butler,
Bishop of Limerick, and Alexander Spaight, Conservative M.P. for Limerick City.
The most prominent members from Ireland on the committee were The O'Conor
Don (Liberal) and Sir Frederick Heygate (Conservative). See below, p. 63.
[2] See above, pp. 56 ff. Blackburn was remarkable in that almost every kind of
corrupt practice was found there to some degree. *P.P. 1868–9*, viii. 146–50.
[3] Ibid. 136.
[4] Ibid. 179.
[5] Ibid. 41.

testified to open bribery at municipal and parliamentary elections.[1] One successful candidate went bankrupt shortly after his election in 1865 and a by-election became necessary. At the by-election neither side could afford to bribe, to the great disgust of the voters.

Liberal and Conservative witnesses charged each other indiscriminately with the corruption at Liverpool. Evidence from other constituencies (not on the petition lists) showed that neither party had the monopoly of undue influence. William N. Hodgson (then Conservative member for West Cumberland) had stood for Carlisle in 1868 against Sir Wilfrid Lawson, and had canvassed the employees of the London and North Western Railway Company of which he was a director. The day after the election those who voted against him were dismissed.[2] On the other hand, a Liberal mill-owner at Ashton-under-Lyne dismissed forty workers who had disobeyed 'instructions' to vote for the Liberal candidate, Milner Gibson, which were boldly posted up at their mill.[3]

Many of the allegations made before the Select Committee concerned intimidation in all its forms. Lurid stories were told of mob violence in many English and Irish borough elections, most of which had not reached the petition courts. The riots at Bristol[4] have been referred to above;[5] but rioting had also occurred in 1868 throughout Monmouthshire (where the damage to property amounted to £5,000) and at Ashton-under-Lyne (where roughs fought each other in the street).

Violence was even more prevalent at Irish elections. The Drogheda and Sligo cases have already been referred to, but additional evidence was furnished to the Select Committee. The General Officer Commanding the troops in Ireland claimed that the purpose of the military was to provide escorts for voters who would be afraid of the mobs that marched the streets in

[1] Ibid. 91–102, 103 ff. Evidence came also from Leeds. All these were large boroughs, but the smaller had their share of bribery too, as was shown by evidence from boroughs as far apart as Windsor, Brecon, and Cambridge.
[2] Hodgson was called before the committee and denied that he had anything to do with the dismissals—they were part of a general reorganization on account of new machinery, he said. See *P.P. 1868–9*, viii. 557–9.
[3] The Conservative agent at Ashton said that workers 'in every department, whether it would be working in the sand, or at a gravel-hole, or sweeping the streets' were influenced politically by their masters. Ibid. 123.
[4] Ibid. 196.   [5] See above, p. 46.

support of popular candidates. But he admitted under question-
ing that sometimes the soldiers escorted voters who did not wish
for this 'protection', although he insisted that as long as open
voting remained, law and order could not be maintained at Irish
elections unless the troops took a hand.[1] Gruesome (though
exaggerated) stories were told by an Irish Conservative member
for Limerick about the trials endured by him and his friends
during elections in the city.[2]

As might be expected, violence and mob rule were exercised
against the unpopular candidates and their supporters; the
Liberals and Irish nationalists had gained accordingly.

When they came to consider the vast nation-wide influence
of landlords in county elections, the Select Committee found
it difficult to draw the line between 'legitimate' and 'undue'
influence, especially since petitions from county constituencies
were so rare. Some interesting stories were told—of a landlord
in mid-Cheshire whose tenants supported a candidate during the
canvass and then unaccountably voted against him; of another
whose tenants asked him if they were free to vote as they
wished, and on his agreeing that they were, voted against his
candidate; and the two cases that caused the greatest stir—the
case of the Marquis of Lothian and the case of the hundred
tenants evicted at Cardiganshire (immediately after an election)
and the fund of £4,000 collected for them, mainly from the
subscriptions of fellow tenants.[3]

The evidence of one other type of undue influence, spiritual
intimidation was confined to Wales and Ireland. The burden of
it was that Welsh Dissenters and Irish Catholics were warned
from the pulpits of their respective chapels and churches that to
vote for certain candidates (always Conservative) would be a
sin and would incur spiritual penalties, if not damnation. No
Welsh minister appeared before the committee, but the Catholic

[1] *P.P. 1868–9*, viii. 513–21. The prominence of the military at every Irish general
election had been the subject of a number of parliamentary inquiries.

[2] Ibid. 285–96.

[3] Ibid. 265–71, 302 ff. The case of the Marquis of Lothian concerned a substantial
tenant who was refused a renewal of a nineteen-year lease because he had voted
against the candidate favoured by the Marquis. In a letter to the *Scotsman* (which
the editor forwarded to the Select Committee on 14 June 1869) Lothian said there
were 'many' reasons why he had not renewed the lease, 'but I should consider
myself acting unfairly if I did not say out at once that among them was the vote he
gave at the election' (ibid. appendix, 613–14).

Bishop of Limerick did, and managed to convince the committee that if secret elections were introduced no priest could force a penitent to reveal his vote, and that the seal of confession was inviolable.[1]

The three English election judges were asked for their opinions on the prevalence of corrupt practices, and to suggest improvements. The aged Baron Martin was of little use to the Select Committee. He said that the interpretation of the law on agency had caused the judges no difficulty. They had held a conference just before the election trials started, and Mr. Justice Willes, having gone into the decisions of House Election Committees 'very carefully', had told them that the relationship between candidate and agent was analogous to that of master and servant, not principal and agent.[2] On the basis of the petitions brought before him Baron Martin said that he thought intimidation hardly existed, and that the general opinion of the prevalence of bribery was 'exaggerated'.[3] Baron Martin's suggestions were that public houses be closed on polling days and that public nominations and, if possible, paid canvassers be abolished. He also suggested that if a candidate's expenses were unreasonably large they should be considered *prima facie* evidence of electoral corruption, even though no positively corrupt acts could be proved, but when questioned on this he admitted that he had derived the idea from Mr. Justice Willes, and referred the Select Committee to him.[4]

The omniscient Mr. Justice Willes endorsed this and also suggested that proof of treating be allowed to cover at least the week before the election, not just nomination and polling days, as was the custom, also that the votes of employed canvassers be disallowed and that no refreshments be provided for them. He pointed out that while bribery had been almost totally absent

[1] Commenting on the bishop's evidence Stanley Hyland, *Curiosities from Parliament* (London, 1955), p. 185, writes: 'It is doubtful whether anyone, at any time, has more skilfully or more courteously handled a Select Committee of the House of Commons.' Hyland gives an interesting, if scrappy, account of the evidence heard by the Select Committee.

[2] *P.P. 1868–9*, viii. 448. Thus the candidate could not evade responsibility for his agent's acts.

[3] Ibid. 445. Martin said that bribery was proved in three cases only out of the thirteen heard by him in 1868. He omitted to mention that Beverley was one of them.

[4] 'He (Mr. Justice Willes) has thought of it a good deal, and will be able to give you much better information than I can upon the subject.' Ibid. 452.

from the cases he had tried many forms of treating had been evident.[1]

Mr. Justice Blackburn believed that treating was extremely prevalent, and pleaded for more extensive discretionary powers for the judges in deciding what constituted a corrupt practice. He thought that a great deal of corrupt expenditure was being kept out of the official returns and advised that the time for petitioning be extended to cover their publication.[2] Curiously enough, each judge relied on his own petitions and ignored those tried by the others.

When the Select Committee came to draw up their conclusions[3] they were able to say that, as far as the English and Welsh counties were concerned, they were satisfied that an influence 'exceeding that which a respected landlord must always exercise in his neighbourhood' was often brought to bear on tenant farmers. In the Scottish counties, on the other hand, the tenants had in some areas been known to vote *en masse* against the landlord's favourites—but the landlord–tenant relationship in Scotland was on a more strictly commercial footing, and the Lothian case was rather exceptional.[4] The Irish counties again were *sui generis*, with the influence of the Catholic clergy set against that of the landlords. The committee, however, were agreed that some urgent change was needed in Irish electioneering and that the regular features of organized mobs and troops to dispel them ought to be replaced. They did not suggest any remedies for the evidence before them was very conflicting, and they did not know whether to believe the landlords' claim that many voters would have supported them through feelings of attachment had it not been for pressure from the pulpit and the mobs, or the priests' claim that their influence was only directed towards strengthening the determination of the voters to follow their own convictions.[5]

---

[1] *P.P. 1868-9*, viii. 458–71.

[2] Ibid. 529–42.

[3] For the report of the Select Committee see *P.P. 1870*, vi. 133–8.

[4] The Select Committee attributed the almost complete absence of bribery in Scottish elections as due 'in a great measure to the superior education of the Scotch people; and partly to the fact that the constituencies being comparatively new, there exists no corrupt class, long familiar with the traditions of bribery, similar to that which in many English and Irish boroughs has not only retained in itself but spread through the constituency the desire for a corrupt expenditure' (ibid. 135).

[5] Ibid. 136.

The final conclusion of the committee on intimidation in English and Irish boroughs was as follows: 'There exists during the canvass in most boroughs a system of working upon voters through private considerations, whether of interest, hope or fear, for political purposes, and this system enables undue influence in a modified form to be constantly practised'—though (they added) it was rarely practised in a manner susceptible of legal proof, and thus there were few cases of elections invalidated on this ground.[1]

The Select Committee carefully considered *four* remedies suggested by their witnesses. The first was that public nominations should be abolished. They split almost equally on this. The report argued that there was 'much to be said in favour both of the retention and discontinuance of the practice'. But in spite of Hartington's opposition, a resolution *not* to adopt this reform was carried, by one vote,[2] on the ground that there was no practicable alternative.

The second remedy, that paid agents and canvassers be abolished, had been supported by some witnesses and was chiefly advocated by Henry Fawcett,[3] but the committee did not entertain it, because they thought it would be very difficult to enforce, and because they could not imagine electioneering without agents.

The third, that the number of polling places be increased, they accepted, but doubted if it would be adequate. The fourth, the use of voting papers or a secret ballot occupied most of their attention.

The idea of voting papers[4] (which were used in the university constituencies) appealed to a few witnesses and members of

[1] Soon after the Select Committee was appointed *The Times* anticipated this finding in a leading article on the 'social mischiefs' of intimidation: 'Very seldom direct threats are offered . . . no actual threats pass, yet a belief exists that a hostile vote will be followed by resentment and revenge. . . . Any one who has passed through a canvass must be aware that this feeling of fear is very general. . . .' *The Times*, 6 Mar. 1869.

[2] The main reasons given in the report were that 'the abolition of the present system would tend . . . to fetter the free choice of the electors, and would deprive a candidate of an opportunity of setting himself right with a constituency' (*P.P. 1870*, vi. 136).

[3] See below, p. 70. Fawcett was generally in favour of reducing the cost of electioneering.

[4] This meant that the voter could apply to the presiding officer for a paper on which he would write the name of the candidate he supported.

the committee, but most were against it. The opportunities they would give for bribery, fraud, and intimidation were quite obvious; and the committee quickly dismissed the suggestion. The Select Committee had thus to fall back on the ballot, and they heard a number of witnesses (all English) who were expert on one or other of the foreign ballot systems. The Greek ball-ballot and the American semi-secret ballot did not occupy them for long, nor did Sir Charles Dilke's account of the French ballot. All of these were considered from the start as unsuitable. Instead they concentrated on the systems within the Empire— in the two Australian states, Victoria and South Australia, which since 1856 had used secret voting for elections to their local legislatures. In both states the presiding officer handed out a paper with the candidates' names printed on it and a space for the voter's mark. There was this difference, however, that in South Australia the voter on establishing his claim was presented with a card which contained no identifying mark, while in Victoria the registration number was written on the back of the ballot, to provide for a scrutiny.

The committee spent a good deal of time discussing the 'Tas-manian dodge',[1] but if they had then consulted (as the Government were to do in 1871)[2] the current authorities in Australia, and not retired politicians, they would have found that persona-tion was practically eliminated in Victoria though still prevalent in three states using the South Australia system.

The evidence on municipal elections convinced the Select Committee that when they were followed by parliamentary elections, as in 1868, corrupt practices were employed at the first election in order to influence the second, and that the methods were much the same. They also agreed that the law regarding destruction of property by rioters should be made more severe; that all candidates ought to make a full statement of expenses incurred since the start of the campaign and that it should be deemed a corrupt practice if they failed in this.

The recommendations of the Select Committee were incor-porated in the report without any indication as to whether they

[1] The 'Tasmanian dodge' worked as follows: A voter smuggled in a piece of paper of the same size as a ballot paper, put it into the box, brought the actual ballot out of the booth and gave it to an agent, who marked it as he pleased and gave it to another voter (for a consideration). The second voter would smuggle out another ballot, and so on.			[2] Cf. *P.P. 1871*, xlvii. 317–36.

were agreed on by a majority or not.[1] Thus the resolution on
public nominations was included, although it had been *defeated*
by a majority of one, together with the resolutions on the ballot
which had been *carried* by a majority of one. Had Sir Frederick
Heygate not been absent through illness on that day the latter
would have needed Hartington's casting vote.[2]

3

The report of the Select Committee was placed before the
House on 15 March 1870, but a month earlier one of the
members of the committee, the radical, E. A. Leatham, anticipated the Government by introducing a private member's Bill
containing a ballot.[3] Leatham got round the problem of reconciling a scrutiny with secrecy by prescribing a ballot card, after
the Victoria model, on which the presiding officer would write
the voter's registration number in invisible ink[4] which would
be brought to light only on the orders of an election judge.
There was an advantage, Leatham claimed, in someone who
was 'not a strong party man' proposing such a measure, in that
partisan jealousy would not be aroused. He also remarked
that the startling evidence they had heard had resulted in a
'progressive softening' of hostility to secret voting on the part of
the Conservative members of the Select Committee.

For the Government Hartington expressed surprise that
Leatham did not wait for the publication of the report, and,
while not opposing the first reading, he asked that the second
reading be deferred until the report was available to the House.
Leatham agreed, but his eagerness was such that he moved the
second reading on the first day after the publication of the report. In his speech[5] he relied heavily on the evidence given

---

[1] *P.P. 1870*, vi. 133.

[2] So Heygate said in the House of Commons. Cf. *3 Hans*. ccvii (29 June 1871),
791–2. He was Conservative M.P. for Londonderry County.

[3] Radical M.P. for Huddersfield and a brother-in-law of John Bright, Leatham
succeeded Berkeley as the chief advocate of the ballot in the House—Bright was
now in the Government. Leatham was sometimes embarrassed by the fact that his
brother, W. H. Leatham, had been unseated at Wakefield by a Royal Commission
in 1859: he sat again for Wakefield (1865–8) and for Yorks S.W. (1880–9). See
above, p. 33, n. 2.

[4] Leatham suggested a weak solution of chloride of cobalt. For his speech see
3 Hans. (14 Feb. 1870), cxcix. 268–77, and for Hartington's, ibid. 278–81.

[5] Ibid. cc (16 Mar. 1870), 10–30. The rest of Leatham's speech consisted of a

before the committee to prove the necessity of the ballot: 'The
Ballot, in fact, teaches, by removing the patron and the pur-
chaser of votes, that the vote is no longer to be considered an
article of merchandise or of favour.' He also stressed that
intimidation prevailed to a greater extent than most members
realized. Again Hartington deplored Leatham's unseemly haste,
but he also gave some indication of government policy about
the report. Since the election of 1868 had involved unprecedented expense and much rioting and disorder, 'a large section
of the public', he said, had come round to the view that if no
other remedy could be found secret voting ought to be tried. For
their part, the Cabinet would consider the report of the Select
Committee and, perhaps later in the session, introduce their
own Bill. On this understanding they would not oppose the
second reading of Leatham's Bill.[1]

Gathorne Hardy from the Opposition front bench, while not
refusing a second reading, reserved their right to oppose the
Bill later on in committee. Other Conservatives, Northcote,
Raikes, and the voluble back-bencher Newdigate, expressed
open opposition—a hint of what was to come later. Bernal
Osborne (who had found a seat at Waterford after his defeat in
the general election)[2] in a characteristically sardonic speech in
support of the Bill, said that he had left Nottingham 'because it
was too lively for me', and gave the House a circumstantial
account of a violent physical attack on Robert Lowe during his
canvass at Kidderminster in 1859, implying that that experience
ought to have made Lowe a convert to the cause of the ballot.

That was virtually the end of the 'Secret Ink Bill'. The
government measure was introduced on 9 May 1870, and it was
not until 27 July, when there was no hope of carrying it during
that session, that the adjourned second reading debate on
Leatham's Bill was resumed.[3] Three speeches only were made,
but two were very important, because they foreshadowed the
main trend of both Conservative and Liberal policies on secret

digest of the evidence of the ballot experts—to show why he preferred the Victoria
type.
   [1] *3 Hans.* cc (16 Mar. 1870), 31–35. For Hartington's reluctant conversion to the
ballot see B. Holland, *Life of the Duke of Devonshire*, i. 75. This debate was adjourned.
   [2] Ibid. 41–42. See also above, p. 46.
   [3] The Bill was read a second time without a division, and having been committed for that day month (which fell during the recess) it automatically lapsed.

voting for the next two years. These were speeches by Gladstone and Disraeli.

Gladstone[1] began by saying that though he had often voted against the ballot he believed that that was the first time he had spoken about it in the Commons.[2] Previously the bulk of the Liberals were content to accept the Palmerstonian 'trustee' doctrine of the franchise. However, their outlook had changed since 1867 because the franchise extension of that year had been in principle unlimited, and the arrival of adult suffrage was consequently 'a simple question of time and convenience'. Thus, since 1867 the arguments against secret voting had either wholly disappeared or lost much of their force. On the other hand, the proper duty of Parliament, having conferred the franchise on so many, was to see that it was exercised freely and fairly, and the evidence adduced since 1867 had given greater weight to the arguments for the ballot.

Disraeli, at the beginning of his speech, confined himself to scoring debating points—Why had this great constitutional question been brought up at the fag-end of the session and in a poorly attended House of Commons? Why was it treated as a 'mere crotchety question' instead of 'in a becoming manner'? His own view was that the franchise was not a trust but a privilege, and as such ought to be freely exercised. Unlike Gladstone, he thought that the wider the franchise the less reasonable was the case for the ballot. He believed that the 'existing constituent body' possessed in itself sufficient 'elements of independence' to resist improper influence by any individual or class.[3]

These opinions, the result of the impact of post-1867 conditions upon traditional Conservative and Liberal theory, were expressed by the two leaders in speeches of unusual clarity and succinctness in a sparsely filled House during the final debate on the first still-born Ballot Bill of 1870. Many changes were to be rung upon them over the next two years.

The first Ballot Bill[4] to be sponsored by a government was

[1] *3 Hans.* cciii (27 July 1870), 1028–34.
[2] But see above, p. 58, and below, p. 72.
[3] Ibid. 1035–8. There was only one speech apart from Gladstone's and Disraeli's—a very short one by a back-bencher. For the development of Gladstone's thought see below, pp. 72–73.
[4] The official titles of the three government measures were: the Parliamentary Elections Bill (1870); the Elections (Parliamentary and Municipal) Bill (1871); and the Parliamentary and Municipal Elections Bill (1872).

introduced on 9 May 1870 by Lord Hartington. The machinery prescribed in several clauses eventually passed into law in 1872 —a 'cheque-book' ballot with the counterfoils filled in by the presiding officer, to be produced only if a scrutiny were ordered by an election judge. The recommendation by the Select Committee that public nominations be preserved was rejected, but in other respects the Bill followed the lines of the report closely enough.[1] In addition the Bill contained a stringent clause prohibiting any expenditure not covered in the official return.

A short debate followed; the only effective criticism of the Bill coming from Henry Fawcett,[2] who since 1867 had been a strong and persistent advocate of throwing the entire administrative electoral expenditure on the constituency rates as the only lasting remedy against corrupt practices. Fawcett expressed bitter disappointment that this solution (which was defeated on the Select Committee only by Hartington's casting vote) was not adopted by the Government. He openly accused the Government of turning to the ballot merely on account of 'party exigencies'. Gladstone answered with some asperity that secret voting was so important that it would be foolish to 'overload the vessel' by bringing in extra questions, which might prevent the Bill from passing into law in that session.[3]

The two Ballot Bills of 1870 excited little attention in the press, partly because of the plethora of legislation in that year —Forster's Education Act (which applied the ballot to elections for the London School Board) and the Irish Land Act were two controversial and very complicated measures, which took up most of the session;[4] partly because of the critical foreign situation, the Spanish succession, and the Franco-Prussian war. *The Economist*, representing the Liberal point of view, rashly asserted, after the Report of the Select Committee had been

[1] Hartington pointed out that the Select Committee had been inconsistent in claiming that the abolition of public nominations would both fetter the free choice of electors and make it difficult to prevent 'nuisance' candidatures (*3 Hans.* cci (9 May 1870), 431. See above, p. 65, n. 2.

[2] Radical M.P. for Brighton and, despite his blindness, a Professor at London University, also a member of the Select Committee. Between 1868, when he entered Parliament, and 1882 Fawcett made eight efforts to carry his pet aim into law. L. Stephens, *Life of Henry Fawcett* (London, 1885), p. 277. See below, p. 163, n. 5.

[3] *3 Hans.* cci (9 May 1870), 451.

[4] The government Bill was withdrawn on 18 July. The Bill for disfranchising Beverley and Bridgwater also helped to crowd it out. See above, p. 55.

presented, that there was no reason why a short Bill prescribing secret voting and abolishing public nominations should not pass into law before Easter.[1] On the other hand, *The Times*, while ignoring Leatham's Bill, condemned the government Bill for being of 'the composite and hybrid character' which so seldom pleases anybody.[2] However, this was the sole comment that *The Times* made on the government proposals, and it was clear that they did not regard them as likely to pass into law in the near future. When they did, in 1871, they devoted a large amount of leader-page space to the subject.[3]

Outwardly, then, in 1870 there was little indication that another great constitutional struggle was looming ahead. The number of petitions for the ballot was not large; such public meetings as were held expressed dissatisfaction with the Government rather than agreement, and the only aspect of secret voting that excited any interest at all was the design and construction of ballot-boxes.[4] One of the earliest letters on the subject appeared in *The Times* (when Leatham's Bill was coming up for its second reading) from a firm which announced that they had taken out a patent for a 'Ballot-voting apparatus' which combined the following 'essentials':

simplicity, certainty, security, absolute secrecy, and public confidence; that it should possess equal facilities for the educated and illiterate, a public check of voters against votes . . . and safety from tampering; that it should contain no detail or consecutive record or trace of votes, that it should be self-acting and trust to no one . . . (and) *that it should give to the public outward manifestation of its internal integrity without disclosing the poll* (my italics).[5]

It was in the Cabinet that the decision was made to reintroduce the ballot at the beginning of the following session. The decision was probably Gladstone's more than anyone else's.[6]

[1] *The Economist*, 19 Mar. 1870. The following prediction could hardly have been more wide of the mark: 'There is no chance of a defeat in the Lower House, and not much of any protracted debating, while the subject is not one which concerns the Lords, or with which they will seriously concern themselves.'
[2] *The Times*, 11 May 1870.
[3] See below, pp. 77 ff.   [4] Cf. *The Times*, 19, 27 May 1870.
[5] Ibid. 10 Mar. 1870. For an amusing account of the ingenious contrivances appearing during these years see Hyland, *Curiosities from Parliament*, pp. 199–201.
[6] In the Gladstone correspondence kept in the British Museum only two letters have been preserved on the Ballot Bills of 1870, 1871, and 1872, both are from Forster to Gladstone and are referred to below.

Bright, the most important radical in the Cabinet, suffered from
a serious illness from February 1870, which to his annoyance
kept him out of the Commons all during the ballot debates. In
November he wrote to Gladstone asking to be allowed to resign
since he was sensitive to charges of clinging to office. Gladstone
demurred at first. He was very anxious not to provoke rumours
of a difference between himself and the radicals and it was not
until 17 December that an agreed statement was issued announcing Bright's resignation. In the reshuffle Hartington was made
Chief Secretary for Ireland, which removed the ballot from his
charge. Instead, W. E. Forster,[1] who as Vice-President of the
Council had piloted the Education Bill through the Commons,
was brought into the Cabinet specifically to carry the ballot
through.

Gladstone's attitude had obviously changed. Like Hartington
and the Whigs he had opposed secret voting until the end of
1868, although in a letter in 1871 he said that his opposition
had never been vehement.[2] While the non-radicals in his Cabinet
were converted to the cause of the ballot through the revelations of the Select Committee, the reasons for Gladstone's
change of heart were more theoretical. In the letter cited above,
he wrote that at any time within the previous twenty-five years
he would have considered the ballot as the legitimate comple-
ment of household suffrage. These ideas were logically presented by Gladstone in his speech of 27 July 1870 on Leatham's
Bill in which he predicted the coming of universal suffrage as
simply a matter of time and convenience.[3] This speech, as has
been said, was made on a day devoted to private members,
during a discussion of a Bill that clearly had no future, and at
a time when the Franco-Prussian war was approaching its
climax, nevertheless, *The Economist* recognized it as a policy

[1] Forster had been at the beginning of his political life an adherent of the
trustee argument. He was not a member of the Select Committee of 1869. (His
Education Bill had included the ballot as the means of electing London School
Boards. See above, p. 70.)

[2] Gladstone to Lord Shaftesbury (11 Dec. 1871), cited in Morley, *Life of Gladstone* (London and New York, 1903), iii. 367–9. The first indication of Gladstone's
changed views was given in a speech shortly after his becoming Prime Minister
(21 Dec. 1868) in which he said that he had always supported open voting, but
with this reservation that whether by open voting or otherwise free voting must be
secured (ibid. 368). But compare the speech quoted above, p. 58.

[3] See above, p. 69.

statement of the highest importance. *The Economist* thought the
time inopportune for such 'extremely wide-reaching' ideas; and
considered that better ways could be found for justifying Gladstone's conversion to the cause.[1]

But although he spoke with such conviction Gladstone was
not quite happy about his change of mind. In his diary for that
night he wrote: 'July 27, 1870—H. of C. Spoke on ballot, and
voted in 324–230 with mind satisfied, and as to feeling, a linger-
ing reluctance.'[2] Gladstone's mind once satisfied, the future
course of official Liberal policy about the franchise, household
suffrage in counties, and the equalization of electoral districts
was assured, as well as secret voting. But it was on the issue of the
ballot that the Liberal party as a whole first came round to the
radical view that the vote was a right, not a trust or a privilege.

The conversion of the Liberal leadership to the ballot did not
provoke any Cabinet crisis. The two radicals, Forster and Stansfeld (President of the Local Government Board), were obviously
for it, while Gladstone and Hartington carried the rest. Lowe
appears to have had some doubts but did not press them;[3] the
Cave had broken up after the election of 1868. When the Bill
came before the Lords in 1871 only Earl Russell, the Earl of
Shaftesbury, and Lord Lyveden brought out the old Palmerstonian arguments on the Liberal side. Russell had not served
in a Cabinet since his resignation in 1866, Lyveden was of little
importance, and Shaftesbury's attitude seems to have been the
result of a chance conversation many years before.[4] But while
they acquiesced in the measure the Cabinet generally did not
show any enthusiasm for it. Apart from Forster, Hartington,
Stansfeld, and occasionally Gladstone, ministers avoided speaking in the debates of 1871 and 1872.

[1] *The Economist*, 30 July 1870.
[2] *Life of Gladstone*, iii. 368. Morley goes on to write that he does not know whether the reluctance was due to misgivings on the merits of the Bill, or the natural anxiety of the head of the Government about the amount of parliamentary time available.
[3] The *Saturday Review* (24 June 1871) said that it was not to be expected that Lowe 'would make a useless sacrifice by resigning office instead of voting for the Government measure'.
[4] In 1839 Shaftesbury met Daniel Webster in London, and the American politician advised him: 'Above all things, resist to the very last the introduction of the Ballot; for as a republican I tell you that the Ballot can never co-exist with monarchical institutions.' Shaftesbury never forgot that advice. E. Hodder, *The Life and Work of the Seventh Earl of Shaftesbury* (London, 1886), iii. 293.

4

The second Ballot Bill devised by the Liberal Cabinet was introduced by Forster on 20 February 1871.[1] It differed from its predecessor in that both the ballot and the abolition of public nominations were extended to municipal elections, and the principle of secrecy was made absolute by abolishing the scrutiny. Another change was that the penalty for omitting part of the election expenses from the official return was made the same as for treating—forfeiture of the seat.[2] The prohibition of public-houses as committee rooms was retained, polling hours were to be extended, and lastly Fawcett's ambition was realized since the 'compulsory expenses'[3] of the election were to be borne by the ratepayers. The reason Forster gave for this change was that the burden of these expenses prevented working-class candidatures.

Forster's opening speech was full of confidence and he ended by asking the Conservatives to discuss the Bill in 'a spirit independent of party'. He hinted that it might be in the Conservative interest to have some safeguard against the tyranny of the mob and he even tried to prove that the bill was the logical extension of the Act of 1867. A perfunctory debate followed, the Bill being greeted with enthusiasm by the radicals, Leatham and James, and with veiled hostility by some Conservatives.[4]

It was not until the second reading debate came up on 3 April that the cause of Forster's confidence was apparent. He had made an agreement with the Conservative front bench that they would let the second reading through without a division, on condition that a full discussion would be granted on each clause during the committee stage. The agreement was reached be-

---

[1] *3 Hans.* cciv (20 Feb. 1871), 529–46.

[2] In the Bill of 1870 the penalty was the same as for bribery—loss of seat plus fine or imprisonment. Forster said that on reconsideration he thought that penalty too severe.

[3] i.e. returning officers' charges and the cost of erecting the hustings. In 1868 these charges (in England) amounted to £92,000—about twice the figure for 1865.

[4] *3 Hans.* cciv (20 Feb. 1871), 547–56. Leatham congratulated the Government on the 'marked' improvement over the Bill of 1870. He was especially glad that municipal elections had been tackled. James said that the Bill was a 'complete and perfect measure'. Beresford Hope, however, complained that the ballot question was mixed up with others of less importance and Scourfield rehashed the 'trustee' doctrine.

cause of the back-log of legislation, but it was querulously opposed by some back-benchers—chiefly Beresford Hope and Colonel Barttelot. Replying to objections, Gladstone denied that this arrangement fettered the freedom of the House. He made it clear that the Government was anxious for the Bill, as one of the 'heavier' measures of the session, to pass into law as soon as possible.[1]

The second reading passed without a division but the attention of the House was then redirected to local taxation and the licensing laws, which took up most of its time in April. Towards the end of the month, Bright, convalescing in Rochdale, wrote indignantly to Forster about the indifference with which he believed the Cabinet were treating the Ballot Bill, and asked what was the good of having two professed radicals in the Cabinet if they did not assert themselves.[2] Forster replied on 26 April, assuring Bright that he was as anxious to get the Ballot Bill through as he had been to get the Education Bill passed in the previous year, that he would not have taken charge of it if he did not believe the Cabinet meant to pass it, and that Gladstone had assured the House that the Bill came next to the Army Regulation Bill.

But the Army Regulation Bill, which abolished purchase of commissions, was held up by the obstruction of the Army officers led by Colonel Barttelot—a worthy successor to Colonel Sibthorp. By the beginning of June Forster was getting seriously worried. He wrote to Gladstone urging strongly that the committee stage of the Ballot Bill be moved during the second week, as otherwise the opposition in the Lords would be able to plead lack of time for proper consideration when the Bill came before them.[3] Lacking this excuse Forster believed the Lords would neither reject nor shelve it. He did not want to be unfair to Cardwell (the Secretary for War) but the consequence of the Ballot Bill not going through in that session would be far worse than any other parliamentary mishap. It would mean a split in the Liberal party, both in the House and the country, and in any case losing the Ballot Bill would help rather than hinder the opposition to the Army Bill.

[1] *3 Hans.* ccv (3 Apr. 1871), 1060–1.
[2] T. Wemyss Reid, *Life of the Rt. Hon. W. E. Forster* (London, 1888), i. 531–2.
[3] Add. MSS. 44,157, pp. 36–37. Forster to Gladstone (4 June 1871).

Forster did not gain his point immediately, but after nearly three weeks had passed during which several meetings of radical and working-class organizations had been held up and down the country, and a deputation from the metropolitan Liberal associations had urged that the ballot should come into law in that session,[1] the committee stage was fixed for 22 June.

It was only then that the difficulties facing Forster were fully appreciated. There were several pages of amendments on the order paper, most of them on the Liberal side. The 'Colonels', worsted over the Army Bill, and the Whigs (who had opposed the Parliamentary Elections Act of 1868) were anxious to whittle down the measure. Irish M.P.s, both Liberal and Conservative, were afraid that the ballot would facilitate 'spiritual intimidation' and help the recently founded Home Rule party. Lastly, it became clear that the Conservatives who, by allowing the second reading through had to some extent lulled ministerial suspicions and acquired credit for themselves, had intended from the first to revive the second reading debate on committee. On the first day Cross, leading for the Opposition in a typical 'second-reading' speech, moved an amendment that the committee be postponed for three months. He summarized the arguments against the ballot: the 'trustee' or 'public duty' argument; the argument that the experience of other countries was misleading since discrepant factors were not taken into account; the argument that such a revolutionary change in political practice ought not to be attempted unless it were conclusively proved that no other expedient would suffice; the argument that the traditional electoral offences were on the decline anyway, and that the Bill would merely change their form and give a new impetus to personation.

The Cross amendment took up three full days of the committee's time.[2] During the debate the Bill was assailed from many angles. Irish Conservatives expressed their fears of an increase in the influence both of the Church and of extremist societies, such as the Fenians.[3] English Conservatives, and some Liberals too, rehashed all the arguments of the past. Hicks

[1] The Times, 5, 21 June 1871.

[2] 3 Hans. ccvii (22 June 1871), 401–90; (26 June), 560–637; (29 June), 746–862.

[3] In reply to this Hartington denied that the majority of the Irish voters would support the nationalist candidates. (In 1871 the Home Rule party was just one year old.)

Beach expanded Cross's argument that the Bill would facilitate personation and condemned the Cabinet for including some provisions that the Select Committee had rejected. Others challenging Hartington's assumption of a clamant public demand pointed out that the more influential newspapers were against the ballot.

Few speeches were made for the Bill: Bernal Osborne and the radical Osborne Morgan censured the Opposition for closing their eyes to the great extent of bribery and intimidation. Stansfeld said that the Cabinet had dropped the scrutiny because it was very expensive, would rarely be used and could not make up for the psychological advantage that a perfectly secret ballot would bring to the voters.

In addition to attacks from their own followers the Cabinet had to put up with some open obstruction from Conservative back-benchers speaking on a wide variety of topics. This earned a rebuke from *The Times* and a bitter attack from Gladstone, who threatened that the rules of the House would be revised if its forms were continually flouted in that manner.

The 'understanding' between the two parties was now in ruins and the fruits of Disraeli's policy of 'reserve in opposition' plainly evident.[1] On 6 July Gladstone summoned a meeting of the Liberal M.P.s at 10 Downing Street to discuss tactics, but the news was leaked to *The Times*,[2] which reported that the party rank and file were advised to make as few speeches as possible and to withdraw all the amendments that the Government was unwilling to accept.

Disciplining the Liberals did not, however, make up for careless drafting. Several of the clauses bristled with complexities which were revealed to Forster only in the course of the debate. The most troublesome was the clause on nominations. As originally drafted it required ten *duly qualified* electors to subscribe the nomination papers, but after it was pointed out that no one could be sure that his qualification was flawless, Forster eventually agreed to substitute a proposer and seconder whose names should be on the register. At the beginning of the fourth

[1] The obstruction to the Ballot Bill was a revolt against the official Opposition line and the leaders allowed themselves to be carried along by it. Cf. Monypenny and Buckle, *Life of Beaconsfield*, v. 172–3.

[2] *The Times*, 6–7 July 1871.

week, a Special Committee of the Cabinet was appointed to go through the Bill and strike out every clause that was not absolutely necessary. Forster wrote on 24 July that even with the barest minimum of clauses it would still not be possible to take the third reading before 8 August;[1] the debate had not progressed beyond the third clause, on secret voting. The Special Committee had 'reluctantly but unanimously' come to the conclusion that the only course open to the Government would be to stop after clause 3 and then announce an autumn session. On the following day *The Times* reported on the suggestion for an autumn session made by Whitbread, and said the Government had the choice of cutting down the Bill to a simple secret voting measure (and so losing the confidence of the working classes who were more interested in abolishing the artificial hindrances to membership of the Commons), or holding an autumn session (and so deferring to the supposed demand of public opinion knowing that it could not be satisfied, since the Lords had still to be considered); or admitting that the Bill could not possibly pass in that session and dropping it.[2]

The Government followed none of these courses. On 27 July[3] Forster announced to the Commons that he was dropping the non-essential clauses[4] and insisting only on those concerning the methods of nomination and secret voting. The debate therefore continued with every available moment given to the Bill, although thirty-nine other Bills and the votes in supply were in arrear. When at last the Bill came up for the third reading, on 8 August, one day later than the deadline set by Forster in his letter of 24 July, it had passed through twenty-seven sittings and seventy-three divisions, more than the Education Bill, and 'the process of evisceration', as *The Times* put it, had cut out the clauses on expenses and the amendment of the anti-bribery laws, while the clause on public nominations had been sensibly modified.[5] But the secret voting clause remained the same as

---

[1] Add. MSS. 44157 (lxxii), 38–39; Forster to Gladstone (24 July 1871).

[2] *The Times*, 25 July 1871.

[3] *3 Hans.* ccviii (27 July 1871), 314–17.

[4] The clause to throw the election expenses on the constituency rates (which Forster also insisted upon) was defeated on 31 July by 256 votes to 160.

[5] On 1 Aug. an amendment by Fawcett to reintroduce the clause which made corrupt every payment not included in the official return (see above, p. 74) was defeated by 181 votes to 84.

when introduced (an absolutely secret ballot) and a Conservative amendment to introduce the cheque-book method had been easily defeated.

On the third reading, Disraeli lamented the disruption of public business on account of a Bill for which there was no overwhelming public demand, as the Liberals claimed. He justified the persistent Conservative opposition by referring to the 'Pythagorean initiation of silence' at the Downing Street meeting and the forced withdrawal of over 100 Liberal amendments. He concluded in a sarcastic vein: no one wanted the Bill, he said, but Gladstone. It was 'one of those nervous eccentricities which too often marred his transcendent abilities'.

Gladstone[1] replied by claiming that the Liberals had followed the Bill through more than seventy divisions with the same perseverance and in as great numbers as they had followed the Irish Church Bill, which was the main issue of the last election. Forster wound up the debate by saying that whatever fate that Bill might have the ballot would be on the Statute Book before many months.

On the same day the Bill received a formal first reading in the House of Lords. The second reading was moved by Lord Ripon in a short speech on 10 August. Lord Shaftesbury, who had given notice of his intentions, moved the rejection of the Bill in a speech full of high principle: he feared that secret voting would have serious and permanent effects on constitutional habits, minds, and thoughts. Lord Lyveden supporting the amendment roundly stated that the ballot was not an integral part of the Liberal creed. He ought to know, he said, since he had been a Liberal when Gladstone was still an 'Orange Tory'. The House divided after a short debate and the Bill was lost by 97 to 48.[2]

The Times had predicted accurately (2 August) what would happen when the Bill left the Commons:

... the Peers will decline to enter upon it; the Bill will be put aside for the year; there will be the customary show of indignation; the question will be asked in the usual inflated manner whether the will of the nation is to be for ever thwarted by a body of reactionary Peers, and then every one who can will depart for the holydays [sic] rejoicing.

[1] 3 Hans. ccviii (8 Aug. 1871), 1114–24. [2] Ibid. (10 Aug. 1871), 1256–1307.

Passions were indeed aroused by the defeat of the Bill. Glad-stone showed greater enthusiasm for the ballot than ever before. In a speech at Whitby on 2 September 1871 he said: 'The People's Bill has been passed by the People's House, and when it is next presented at the door of the House of Lords it will be with an authoritative knock.'[1] The *Daily News* pained Lord Shaftesbury by labelling him as 'an obtrusive professor of street-corner piety' and of 'Pharisaism unimpeached and unimpeach-able'.[2] Even among the Conservatives a subtle change of attitude was noticeable. The Conservative candidate in a by-election at Stockport felt obliged to pledge himself to the ballot, and thereby caused his leaders and the Conservative press much embarrassment. The change had affected the newspapers also. Although the *Daily News*, *The Economist*, and the *Fortnightly Review* were still vehemently pro-ballot, and the traditional papers of the Right equally firm against it,[3] the most influential daily and the most influential weekly shifted their line during the long and tortuous debates in committee. At the beginning of the session *The Times*[4] treated the whole subject with lofty scorn as if the Government were not really serious about it, and the inconsistencies, both in the Bill itself, and in the manner in which it had developed from the Select Committee's Report, were duly recorded.[5] When it became obvious that the Bill would be passed they complained of its inexpediency, and then pleaded for an appeal to the constituencies.[6] Then, when the attitudes of the two parties had further hardened, *The Times* rebuked the Conservatives for their destructive tactics:

The Government have introduced the Ballot Bill on the plea that bribery and intimidation are so rampant that it is necessary to resort to secret voting as a lesser evil. We deny and have denied the assumption of fact involved in this plea, but it is the basis of Mr. Forster's argument, and as such cannot be overlooked.[7]

At the very end of the session *The Times* admitted that the

---

[1] Morley, *Life of Gladstone*, ii. 369.

[2] *Daily News* (12 Aug. 1871). Shaftesbury wrote sadly in his diary on reading this: 'Such honours Ilion to her hero paid!' Cf. Hodder, *The Life and Work of the Seventh Earl of Shaftesbury*, iii. 297.

[3] Especially the *Standard*. See below, p. 85, n. 4.

[4] *The Times*, 21 Feb. 1871.   [5] Ibid.

[6] Ibid. 27 June 1871.

[7] Ibid. 14 July 1871. This editorial clearly shows the change of front.

principle of secret voting had received 'the fullest sanction from the popular branch of the Legislature',[1] and having acknowledged this as a *fait accompli*, in the following year they concerned themselves merely with details and used all their influence to prevent an out-and-out conflict between Lords and Commons.

The *Saturday Review*, while scoffing at the sincerity of Gladstone and Lowe, realized as early as June 1871[2] that the Bill would get through, and in 1872 accused the Conservatives of flogging a dead horse.[3] The antagonism of both papers to the principle in spite of their acceptance of its inevitability was well summed-up in the *Saturday Review* of 17 February 1882: 'For good or for evil, it is an experiment which is going to be tried . . . all that wise men can do is to make the measure passed as perfect, as effectual, and as little objectionable as possible.'

5

The persistence of the Government, and especially of Forster, had by now made it quite plain that another Ballot Bill would be introduced in the following year. It was certain to pass the Commons and considerable pressure would be exerted on the Lords to get it through. This did not mean that the Liberals themselves were now quite happy about it. The old Whigs had obediently trooped into the lobbies—as Gladstone boasted they would—but they left on Forster's shoulders the burden of carrying the Bill through the long sessions in committee,[4] nor could they muster up sufficient enthusiasm to speak in its favour. The radicals, on the other hand, were angry with Forster for sacrificing the clauses on election expenses—which they considered to be the most needed reform—for the sake of the clauses on secrecy. In an outspoken article written in November 1871[5] Fawcett said that the ministry relied on the ballot to restore them to the popular favour they had forfeited by Bruce's Licensing Bill and the continued shelving of the Mines Regulation

---

[1] Ibid. 25 July 1871.   [2] *Saturday Review*, 24 June 1871.
[3] Ibid. 6 July 1872.
[4] Wemyss Reid, *Life of the Rt. Hon. W. E. Forster*, i. 530–3.
[5] H. Fawcett, 'The Present Position of the Government', the *Fortnightly Review*, x. 544–58. Fawcett also referred to the clause on extension of polling hours (which had appeared in the original Bill but was struck out in committee) as the next reform most desired by the working class.

G

Bill, but that the working classes had lost interest when the clause they most desired was struck out, and many advanced Liberals felt like thanking the Lords for rejecting a measure so mangled and incomplete.

It was certain, then, at the beginning of the 1872 session that the Cabinet would bring in a Bill containing at least the clauses which had been approved by the Commons in the previous year. The only question was what the attitude of the Opposition would be, since all possibility of a further arrangement had been sabotaged by the obstruction of 1871.

Disraeli hoped that 'reserve in opposition' would work again and that the Whig peers would once more lead the attack. On 11 January 1872, however, he wrote to the Duke of Richmond that he had heard that 'our party in the Lords' could no longer count on Earl Russell, the Duke of Somerset, and Lord Lyveden as opponents of the Government.[1] In another letter of 16 January Disraeli wrote that he was undecided as to the course to pursue until he knew the ministry's exact proposals. He added: 'We must not conceal from ourselves that the Tory party in the Ho. of Commons is not united on the question, and tho' I am not myself prepared, under any circumstances, to concede the principle of secret voting, as at present advised, I fear our ranks may be broken.'[2]

Disraeli could see no possibility of a compromise, although Richmond seemed to think that one might be arranged on the issues of the scrutiny and the abolition of personation.

On 8 February 1872[3] Forster moved for leave to introduce the third government Bill for secret voting. It was substantially the same as the Bill of 1871 had been when it went to the Lords, providing for vote by ballot without a scrutiny, an increase in the number of polling places, and the abolition of public nominations. The main alterations were that municipal elections were no longer covered by the Bill,[4] and that the clause on expenses

---

[1] Monypenny and Buckle, *Life of Beaconsfield*, v. 176. Richmond was the Conservative leader in the Lords. Disraeli's letter was by way of reply to a letter from Richmond which stated that Earl Russell now believed the country would support the Liberals on the ballot. In his letter of 16 Jan. Disraeli told Richmond that some Lancashire borough members were being pressed by their constituents to support the ballot.

[2] Ibid.   [3] *3 Hans.* ccix (8 Feb. 1872), 172–8.

[4] Forster admitted that when drafting the 1871 Bill he had overlooked the fact that there were no public nominations at municipal elections.

was left out; the former because Forster now felt that they deserved a separate Bill, the latter because the sense of the House
had been strongly against it. On the same day the Attorney-
General introduced a short Corrupt Practices Bill comprising
the extra clauses which the pressure of time had forced the
Cabinet to drop from the Bill of 1871.[1] The two Bills were to be
taken concurrently.[2]

Leave was granted without a division and the second reading
was taken on 15 February in a 'thin and inattentive house',[3]
with the leaders of the Opposition absent. A hostile amendment
by Colonel Barttelot and Liddell was defeated by 109 votes to
51. The order for committee was taken on 29 February. Forster's
hope that the Bill would this time get a speedy passage was disappointed[4] for it stayed in committee until 13 May. The most
animated discussions centred on a Leatham amendment to
punish 'wilful' disclosure of a vote at the polling-booth by six
months' imprisonment. It was opposed by Fawcett and Harcourt
(who moved a further amendment to substitute 'with corrupt
intent' for 'wilful'), but supported by Forster and James, who
asserted that the ballot would be useless if a voter could *prove*
how he had voted. Leatham accused Fawcett of turning his
coat. Eventually, after two divisions on separate days, Forster
accepted a modified form of Harcourt's amendment.[5] Fawcett
made yet another effort to throw the necessary election expenses
on the rates, but although the Government were willing to
accept it, it was heavily defeated.[6] There was some justification

[1] This Bill provided (1) that personation was a misdemeanour, and the returning
officers were obliged to prosecute anyone found guilty of it; (2) that the vote be
struck off where personation had been instigated by a candidate or agent; (3) that
payments not officially returned be deemed corrupt; (4) that public-houses might
not be used as committee-rooms; (5) that the Parliamentary Elections Act (1868)
be made permanent—it was to expire in 1871.

[2] The two Bills passed through every stage at the same time. For convenience the
two are referred to below as one.

[3] *Annual Register 1872*, p. 62; *3 Hans.* ccix (15 Feb. 1872), 470–517.

[4] His temper got shorter, especially on account of jokes about his 'Siamese twins'.

[5] In the second division Leatham's amendment, though supported by the
ministry, was defeated by 274 votes to 246, forty Liberals voting with the majority
and twelve abstaining. The compromise amendment read: 'No person shall
directly or indirectly, induce any voter to display his ballot paper after he shall
have marked the same, so as to make known to any person the name of the candidate for or against whom he has so marked his vote.' (The penalty proposed was
three months' hard labour.)

[6] By 261 votes to 169, on 25 Apr.

for *The Times* writing on 10 May that Forster had to contend with 'the open opposition of nearly half the House of Commons, and the more dangerous secret dislike of half the remaining half'.

After twelve nights in committee and two on the report stage five alterations, none of them significant, were made in the Bill, and the Government fixed the third reading for 30 May, the off-day between the Derby and the Oaks. It passed the third reading despite an attempt by a Home Ruler, John Francis Maguire, to get a recommittal;[1] and on the following day was read a first time in the Lords.[2]

So far, the Conservatives in the Commons had contented themselves with reiterating the age-old arguments on principle, and most of the suggestions made in committee had come from the Liberal side. However, it soon became clear that Disraeli and Richmond had agreed to pretend to accept the principle of the Bill and allow it through the second reading in the Lords, but to blunt its edge by amendments in committee.[3] A hostile amendment by the Whig, Lord Grey, was defeated by 86 to 56 votes and the Bill passed its second reading on 10 June. But after two days in committee[4] it was sent back to the Commons with eight amendments, one providing for a scrutiny by pre-scribing a 'cheque-book' ballot, and another giving every voter an option between secret and open voting.[5]

The restoration of the scrutiny was bad enough, but the optional ballot was quite unacceptable to the Government. For them the whole value of the Bill lay in the complete suppression of evidence as to how a voter had cast his vote. If the evidence

---

[1] *3 Hans.* ccxi (30 May 1872), 843–85.

[2] By the time that the Bill went to the Lords Conservative candidates in five by-elections had found it expedient to pledge themselves to support the ballot.

[3] These tactics resembled the 'reserve in opposition' of the previous year. See above, p. 77.

[4] *3 Hans.* ccxi (17 June), 1800–47; ccxii (25 June), 157. There was no division on the report stage; but Lord Denman filed a 'protest' on several grounds, none of them original.

[5] The other amendments were: (1) returning officers and agents relieved from penalties if they disclosed votes; (2) polling stations not to be more than two miles apart; (3) no school in receipt of a parliamentary grant to be used as a polling station; (4) illiterate voters to be empowered to declare their identity before the returning officer (a magistrate in the original Bill); (5) the Act to expire on 31 Dec. 1880 (Beauchamp); (6) polling hours to be extended to 5 p.m. in winter and 9 p.m. in summer (Ripon).

could be produced then bribers and intimidators would be as well off as before. Moreover, the Beauchamp amendment, under which the Act would expire in 1880, would encourage those so minded to spoil the next election for the ballot supporters. *The Times* and the *Saturday Review* joined in the Liberal outcry against the perfidy of the Lords, the former earnestly pleading for all parties to 'look upon further controversy as useless, and to give an honourable assent to what the Government has proposed and the House of Commons has accepted'.[1]

Gladstone arranged the business of the Commons so that the Lords' amendments could be considered immediately. By 1 July the Commons had completed their review and at the instance of the Government sent a message to the Lords rejecting all the amendments. On 8 July the Lords met and decided to 'insist' on all their amendments, except the one on school rooms, and sent a message accordingly. Whereupon Gladstone decided to ask the Queen for a dissolution[2] if the Lords continued to insist on a matter affecting the electoral system. *The Times*, which was always well informed at this period, had predicted that the Conservative majority in the Lords, if faced with the alternative of a dissolution, would concede every other point, provided the Government accepted the Beauchamp amendment.[3] On 12 July the Commons met again to consider the 'reasons' offered by the Lords for insisting on their amendments and stood firm on every point, except the Beauchamp amendment, which they accepted. Disraeli and Richmond saw that there was now nothing more to be gained and, despite the indignation of the Conservative press, which had been clamouring for a general election on the ballot issue,[4] decided 'not to insist upon' their other amendments. The Ballot Act and the Corrupt Practices Act received the royal assent on 18 July 1872.[5]

The new legislation was put to the test sooner than had been expected. Hugh Childers, for twelve years Liberal M.P. for the

---

[1] *The Times*, 19 June 1872. See also *The Economist*, 6 July 1872; *Daily Telegraph*, 13 July 1872; *Saturday Review*, 13 July 1872.

[2] Morley, *Life of Gladstone*, ii. 369.

[3] *The Times*, 2 July 1872.

[4] The *Standard* had warned the House of Lords that for it to give way would be to 'abdicate its position as an independent branch of the Legislature and to betray the country' (18 July 1872).

[5] 35 & 36 Vict., c. 33. It was also to apply to municipal elections.

small north-country industrial borough of Pontefract,[1] was brought into the Cabinet as Chancellor of the Duchy of Lancaster and had to vacate his seat. The by-election took place on 15 August. *The Times* sent a special correspondent to cover the contest and he had to report the unexpected news that the conditions in the borough were remarkably quiet: 'No bands of music paraded the town. No colours or banners were seen in procession. The church bells were silent. . . . Both at Pontefract and Knottingley the topic was the dullness of the election. "It hardly seemed like an election," the tradespeople said; and they were right.'[2]

6

The Ballot Act is regarded by the constitutional history textbooks as next in importance to the Reform Acts in the remodelling of the electoral system. It is hard, however, to see just how some of the effects that are attributed to it can be proved. The period during which the Act (together with the Acts of 1854 and 1868) operated as the main check on corrupt practices was a mere eleven years, covering two general elections, and (as will be shown) the offences of bribery and treating continued in a slightly different form in spite of it. On the other hand, undue influence, violence and intimidation figured much less in later elections, and the substitution of the polling-booth for the hustings made the casting of a vote seem more of a deliberate political act and less of a social occasion. The Pontefract election was the prototype of those that followed.

It is easy to see the introduction of the first Ballot Bill as a direct consequence of the report of the Select Committee of 1869–70, and the motive of the majority of M.P.s is clear— disgust at the persistence of corrupt practices in spite of the high hopes placed on the Parliamentary Elections Act. Once the report of the Select Committee is taken into account the causal chain leads back to the 'Screw Circular', the Lothian letter, the riots at Bristol and Ashton, and the unregenerate bribery of Bridgwater and Beverley.

There was, however, another reason why the years 1870–2

---

[1] Baron Martin's former constituency. Its electorate in 1872 was 1,916.

[2] *The Times*, 16 Aug. 1872. In spite of the novelty the poll was only 65 per cent. Childers won by a narrow majority.

were especially suitable for the passing of the Ballot Act. The Corrupt Practices Prevention Act of 1854 became law in the same decade as the Northcote–Trevelyan report appeared and the first University Commission was set up. These were the first steps in the struggle of the Victorian middle-classes for intellectual freedom and equality of opportunity. They took over an increasing amount of the patronage so long enjoyed by the nobility and landed gentry and by the late 1860's there were probably more bishops, generals, and dons of middle-class origin than ever before. The years 1870–1 witnessed the 'Glorious Revolution' of the new middle class with the final abolition of purchase of army commissions, privileged entry to the public service, and religious tests at the universities.

The Ballot Act formed part of this changing social pattern, since its main effect was to strike at yet another form of influence and privilege—the rule of the wealthy landlords and factory-owners over the political consciences of their tenants and workmen. But a long time was still to elapse before an intelligent man without means could become a member of Parliament. The Select Committee of 1869 had ventured to tackle many problems, but not the high cost of electioneering, and Fawcett's amendments were unsuccessful.

Many of the chief actors in the parliamentary drama were unaware of the deeper implications of their aims and attitudes. With one notable exception the same was true of the press. In June 1871, at a time when Conservative obstruction was holding up the current Bill in the Commons, Bagehot's *The Economist* wrote that the secret opinion of the Conservatives that the classes could govern better than the masses might be true, but it was beside the point: [They] 'have parted with their power to govern, and the only question is, whether . . . the classes really in possession of power should exercise it honestly, or under a perpetual sense of pressure and of guidance.'[1]

[1] *The Economist*, 24 June 1871. Gladstone's speech in 1870 (see above, p. 69), went some distance with *The Economist*, but not the whole way.

CHAPTER IV

1874–1880

I

THE general election of 1874 was sprung as a surprise. After five years of intense administrative activity Gladstone decided to go to the country rather than wait for another year. Writs were issued at once, and the time allowed for the campaign was a mere three weeks.

It was waged vigorously with thirty more contested seats than in 1868.[1] The election addresses and speeches of Gladstone and Disraeli were concerned mainly with matters of *haut politique*—the Straits of Malacca, the engagements in West Africa, the disposition of budgetary surpluses, the possible abolition of income tax. Electoral questions were (unlike 1868) ignored, apart from a half-hearted advocacy of household suffrage, and a few pious expressions of hope that the first general election with secret voting would not be marred by any untoward incidents. The other leaders followed suit.

Secret voting, however, did not rule out violence during the campaign. There were ten cases of serious rioting—the worst at Willenhall near Wolverhampton where the local colliers and lockmakers armed themselves with staves to meet thirty 'roughs' (supporters of C. P. Villiers) who had come by train from Wolverhampton to create a disturbance. An eyewitness account shows this clash to have been as bad as any election disturbance since the riots at Coventry in 1832.[2]

Blood flowed freely and they [the 'roughs'] were terribly kicked, one so shockingly about the head and face that his life is in much jeopardy. . . . So soon as the roughs were able they got back to the railway station, where the profuse flow of blood has left painful evidence of the extent of the injuries the most injured have sustained.

---

[1] In 1868, 211 seats were uncontested; in 1874, 181 seats. See below, App. II.
[2] See above, p. 16.

The victorious mob then paraded the streets, smashing the windows
of three publichouses where the landlords are Tories, and similarly
attacked the residence and factory of the chairman of the Conservative Committee.[1]

Serious riots took place also at Stourbridge in East Worcestershire, where 60 police and 100 yeomanry restored order with
difficulty, since some of the police were stoned halfway from
Lye to Stourbridge and suffered severe injuries; at the Forest of
Dean, where the military were also called out; and at another
district in Wolverhampton where the Chief Constable and
twelve of his men were forced to beat a retreat and a magistrate
was threatened with death if he read the Riot Act.[2] Rioting also
occurred at Barnsley, Newcastle, Nottingham, North Durham,
Sheffield, Thurles (Tipperary), Dudley, and Holybridge. Out
of all these cases, however, only two petitions (Dudley and North
Durham) were presented alleging rioting and intimidation.

In spite of these incidents, at the end of the campaign *The
Times* could write (apropos of Sydney Smith's famous dictum
that the ballot would be accompanied by 'a scene of wholesale
bacchanalian fraud, a *posse comitatus* of liars which would disgust
any man with a free Government') that it had never occurred to
Smith that the departure of open voting would also mean the
disappearance of its concomitants: 'Mobs, processions, favours,
free fights, and punch-drinking have become for the most part
things of the past, and where rioting did occur during the late
Elections it was probably not aggravated by any political du-
plicity.'[3] In fact, sporadic rioting had been the common form of
previous elections. It is not surprising that it had not disappeared
as soon as open voting was abolished, since the riots that occurred in 1874 took place (as before) during the campaign, not
on polling day.

The days of polling were remarkably free of incident. In the
county constituencies even with open voting polling days had
generally been quiet. But the improvement of conditions in the
large cities was emphasized by the Commissioner of the Metropolitan Police when giving evidence before a Select Committee

[1] *The Times*, 5 Feb. 1874.
[2] Some of these men were summarily convicted and sentenced to 4 months' and
8 months' hard labour. Ibid., 19 Feb. 1874.
[3] Ibid., 11 Feb. 1874.

in 1877: 'Since the passing of the Ballot Act we have never had the slightest trouble at any election that has taken place in London, and the places that used to be the worst are now the best. . . .'[1] A prominent member of the Sheffield Town Council recalled in 1878 that during forty years' experience of elections he had seen windows broken and dead cats hurled at the candidates, but all that had changed since the ballot was introduced.[2]

Considerable interest was directed during the campaign to the technicalities of the Ballot Act, and many a puzzled election official wrote to the papers to air a grievance or ask for advice. It soon became clear that Forster and his supporters, though strong on theory, had overlooked a number of practical difficulties. Only three days were allowed for the preparation of boxes and ballot papers, even in the large metropolitan constituencies. The firm producing them at Lambeth[3] wrote that it took six of their staff, working non-stop, two days and a half merely to number the papers. Hackney was less fortunate. Ballot papers and boxes arrived on time at only eleven out of the nineteen polling stations; at two others they arrived an hour late, and two more received no papers at all. But this was the only example of a breakdown in the arrangements.

Other problems of interpretation were whether presiding officers could personally fill in any ballots other than those specified in the Act;[4] whether the official stamp was to be placed on the face or the back of the paper; whether at the close of the poll people in the polling station were entitled to vote after 5 o'clock had struck, and whether the returning officer could reject ballot papers on the ground that they were imperfectly marked. The Act specified four grounds for rejection: (1) lack of the official stamp, (2) more than one cross, (3) the presence of an identifying mark, (4) uncertainty. The first three problems were comparatively trivial although they provoked a good deal of learned discussion.[5] The last raised the whole question

[1] Lt.-Col. Edmund Y. W. Henderson's evidence before the Select Committee on Parliamentary and Municipal Elections (Hours of Polling), *P.P. 1877*, xv. 32.

[2] John Wilson's evidence before the (second) Select Committee on Parliamentary and Municipal Elections (Hours of Polling), *P.P. 1878*, xiii. 465. For these committees see below, p. 108.   [3] With a registered electorate of 40,000.

[4] The Ballot Act empowered presiding officers to mark the ballots only of (1) illiterates, (2) people physically incapacitated, and (3) Jews of the strict observance when polling day happened to fall on a Saturday.

[5] *The Times*, 6–14, 18, 21 Feb. 1874.

whether the 'Directions for Guidance of Returning Officers and Voters' in Schedule II of the Ballot Act were imperative or advisory. That question had to be reserved for the election judges.[1]

If we discount errors and questions referred to the petition courts, the new voting methods were applied for the first time on a large scale with remarkable success. Some officials even improved on the intentions of the framers of the Act. The Act prescribed that presiding officers should both stamp the papers and check them before they were put into the box,[2] but in many large boroughs such as Liverpool and Manchester the presiding officers were so busy stamping the papers that they had no time left to supervise the casting of votes. The practice in Leeds, which afterwards became the standard, was to restrict the presiding officer's duties to checking the ballots and keeping order in the polling station while two clerks, one of whom stamped all the papers, assisted him. This practice, though not envisaged by Forster, proved highly efficient.[3]

At the close of the poll the presiding officer had to send the ballot box[4] with an account of the number of papers issued, a copy of the register, and the counterfoils (all in separate parcels) to the returning officer's headquarters. In most constituencies the returning officer first checked the contents of the boxes with the 'ballot account', then the count began. The Act (for no apparent reason) prescribed that the papers be checked at the *end* of the count.

No uniform method of counting was prescribed: in most constituencies ballots were counted by the hundred without any further check. Leeds, however, again led the way. The Town Clerk,[5] who managed this first secret election with considerable ingenuity, later explained his method:

I have every vote recorded upon a sheet; I have the names of all the candidates upon the sheet with 100 squares to each name, all

---

[1] See below, p. 95.

[2] So as to recognize the official stamp—a precaution against the 'Tasmanian dodge'. See above, p. 66, n. 1.

[3] Evidence given before the Select Committee on the Working of the existing Machinery of Parliamentary and Municipal Elections, *P.P. 1876*, xii. 362, 364, 379, 399.

[4] The Leeds practice provided only one ballot box to every polling station.

[5] Capel Augustus Curwood. He had been an advocate of the ballot for many years and a friend of Henry Berkeley.

ruled. Then they are filled in from the papers by two clerks, and then they are checked at another table by other two [clerks], and then they are checked by the candidates' agents, if they wish to do so, and the whole process is supervised by the returning officer and his clerks, and by the candidates.[1]

Although Leeds was one of the largest boroughs in the country, with three seats since 1868, the Town Clerk claimed that his painstaking method not only satisfied all the candidates but enabled the count to close before one o'clock in the morning.

When the count was over the returning officer declared the result publicly (as before), and then sealed up the valid and rejected ballots in separate envelopes, which together with the marked registers and the counterfoils were sent to the Clerk of the Crown in Chancery, in whose custody they would remain for a year and a day (to provide against a scrutiny) and then be destroyed. These practices have continued in Britain to the present day.[2]

2

The number of petitions that were brought to trial after the election of 1874 was twenty-two. This reduction led some observers to presume an all-round improvement in electioneering morals, but the next general election was to show that this was illusory. Expense was the most probable cause of the drop in petitions. Agents had now discovered that the services of election lawyers were much more expensive than in the days before the transfer of jurisdiction. Comparable figures are difficult to find, but Spofforth, an authoritative witness, told the Select Committee of 1875 that in his experience the cost of petitioning had risen by nearly five times since 1854.[3] It was common knowledge that Henry Hawkins charged 500 guineas basic fee per petition until he became a judge in 1876.

With the 1874 petitions may be conveniently considered the two petitions of 1873, which were the first after the passing of the Ballot Act.

[1] *P.P. 1876*, xii. 399.

[2] The Registration Act (6 & 7 Vict., c. 18) gave the Clerk of the Crown in Chancery custody of the poll books. The Representation of the People Act of 1949 continued the procedures described above, with some modifications.

[3] *P.P. 1875*, viii. 556. The Beverley petition trial (1869) had cost £3,000, while the Cambridge petition trial (1857) which lasted just as long cost a mere £557. (See also *P.P. 1883*, liv. 285–91.)

The first was from Gloucester City. After the election of 1859 William Price and Charles James Monk (both Liberals) were unseated by an Election Committee of the House which afterwards moved for a Royal Commission. The Commissioners found that in general bribery had prevailed in the borough for a long period and judged the two members to have been among the guilty. Price and Monk were debarred from representing the constituency for the lifetime of that Parliament, and the writ was suspended until 1862. From 1862 two other Liberals filled the seats, but these stop-gaps moved out in 1865 when Monk and Price, their disqualification having expired, were again returned. They were re-elected in 1868. In 1873 Price was appointed a Railway Commissioner and had to resign his seat. The Liberals chose as their candidate Thomas Robinson, a corn merchant who was an alderman and had been four times mayor. The Conservatives put up William Killigrew Wait who defeated Robinson by a small majority.

After the election the Liberals petitioned on the usual grounds of bribery and treating (both of which failed) and two further charges, colourable employment and personation, based on the Ballot Act.

The charge of colourable employment arose out of a bargain between the two parties that the polling stations should be guarded by twenty-four 'special constables'—party supporters who were paid for this duty. There were, however, five other Liberal partisans who expected to be appointed but were not, and after the election boldly claimed payment from the Liberal agent. He weakly consented and the news got to the other side.

Mr. Justice Blackburn held this to be a foolish but not a colourable act, and gravely admonished both parties that it would be better to leave such arrangements to the local authority. He had some doubt as to the validity of these five votes, but in the event he allowed them.[1]

The charges of personation were of the sort that might be expected when the ballot was an innovation—a son voting instead of his father as both occupied the same house; a non-voter with the same name as a voter living in the same street and thinking the name on the register was his. These were perfectly

[1] *P.P. 1874*, liii. 193 ff. See below, p. 142, for the opinions of the 1880 Royal Commission on the by-election of 1873.

understandable mistakes, said Mr. Justice Blackburn, and dismissed the petition with costs.[1]

The second case was the petition following the Taunton[2] by-election, in October 1873, caused by the appointment of Sir Henry James, Q.C., as Attorney-General. James had won the seat on a scrutiny after the 1868 election, when the local Conservative Association was proved to have paid out a large sum of the so-called 'Barristers' Court Money' (i.e. payment for loss of time in attending the registration court[3]) two months after the registration when the election was on the way. This time the issue of agency came up under a different form, and showed the increasing importance of the national political associations. The London Labour Representation League, then in its infancy, sent two delegates down to Taunton to support James's candidature. They collaborated with one Rollings,[4] President of the Taunton Agricultural Labourers' League, who said he supported James because he thought his candidature was 'most in favour of working men's interests'. The Londoners and Rollings had actively assisted James's agent Burman. One of them paid some of the petty cash account for Burman, and both ran up in James's name an account for election literature with a printer. The connexion between Burman and Rollings was so close that several people who had applied to Burman for jobs during the campaign were referred by him to Rollings. This agricultural labourer, in his zeal for the return of the Liberal minister, gave half-crowns to a few people in public houses, and this formed the main charge against James. It was also alleged that the London delegates had given £5 to a timber merchant to distribute in bribes.

In their defence James and Burman denied any connexion with Rollings and his friends (even though they had been seen accompanying James in his canvass), and the fact that the printer's bill which was run up by the Labour Representation League was afterwards paid by Burman was explained away as an oversight.

Mr. Justice Grove's judgement did not add another interpretation to the conflicting doctrines on agency; he merely remarked that the other judges were agreed that it was a very

[1] P.P. 1874, liii. 195.   [2] Ibid. 463–7.
[3] See above, pp. 16–17.   [4] A local saddler.

difficult question to settle. His decision was reached rather on personal impressions than on construction of the law. Admitting that there were in Taunton a certain number of voters who would for a consideration promise their votes to either candidate ('some of whom had reached that lowest stage of degradation that they gloried in their shame')[1] the judge was unfavourably impressed by the way in which the Conservatives had 'fished' for evidence for the petition (their solicitor was not called into the witness box) and, on the other hand, found Burman a transparently honest witness. He dismissed the petition with costs, but although Sir Henry James retained his seat he did not forget the circumstances of the trial when steering the Corrupt and Illegal Practices Bills through the Commons in 1881, 1882, and 1883.[2] If the law of agency had been held in 1873 (as it was later) to cover the activities of the national as well as the local political associations, James would have lost his seat.

The petitions that came to trial in 1874 made rather a mixed bag. Twelve[3] involved technical breaches of the law (mostly of the Ballot Act), three were based solely on intimidation, and the remainder involved the traditional electioneering offences.

Five[4] cases turned on the Ballot Act and three of them (Athlone, Renfrew County, and Wigtown) on the admissibility of certain votes that had been rejected by the returning officer. The Irish Court of Common Pleas, to which the case at Athlone was referred as a special case, decided to allow votes marked on the right-hand side but 'within the same compartment as the name of the candidate', but avoided the question whether votes marked on the left-hand side of the paper would be valid.[5]

This question, which involved deciding whether the 'Directions for the Guidance of Voters' appended to the Act were mandatory or advisory, was settled by the Scottish Court of Session in their judgement on the Wigtown case. They decided,[6] with one dissenting voice, to reject the disputed votes as not

[1] *P.P. 1874*, liii. 463.   [2] See below, Chap. VI.
[3] In one case where unqualified voters had inadvertently been registered the judge ruled that the fact of registration was conclusive evidence of a title to vote.
[4] Athlone, Renfrew County, Wigtown, Hackney, Drogheda.
[5] *P.P. 1874*, liii. 117–20.
[6] Ibid. 278–90. Lord Ormidale and Lord Neaves delivered the judgement. Lord Benholme dissenting said that if a proper cross had been made leaving no doubt as to whom the vote was intended for, neither the placing of the cross nor the addition of extra marks ought to affect the result.

marked in conformity with the Act, although it was quite clear
for whom the votes were intended (some with a cross on the left-
hand side, others with an additional mark beside the cross) and
it was extremely unlikely that the votes could have been identified as a result of the extra marks.

The Athlone decision elected the petitioner, when the thirteen rejected votes had been cast.[1] The Wigtown decision gave
the seat to George Young, Gladstone's Lord Advocate, by a
margin of one vote, after he had been beaten in the original
result by two votes. But after the petition had been lodged he
was appointed a judge of the Court of Session, and a by-election
was immediately ordered.

In the Renfrew case Lord Ormidale rejected twenty-two
votes as not properly marked, but as more of them were cast
for the petitioner than for the respondent the result was not
affected.[2]

The Drogheda case showed how the fundamental principle of
the Ballot Act could be violated, apparently in good faith.[3] In
this small borough seven polling stations were set up in private
houses. Each station consisted of two rooms connected by a
passage, the presiding officer in one guarding the ballot box,
and the voter in the other marking his ballot. In the passage
through which the voter would have to return with his marked
ballot were a policeman and party officials. There was no specific
charge that any particular vote had been disclosed, but quite
obviously there were plenty of opportunities for a breach of
secrecy.

As was the common practice with Irish election judges when
faced with any new difficulty,[4] the case was referred to the full
Court of Common Pleas by Mr. Justice Barry. This was of
little use as they divided evenly on the question and referred it
back to him. Mr. Justice Keogh and Mr. Justice Lawson held
that the Act enjoined on presiding officers the positive duty of
ensuring secrecy which the two-rooms-with-passage arrangement could not possibly provide. Lord Chief Justice Monahan

[1] The sheriff had certified that Sir John Ennis and Edward Sheil had each
obtained 140 votes, and he, not being a registered elector, had no authority to
decide between them. Then Sheil lodged the petition claiming the thirteen rejected
votes and was returned. See below, p. 129.

[2] *P.P. 1874*, liii. 259.   [3] Ibid. 149–66.

[4] Three of the four Irish petitions in this year were heard as special cases.

and Mr. Justice Morris interpreted the secrecy clauses nega-
tively; all that was needed was the *opportunity* of secrecy, and as
there was no proof that any vote had been divulged, they were
in favour of rejecting the petition. The latter view was plainly
opposed not only to the provisions of the Act—in this case the
'Directions for the Guidance of Voters'—but also to its under-
lying spirit. Nevertheless it satisfied Mr. Justice Barry, who
reached the same decision, justifying it on the ground that
he must be convinced that a positive breach of secrecy *had*
occurred before he could invalidate the election. The petition
was dismissed and another eccentric judgement was registered,
to the further confusion of election lawyers.[1]

Another technical petition arose out of the returning officer
exceeding his functions. In Mayo the sheriff, on being informed
that one candidate had not complied with the Act of 1868,[2] took
it on himself to refuse a poll and declared the other candidate
elected.

The successful petitions of 1874 brought to light much the
same offences as in 1868, but under subtler and more devious
forms. The unique series of petitions from Stroud deserves some
attention, since it is the only British constituency ever to have
had four elections in one year. In December 1873[3] H. S. P.
Winterbotham, one of the two Liberal members, died. At the
by-election in January 1874 a Conservative, J. E. Dorington,
won by a comfortable margin after a rather unexciting contest,
but immediately after the return the Liberals lodged a petition
on the usual grounds.

This petition lapsed when Parliament was dissolved and the
borough warmed up for the February general election. Dorington stood again, against S. S. Dickinson (the sitting Liberal) and
W. J. Stanton. The agents on both sides seemed to think treating
quite permissible; the Conservatives gave a number of break-
fasts to the well-to-do voters, and the Liberals gifts of food
and drink to the poor—the poorer voters of this agricultural

[1] *P.P. 1874*, liii. 163–7.
[2] By not appointing an election agent before 1 o'clock on polling day. Mr.
Justice Keogh said of the sheriff's action: 'The case would be serious if it were not so
intensely ludicrous.' Ibid. 240.
[3] For the reports of the Stroud cases see *P.P. 1874*, liii. 260–7 and *P.P. 1875*, lx.
431–45. For a summary of the legal issues see O'Malley and Hardcastle, *Election
Petitions*, ii. 107–14, 179–85; iii. 7–12.

borough were mostly illiterate and 'knowing little of the matter than that one party was called yellow and the other blue'. Both sides contravened the Act of 1854 by displaying large numbers of flags and banners.

Stanton and Dickinson were easily returned, but the Conservatives lodged a petition claiming widespread treating by the Liberals as well as specific acts of bribery. The Liberal agent against whom bribery was charged and the five voters whom he was alleged to have bribed vanished mysteriously just when the trial was due to begin. However, Baron Bramwell found enough evidence to unseat the Liberals on the ground of general treating, but said that it had been carried out so openly that he presumed the agents were not conscious of wrong-doing; he reported to the Speaker that corrupt practices had extensively prevailed.

Such a report in other cases had resulted in the Government moving an address for a Royal Commission. In this case they made no move; it was explained afterwards that the law officers were uncertain whether treating by itself was a sufficient cause (under the Act of 1854) for a Royal Commission.[1]

The campaign for the double by-election in May went on unimpeded. Before the election the agents of both parties reached a compromise in that neither would object to the other paying travelling expenses to out-voters, of which there were a large number in Stroud. However, as the campaign progressed partisan feeling rose to what the Liberal agent afterwards described as 'lamentable bitterness'.[2] The result was that Dorington came first and A. J. Stanton[3] (not to be confused with the candidate of the February election) second, but this pleased neither side: the Liberals lodged a petition against Dorington's return and the Conservatives simultaneously petitioned against Stanton. Again neither side claimed the seat, showing that the petitions arose largely through spite. Baron Bramwell came down again and tried the two petitions together from 2 July to 13 July 1874. In their case against Dorington the Liberals revealed the compromise arrangement about travelling expenses and claimed that the Conservatives had sent, in the form of postage stamps,

---

[1] *3 Hans.* ccxxii (9 Feb. 1875), 163–89.   [2] See below, p. 100, n. 1.
[3] His nephew. Another nephew stood in July as a Conservative. The Stantons were the leading wool manufacturers in Stroud.

sums far beyond the mere railway expenses. Bramwell admitted that the lower class of voters in Stroud would probably be so irritated by an offer of the bare railway fare that they would vote for the other side. Nevertheless, he censured both parties for agreeing to 'the unpunished doing of an illegal act'.

Although systematic treating seemed absent from the by-elections (and this counted as an improvement) there were some charges of individual treating and one or two of bribery. Bramwell gave the accused the benefit of the doubt in these cases. Offers of payment for travelling expenses were also raked up from the February election, and also one promise of payment for 'time lost' at the January by-election. These Baron Bramwell considered to be 'as operative as though they had taken place in May',[1] and although he considered that Conservative agents had in general 'not intentionally misconducted' themselves during the May election the judge decided that Dorington must lose his seat on account of the payment of travelling expenses in February and May.

The petition against Stanton covered much the same ground but although it was proved that railway fares were paid by Stanton's friends, Bramwell held that they were not agents. The only original feature of this petition lay in the payment of work-men for their absence on the polling days in January, February, and May by several pro-Liberal mill-owners. The payment for January was made retrospectively when the February election was coming up, the others had been made promptly. These employers had never paid for absence before and Serjeant Ballantine, the counsel for the Conservatives, claimed that it was a corrupt payment; although the May election was the one in question, the payments in January and February had led the workers to expect the same in May.

Baron Bramwell held that this 'somewhat . . . mischievous practice' nevertheless did not involve an agreement to vote or to refrain from voting, and thus did not come within the Act of 1854, nor could the workers claim in the courts to be paid in future on every election day. He dismissed the petition against Stanton, but refused costs, and ended by expressing a hope that this would be the last visit of an election judge to Stroud.

This hope, expressed by many, was not to be realized. The

[1] Cf. Mellor's decision at Barnstaple, below, p. 106.

fourth election (for Dorington's seat) was held in July, a few weeks after the conclusion of the previous trial. H. R. Brand, the defeated Liberal candidate at the May by-election, won the seat; once again a petition was lodged, again the seat was not claimed, and again the respondent's return was impugned not only on account of malpractices (bribery, treating, and personation) at the July by-election, but at the earlier one also.

This time Baron Pigott heard the case (his first, since he had just been appointed to the election rota) which lasted from 23 November till 10 December 1874. Like Bramwell in the three previous petitions Pigott was handicapped by having to restrict his inquiry to the electioneering behaviour of the respondent (since the seat was not claimed), and his report was to that extent one-sided. However, a clearer picture of the undercover party activities in the borough emerged than at the previous trials.

Firstly, the dominant political organization in the borough, the Liberal party, was shown to be very loose-jointed. There was no responsible head agent, but several co-ordinate agents; the actual expense agent was a different person from the nominal head agent Samuel Leech,[1] and at least one of them had not been appointed at all, but was foisted on to the head agent as a survivor of the management of the previous elections. Brand and Leech apparently disliked the tradition that was now associated with Stroud but were not strong enough to sweep entirely clean. The next disclosure concerned party finance, and explained how the Liberal organization was able to stand the cost of four successive elections. After the by-elections in May a secret fund was started among Liberal supporters in the borough. It was not wholly subscribed until after the July by-election, but it was probably common knowledge that it would be fully utilized. Eventually it amounted to £1,200 and was handed over to the actual expense agent, Mr. Witchell. In the party accounts the fund was camouflaged as a 'Decoration Fund' to pay for the flags and banners used at the general election five months earlier, but these could not have accounted for more than a small portion of it.

[1] Leech (previously agent for the Liberals in Derbyshire for many years) told the Select Committee of 1875 (see below, p. 107) that during the petition hearings feeling in the borough rose so high that business men did only half their usual trade, because political opponents would not deal with them, and even ladies refused to speak to their own sisters in the street. *P.P. 1875*, viii. 465.

The manner in which the party funds were spent explained the unflagging public interest in the elections and the promptness with which petitions were presented. It was revealed that certain partisans were kept in nominal (or colourable) employment during the long petition trials so that their loyalty might not weaken—one man, a baker, had been employed by the Liberals for nearly the entire year at the very generous rate of 25s. per day. Likewise, several men, including some who absconded when the trial was due, were employed to 'get up evidence for the petitions'.

This was linked to what might be called an exchange scheme for importing strangers (especially from Taunton) to offer travelling expenses and straightforward bribes during the elections, and for exporting local bribers when the petitions came up for hearing. The sums mentioned were not large; as far as the evidence went they ranged from 2s. 6d. to £2, but it was impossible to estimate the number of people, both voters and non-voters, affected. Baron Pigott reported thirteen known cases of people who accepted bribes and five, of whom three came from Taunton, who offered them. As might be expected Brand and his nominal agent denied any connexion with the strangers, although some of them had clearly been directed to the homes of voters by the local agents.

In his judgement Baron Pigott concluded that Brand must lose his seat on the ground of bribery by agents. He added somewhat gratuitously that he had no reason to believe that corrupt practices had extensively prevailed, though in the next breath he admitted that the evidence heard was 'necessarily confined' to what could be proved against the Liberals.[1]

The unique electoral history of Stroud during these twelve months gave rise to much comment, but what is perhaps the most plausible explanation appeared in *The Economist*.[2] *The Economist* pointed out that the stream of corruption in this borough, although tending to widen, did not wholly engulf it, as had happened in Sudbury, St. Albans, Totnes, and Reigate. Furthermore, this stream had sprung up very recently; there had scarcely been a sign of it when Winterbotham died in December 1873. The unstable element in the electorate was the

[1] Ibid., lx. 444–5.
[2] *The Economist*, 19 Dec. 1874. See also *The Times*, 11 Dec. 1874.

workers (enfranchised in 1867), who had no opinions about politics one way or the other, and 'not being bred to have a nice sense of public honour', might easily be swung one way or the other by small bribes. The decisive factor was the election agents and their minions, who might think twice before spending large sums on doubtful voters but would not mind risking a few shillings. *The Economist* gloomily predicted that it would take the 'residuum', as Bright had called them, a generation at least to develop into a political class; until then every shift of power from upper and middle classes must involve some use of the weapons of corruption.

Two other interesting cases came from Norwich and Boston. After the Royal Commission of 1870 had completed its report a double by-election was ordered at Norwich. The defeated candidate Jacob Henry Tillett, solicitor and newspaper owner, stood again, with Sir William Russell for the Liberals, while the Conservative candidate was a well-known lawyer, J. W. Huddleston, Q.C.[1] The Liberals won again by a comfortable majority. Tillett appears to have desired quite sincerely that his campaign should be fair. Nevertheless, when a petition was lodged, an agent of Russell was proved to have bribed some voters and since Tillett *indirectly* benefited from this act he was unseated for a second time.[2] At the ensuing by-election of 1871 the Liberal, Jeremiah Colman (of Colman's mustard) won easily.

All this time Norwich was undergoing a rapid social change. The electorate had been extended in 1867 but the new voters were considerably poorer than in other manufacturing towns. Since the boot and clothing industries, on which the town largely depended, were turning to mass production the craftsmen were forced to rely on casual work—the proportion of the electorate so affected was estimated in 1875 to be as high as 30 per cent. On the other hand rents were low owing to a speculative building boom in the forties and fifties, and this encouraged mobility among the poorest classes; in one year 3,000 electors (25 per cent. of the electorate) changed their dwellings.

Although the 'cash in hand' bribery of former years seemed

---

[1] Unsuccessful at Canterbury in 1868. See below, p. 148.

[2] Tillett had also been so careless as to employ as agent a man scheduled for bribery by the Royal Commission of 1870; this alone would have unseated him. *P.P. 1872*, xlvii. 347.

until 1874 to be on the way out except at municipal elections, colourable employment was still rife, and the existence of a large and mobile depressed class put a strong temptation in the way of candidates and party organizations.

Four candidates entered the field in 1874. Sir Henry Stracey[1], who had been unseated in 1868, and J. W. Huddleston stood again for the Conservatives; Colman and Tillett, the latter making his third attempt, for the Liberals. It was expected that the contest would be keen.

No sooner had the campaign begun than flocks of voters besieged the committee rooms of both parties for jobs. They were hired at rates of 3s. 6d. a day and 5s. on polling day, which would obviously not appeal to men in regular employment. The official election agent for the Conservatives, an inexperienced gentleman named Mr. Sparrow, sent a circular to the 'managers' of the eighteen polling districts authorizing them to employ whoever they liked as messengers, subject only to 'a reasonable discretion'. How this discretion was exercised may be seen from the fact that the total number of messengers, &c., employed by the Conservatives was well over 2,000, while the Liberals employed nearly 3,000.

The other feature of Norwich elections, public displays, was more extravagant than in previous election years—very large processions, bands, blue (and pink) lights, and even a local circus, which the Conservatives hired to enhance one of their processions. In addition, the two parties between them hired over a hundred public houses as committee rooms, although in 1868 less than a quarter of that number had been used.

The rate of expenditure on the election was decided by the Conservative agents Sparrow and Pattison, the latter a brewer, whom Huddleston knew and brought into the election as 'expenses agent'. Pattison was also the president of a local building society and his secretary, Buttifant, was employed as assistant election agent. Between them Pattison and Buttifant set the pace which the Liberals had to follow willy-nilly.

Colman and Huddleston won the two seats, Tillett being beaten by 47 votes, and Stracey far behind. When the accounts were presented Huddleston was aghast, forced his agents to reduce their bill from £4,089 to £3,548, and refused to pay any

[1] A great local landowner.

other claims. He was so shaken by this that he resolved never again to stand for Norwich. After the election when Disraeli offered him the Solicitor-Generalship, he sounded Colman to see if the inevitable by-election would be opposed. As neither Colman nor any other Liberal would give the assurance, Huddleston refused the office. The Liberal expenses were £4,407 which Colman and Tillett paid without demur.[1]

In February 1875 Huddleston was raised to the bench. At the by-election in March Tillett stood once again for the Liberals. The Conservative candidate, Wilkinson, was a solicitor and, like his predecessor, a stranger to the borough.

The Conservative organization was then bearing the brunt of a grave local scandal. In the summer of 1874 Buttifant absconded from Norwich after the discovery that he had embezzled £20,000 from the building society of which he was secretary and Pattison president. He returned later, was tried and sentenced to 15 years' penal servitude. While the proceedings were pending Buttifant's relatives brought strong pressure to bear on Pattison by threatening to expose the Conservative electoral malpractices if he did not withdraw the action. Pattison refused and the trial went on. After his elevation to the Bench—in April 1875—Mr. Baron Huddleston received a letter from a relative of Buttifant to the effect that Buttifant's papers afforded 'most abundant evidence of a criminal nature, implicating many of the leading members of the Conservative party, as well as their candidate, the present Mr. Justice Huddleston'. Unless the Conservatives handed over £1,000 the Liberals would be informed of the scandal.[2]

During the by-election campaign the new Conservative candidate hired another agent, but the same helpers and organizers as in the general election, and the efforts of the agent to cut down expenditure were in vain. The same was true of the Liberals,

[1] It is interesting to note that the *real* Conservative expenditure (£3,548) was given both in the official return (*P.P. 1874*, liii) and in the newspaper, the *Norfolk Chronicle* (18 Apr. and 2 May 1874). The real Liberal expenditure, was £4,407, but was officially returned, and also published in the *Norfolk News*, as £3,436. Outstanding claims amounted to £725. *P.P. 1876*, xxvii (app. B), 36.

[2] Two letters were sent; the first, before Buttifant was sentenced, might have been designed to get him off as lightly as possible. The second clearly could not do him any good and must have been intended to cash in on Huddleston's delicate position. Huddleston ignored the letters, which were not made public until the Royal Commission was sitting. *P.P. 1876*, xxvii 22–23.

and the final expenses were at nearly the same level as in 1874. Hundreds of voters employed at very attractive rates, bands and processions were again in evidence.[1] Tillett won for the third time and the Conservatives once again petitioned.

Mr. Justice Lush, who tried the petition, believed in Tillett's vehement protestations of innocence but when it was proved that 150 voters had been employed in two wards—and six more remained to be investigated—he declared the election void, reported that corrupt practises were extensive, and a Royal Commission was appointed.[2]

Before the Commissioners, Tillett, Colman, and Mr. Justice Huddleston expressed their belief that it was futile to hope for an improvement in Norwich electioneering until the laws were drastically changed; even if both parties agreed to fight clean an independent might come in and capture the venal voters. The Commissioners found that although bribery in the form of colourable employment had spread over a much wider area of the electorate than before 1868 there was less money involved. They estimated that the corruptible element amounted to 4,000 of the poorer class,[3] but scheduled a mere 106 of them.

Another Royal Commission was appointed for Boston after a long-drawn-out legal battle between the two parties.[4] Their conclusions were more reassuring. There was no territorial influence; the electors were quite independent; and though bribery had occurred it was not prevalent and the reports of treating given at the election trial were exaggerated. They scheduled six people.

[1] The Conservatives hired 683, the Liberals 1,611. The expenses were four-fifths as high as in 1874. The jobs were very simple, e.g. carrying circulars or messages and the remuneration was over twice what the voters were accustomed to. *P.P. 1875*, lx. 503–64.

[2] Cf. *P.P. 1876*, xxvii. (The entire volume is devoted to the Norwich Royal Commission's Report and Minutes of Evidence.)

[3] Despite all his previous protestations Tillett told the Commission that he knew (from thirty-five years' experience) that eight out of ten wards were 'pretty well riddled with corruption'.

[4] The issue was whether a Christmas gift of coal made to the poor of Boston by a Liberal candidate and organized by his local association (which the judge regarded as bribery) not only affected his seat but that of the other candidates as well, since the association was acting for both. The Court of Common Pleas decided that this would carry the doctrine of agency to unheard-of lengths, and they allowed the second Liberal to keep his seat. Cf. *P.P. 1874*, liii. 343–417 (Minutes of Evidence at election trial), 133–48 (Report of Special Case); *P.P. 1876*, xxviii. 5–12 (Report of Royal Commission), 17–284 (Minutes of Evidence).

The remaining cases may be briefly summarized.[1] The election at Dudley, a normally peaceful borough, was invalidated because of rioting by 'an imported Irish mob'. The Durham county election was invalidated on similar grounds—general intimidation by brickmakers from Manchester and miners during demonstrations in favour of household suffrage for the counties. The future Conservative Home Secretary, R. A. Cross, nearly lost his seat at Bolton because his agent had sent railway passes to outvoters, but Mr. Justice Mellor ruled that there was no conditional promise and that the *Cooper* v. *Slade* precedent did not apply.[2] The same judge held at Barnstaple that bribes given by an undoubted agent at the election of 1865, which the agent had vindictively revealed to the court because the candidate refused to reimburse him, ought not to affect the result in 1874—a decision which conflicted with Bramwell's at Stroud.[3] Altogether fourteen petitions were successful out of twenty-two.

3

Further attempts to improve the electoral law were made between 1874 and 1880. In 1874 Sir Charles Dilke introduced a Bill to extend the hours of polling in London from 4 o'clock in the afternoon until 8 o'clock in the evening, as was the practice at London School Board elections, on the grounds that no untoward results followed those elections, and that the extension would enable unskilled labourers and professional men not prepared to sacrifice part of their working day to exercise the franchise. Curiously enough Forster joined with the Government in opposing it, on the ground that extra policemen would be needed, and the Bill was easily defeated.[4]

In 1875 the House set up a Select Committee under Lowe's chairmanship to report on the working of the Acts of 1854 and 1868 and the Ballot Act. The most interesting part of the evidence consists of the opinions on the election courts given by agents, lawyers, and the judges themselves. There was some criticism of the discrepancies between the judicial decisions—of

---

[1] In Windsor Baron Bramwell dismissed a petition against Colonel Richardson-Gardner who had evicted 20 tenants for having voted against him in 1868. Cf. *P.P. 1874*, liii. 549–54.

[2] See above, p. 56, n. 5.   [3] *P.P. 1874*, liii. 120–5.

[4] *3 Hans.* ccxviii (25 Mar. 1874), 315 ff.

which the Galway and Launceston judgements were the most glaring examples. It was pointed out that there was no provision to reconcile conflicting judgements since the Court of Common Pleas could be appealed to only on questions of law, not fact.[1] The election lawyers generally were satisfied with the working of the system since 1868, although Henry Hawkins strongly advocated that the tribunal be broadened and Serjeant Ballantine wished it to be strengthened by lay assessors.[2] The judges themselves refuted the prediction made in 1868 that the public canvassing of their decisions would impair their prestige. Their decisions were certainly canvassed in the press,[3] but Baron Bramwell stoutly denied that that was 'in anywise derogatory to us',[4] and Mr. Justice Keating said that he had never heard the slightest complaint by the judges that they were being treated disrespectfully. Bramwell's final judgement on the Act of 1868 and the election courts expressed the general opinion of the witnesses: 'I daresay it has not been perfect; it would be a very remarkable thing if it was so; but if I compare the results with what I have heard of the results of the former tribunal, I should say that the present tribunal is a preferable one.'[5] Only one witness recommended a return to the House Election Committees—Markham Spofforth the former Conservative principal agent.

The Report of the Select Committee[6] contained eleven resolutions of which the most important were that election petitions should be tried by two judges instead of one; that no respondent could be deprived of his seat or punished unless the judges agreed; that a representative of the Attorney-General should attend every trial and at the end prosecute those against whom corrupt practices had been alleged; that the penalty on

[1] Nor was there any provision for reconciling conflicting decisions of the full courts, since the two Courts of Common Pleas in Dublin and London and the Court of Session in Scotland held co-ordinate jurisdiction. See above, p. 57.

[2] For the proceedings and evidence before the Select Committee see *P.P. 1875*, viii. 441–637.

[3] Cf. *The Times*, 1 May 1874, pointing out that Bramwell's second Stroud decision was more severe than Willes's at Windsor in 1869.

[4] Bramwell also said that the judges did not find the election duties so unfamiliar: claims for seats resembled ejectment suits, bribery charges, criminal offences. *P.P. 1875*, viii. 577.   [5] Ibid. 572.

[6] Much of the evidence on corrupt practices before the Select Committee consisted of a rehash of the petition trials. The general conclusion of the committee was that corruption was not on the increase.

conviction should be three months' hard labour; that if a candidate were disqualified the votes cast for him would not be considered void unless the disqualification be notorious at the time
of nomination; and that more polling places be provided, since
the law on conveyances was frequently broken.

The resolutions of the Select Committee would have reduced
the possibility of judicial disagreements had they been implemented but Disraeli's Government merely set up further Select
Committees to report on various aspects of the electoral system.
The Dilke Committee of 1876 recommended that the Leeds
procedures for checking and counting the ballots should become
the standard practice, and that votes should be rejected only
when the intentions of the voters could not be ascertained.[1] In
1877 another committee under Sir Charles Adderley, inquiring
into the extension of polling hours, recommended an extension
in London on the lines of the Dilke Bill of 1874.[2] A third
committee (1878) under the chairmanship of Sir Matthew
White Ridley was unable to come to a decision regarding
extension in other boroughs.[3]

In spite of the four Select Committees it was not until 1879
that the Beaconsfield Government, which during its last years
was preoccupied with foreign affairs, introduced any electoral
legislation.[4] This was the Parliamentary Elections and Corrupt
Practices Act of 1879, which carried out the 1875 Select Committee's recommendations that petitions be tried by two judges
instead of one and that no election be invalidated unless the
judges agreed, though the Government refused to accept the
recommendations for prosecution of offenders before the election
judges, or that votes should be valid unless the disqualification
was notorious.[5] The bill (which also extended the Acts of 1854
and 1868 to 31 December 1880) had an uneventful passage
through both Houses.

[1] *P.P. 1876*, xii. 359–538, esp. 364.
[2] One witness estimated that one-third of the Westminster constituency could not
vote since employers would not give them time off. *P.P. 1877*, xv. 3–73, esp. 46–47.
[3] The police were not apprehensive but the civic heads feared drunkenness,
rioting, and increased public expenditure. *P.P. 1878*, xiii. 544–6.
[4] Apart from the Norwich and Boston Corrupt Voters Act (1876) which disfranchised the 106 voters scheduled by the two Royal Commissions.
[5] See *3 Hans.* ccxliv. (20 Mar. 1879), 1363–5. The Bill was introduced by the
Attorney-General, Sir John Holker.

4

When the results of the 1874 election came in Gladstone wrote, 'we have been swept away, literally by a torrent of beer and gin'.[1] Apart from the opposition of the licensed trade, he blamed educational discontents (especially in Ireland) and the 'multiplication of Liberal candidates or their egotistical or crotchety obtrusion' for the fact that the Conservatives had gained their first overall majority since 1841.[2]

Other explanations were offered for the massive swing,[3] but nowhere was it mentioned that since 1868 the Conservatives had developed a national organization and the Liberals were still without one. The National Union of Conservative and Constitutional Associations had grown out of a working men's association at Westminster financed by W. H. Smith. During its first two years it led a very precarious existence and was kept alive by the efforts of the new principal agent, Gorst, and F. Sedgwick, but after 1872, when the offices were moved to the party headquarters in Parliament Street, the National Union prospered.[4] Disraeli saw the need for organization and encouraged them. During the election they produced over 150,000 pamphlets and posters and a news-sheet, *The Sun*, which contained intelligence reports on the state of each constituency. After the election triumph the Council of the National Union reported to the eighth annual conference that local associations were flourishing in 65 out of 74 English and Welsh constituencies won from the Liberals, 'a remarkable fact . . . which appears to them to prove, in an unanswerable manner, the great value even for electoral purposes possessed by political associations'.[5]

If its immediate electoral potentialities came as a surprise to the promoters of the National Union their purpose was clear

[1] Add. MSS. 44543, f. 62 (6 Feb. 1874, Gladstone to Spencer). Gladstone used almost the same phrase in another letter.
[2] Ibid. 60 (5 Feb. 1874, Gladstone to Bright).
[3] *The Times*, 11 Feb. 1874, conjectured that with the ballot elections would always go against the party in power. 'It was for black balls, not white, that the Ballot was invented.' See also *The Economist* and *Spectator*, 7 Feb. 1874.
[4] For the foundation and early history of the National Union see R. T. McKenzie, *British Political Parties* (London, 1955), pp. 146–85, and the *Minutes and Proceedings* of the Annual Conferences of the National Union from 1868 (bound in manuscript at the Conservative Central Office).
[5] *Minutes of the Eighth Annual Conference* . . . (London), p. 8.

enough; to found as many local associations with a working-class basis as possible in the belief that unless they appealed to the new mass electorate the party would be for ever out of power.[1] Gorst, with H. C. Raikes[2] and Sedgwick, was the mainstay of the National Union and as long as he had the confidence of Disraeli all went well. Together with the former Whip, he virtually ran the election campaign of 1874.[3] But after 1875, with Disraeli's attention turning to foreign affairs and the rest of the leaders apathetic, Gorst felt frustrated,[4] since he could see that the mere enrolling of 'Constitutional Associations' and even the social bait of 'Conservative Clubs' was not enough to obtain the solid backing of the masses.[5]

The Liberals started some way behind the Conservatives in this field, but they quickly caught up with and outdistanced them. Again Chamberlain led the way.[6] The 'caucus' machines had been established in a number of large cities but they lacked co-ordination. This was provided in 1877 by the National Liberal Federation which Chamberlain[7] virtually called into existence; he drafted its constitution and formulated its policy. In his speech to the opening conference he said that under the new electoral conditions the party must broaden its appeal and let 'the people at large' into its counsels.[8] With Gladstone's blessing and the exhortation to 'organize, organize, organize', the N.L.F. promoted the foundation of Liberal 'Hundreds' throughout the boroughs; they did not attack the counties until after 1880. They had the advantage over the Conservatives of a much more compact and democratic structure at all levels of

[1] The National Union must not be confused with the Conservative Central Office, which financed candidatures. The Party Whip dominated Central Office, the party agent, the National Union, but there were many contacts between them, as during the 1874 election.

[2] Cf. Raikes's 'highly perceptive analysis' of the new functions of a mass party, McKenzie, op. cit., p. 158, citing *Minutes of the Seventh Annual Conference* . . . (1873), pp. 9–10.

[3] H. E. Gorst, *The Fourth Party* (London, 1906), p. 33.

[4] Ibid.

[5] By the end of 1878, 950 associations were enrolled. The variety of entertainment at the Conservative Clubs provided plenty of material for the 1880 election trials. See below, pp. 132 ff.

[6] See above, p. 45.

[7] Chamberlain became the first president and Schnadhorst the first secretary of the N.L.F.

[8] *Proceedings attending the Formation of the National Federation of Liberal Associations* . . . (Birmingham, 1877), pp. 14 ff.

which the non-representative element was very small.[1] They had the advantage too of the support of the real leader of the party, although Hartington ignored them.

At all levels the Liberals prepared for the next election with more skill than the Conservatives. Adam, the Chief Whip,[2] kept a ceaseless watch on the constituencies, insisting that the new associations canvass rather than attend to registration, and encouraging them to select candidates, with the result that by the end of 1879 very few boroughs were without a prospective Liberal candidate.[3] Lastly, came the innovation of the Midlothian campaign which gave Gladstone a popular success such as no political leader had previously enjoyed and promised well for the future. All in all it looked at the end of 1879 as if the previous election had been the last of the old style.[4]

[1] There were three bodies within the Federation—the *Committee of 600* (ward delegates), the *Council* (officers and 10 elected constituency delegates) and the *General Committee* (the officers, 25 co-opted members, and 35 constituency delegates).

[2] Add. MSS. 44095, pt. i, ff. 23–28.

[3] The N.L.F. produced a stream of propaganda during the years preceding 1880. Much of it is now preserved in boxes in the National Liberal Club.

[4] As a tailpiece it may be mentioned that of two learned articles appearing in 1878 on the subject of party organization one makes the barest reference to the National Liberal Federation and both ignore the National Union. Cf. W. F. Rae, 'Political Clubs and Party Organization', *The Nineteenth Century*, iii (May 1878), 908–32; E. D. J. Wilson, 'The Caucus and Its Consequences', ibid. iv (Oct. 1878), 695–712.

CHAPTER V

The General Election of 1880

I

On 5 February 1880 the Parliament elected in 1874 entered its seventh session—the first in the nineteenth century to do so. Its legislative programme gave pride of place to the Budget, the Water Bill,[1] and the necessary measures to extend the life of the Ballot Act for another year. Since the limit set by the Septennial Act was approaching, the newspapers speculated on whether the dissolution would take place at the end of the session or before. None predicted that the session would last a mere six weeks.

Lord Beaconsfield was awaiting a favourable opportunity to counterbalance the effect of Gladstone's Midlothian campaign —the first example of British 'whistle-stop' electioneering. Two by-election victories in mid-February, one in a former home of radicalism,[2] convinced Beaconsfield that the time had arrived. Moreover, the Conservative Central Office were assuring him that the party would not lose more than eighteen seats.[3]

On 8 March the dissolution was announced in Beaconsfield's famous 'manifesto'[4] setting the integrity of the Empire and the maintenance of British ascendancy in Europe as the electoral issues. The Liberal newspapers were at first taken aback, then after condemning the Government for their 'farcical' behaviour in making arrangements for the session knowing that they would never have to carry them out, they plunged into the electioneering whirlpool. The main attack was on the Prime Minister himself. The 'ascendancy of England in the councils of Europe' was

[1] An unimportant measure to buy out private water companies. Its slow progress was later made the excuse for the dissolution.
[2] Southwark. The other victory was at Liverpool, which had generally gone Conservative. In 1878 and 1879 the by-elections had favoured the Liberals.
[3] Monypenny and Buckle, *Life of Beaconsfield*, vi. 520–2.
[4] A public letter to the Duke of Marlborough, Lord-Lieutenant of Ireland, calling on 'all men of light and leading' to resist the 'destructive' doctrine of Home Rule.

bitterly attacked as a foil for Beaconsfield's vanity and machia-
vellianism, designed to divert attention from bad harvests and
budgetary deficits at home.[1] In spite of their strength of party
conviction the Liberal organs did not venture at the beginning
to make predictions about the result. The *Spectator* cited the
Southwark and Elgin[2] by-elections as evidence that 'under the
ballot calculations are at fault and pledges very frequently
broken'.[3]

No such hesitancy characterized the pro-government press.
The *Daily Telegraph*, *Standard*, and *Morning Post* took for granted
that the Government would be triumphantly returned. The
Pall Mall Gazette wrote: 'Nobody need be told, we suppose, that
the Liberal party has not the faintest hope of success except
through favour of the Irish party.'[4] *The Times* was apprehensive
about the effect that an electoral debacle *for the Liberals* might
have on the country: 'Nothing is ever more unfortunate, in the
general interests of the country than that one of the two parties
should be reduced to this helpless condition.' It earnestly hoped
the Liberals would not throw away the opportunity of making
a 'fresh start', i.e. by accepting Conservative imperialist doctrine
and firmly refusing any association with the Irish Home Rulers.[5]
The *Statist*, an advocate of moderate Conservatism, asserted
that the Liberal leaders unlike their opponents had failed to
read the signs of the times.[6]

Whatever its misgivings about the result may have been *The
Times* prophesied correctly: 'Never, perhaps, since the passing
of the Reform Act of 1832 has an electoral battle been fought
out in the United Kingdom with more determination than
is likely to be now displayed.'[7] But before considering the
course of the campaign some attention must be given to the

[1] The following extract from the *Spectator* (13 Mar.) is typical of the attitude of the
Liberal organs towards Disraeli. It would be hard to find in modern electioneering
a match for its concentrated venom: 'It is for the country to choose . . . between the
old statesmen who, by the continuous improvements of half-a-century, have made
England what it is, . . . and the flashy Oriental who offers it notoriety, and who has
in every quarter of the world destroyed its reputation for fair dealing, unselfishness,
and respect for the rights of the weak'.
[2] Where the Liberals had won in 1879.
[3] *Spectator*, 13 Mar. 1880.   [4] *Pall Mall Gazette*, 11 Mar. 1880.
[5] *The Times*, 10 Mar. 1880.
[6] *Statist*, 13 Mar. 1880.
[7] *The Times*, 10 Mar. 1880. Only *Fraser's Magazine* (Mar. 1880) predicted for
the Liberals a clear majority based on Irish support (xxi. 421–32).

Parliamentary Elections and Corrupt Practices Bill, which, with the Budget,[1] was rushed through in the last two weeks of the session.

2

As has been seen, Holker's Parliamentary Elections and Corrupt Practices Act of 1879[2] had continued the Parliamentary Elections Act of 1868 until December 1880, with two judges instead of one and some minor procedural changes.[3] It was then understood that another continuance Bill would be introduced during the 1880 session. On 4 March, Sir Charles Dilke asked the Attorney-General whether the Cabinet intended merely to reintroduce the 1879 Bill: if so, he would (as before) introduce a resolution on employment of vehicles since that law was universally broken. In reply Sir John Holker moved that the government measure (a simple continuance Bill) be ordered, but the House was counted out. On the following day the Bill received a first reading, but was withdrawn on 8 March.

On the same day it fell to Sir Stafford Northcote to give the news of the impending dissolution to the unsuspecting House of Commons. He assured the House that not only the Water Bill but the matter of conveyance of voters in boroughs would be dealt with before the end of the session, provided that the Opposition gave 'that assistance without which it will be impossible to carry through our business'.[4] Forster, following immediately afterwards, said he had heard Northcote's announcement with 'great satisfaction' and promised co-operation by the Liberals. They clearly expected the Government to put further restrictions on the employment of vehicles for election purposes.

They were to be swiftly disillusioned. The new Bill made its

[1] The Budget which involved a large deficit gave great satisfaction to Liberal campaign orators, and considerably embarrassed the Government, especially Northcote, the Chancellor of the Exchequer.
[2] 42 & 43 Vict., c. 75.   [3] See above, p. 108.
[4] Since Northcote was afterwards charged with bad faith, it is as well to quote his own words on the subject of the forthcoming Corrupt Practices Bill: 'I do not think it would be at all impossible for the House to deal with that Bill [i.e. the Water Bill], and also with the particular question to which the hon. Baronet the Member for Chelsea [Dilke] called attention the other night; I mean the question of the conveyance of voters in boroughs. That is a question which we feel ought not to be left in the uncertain state in which it is at present.' 3 Hans. ccli (8 Mar. 1880), 559–60.

appearance on 10 March, when many members were already
en route to their constituencies. It was in exactly the same form as
the Bill of the previous year but for a clause repealing section 36
of the Representation of the People Act 1867, which made it an
illegal practice to pay for conveyance of voters in boroughs with
the exception of the five large rural boroughs. The effect of this
clause would be to assimilate the borough and county electioneering practice by removing all restrictions on conveyances.
Holker explained that section 36 had been utterly disregarded
and the Government wished to get rid of the anomaly.[1]

This unexpected move was not fully understood at first.
Holker's speech was followed by a very short debate. Dilke
merely said that he had wished the practice to be entirely
abolished, but that he knew the Government could not carry
such a proposal, and Stanton, the member for the litigious
borough of Stroud, hoped that the practice of issuing railway
tickets to voters would also be legalized.[2] The newspapers either
ignored or misunderstood the Bill; *The Times* in a short note
stating it was 'simply a Continuance Bill for 1880 and 1881'.[3]

The second reading debate opened on the following day when
the Liberal attack was launched by the two members for Glasgow, Dr. C. Cameron and G. Anderson.[4] They condemned the
Government for trying to make legal an illegal practice, which,
though widespread, was not universal (it had rarely been heard
of in Scotland or Ireland), and also because of the unseemly
haste with which the Bill was introduced at the fag-end of the
session. The 1875 Committee had discovered a great number of
examples of evasion of the law but that was no reason why the
Government should go in the opposite direction. In any case,
the Bill of 1879 would not expire until the end of the year, so
why was the matter not left to the next Parliament? Other
Liberals and Irish Home Rulers reinforced these arguments:
the inevitable consequence of the Bill would be an increase,
probably of vast proportions, in the cost of elections generally
and certainly in the incidence of bribery; it would discriminate
against poor candidates and make a seat in the House even

[1] *3 Hans.* ccli (10 Mar. 1880), 777–8.
[2] Ibid., 778–80. Leave to introduce was granted without a division.
[3] *The Times*, 11 Mar. 1880.
[4] *3 Hans.* ccli (11 Mar. 1880), 859–63.

more 'the rich man's privilege and perquisite'[1] than it was; if there were an anomaly in the absence of a penalty for conveying in boroughs then a penalty should be introduced rather than the entire law repealed; all conveyance money ought to be made illegal.

The Attorney-General made no attempt to answer these detailed charges. He confined himself to a general plea that it would be 'monstrous' to make a candidate lose his seat for so innocent an act as paying for a cab, while the legalizing of such an act, on the contrary, would do nobody any harm. He stated that by a draftsman's error the Bill applied only to England but that in committee it would be extended to Scotland and Ireland. Only three Conservatives spoke.[2] They argued that the practice, if legal in counties, ought also to be legalized in boroughs; the practice was so widespread that it was no longer regarded as an offence against the law; the feeling of the country was in favour of this change; even if a candidate were poor he could always get plenty of backers ready to pay for his conveyances. Mark Stewart, M.P. for Wigtown Burghs, probably summed up the Government's case as succinctly as anyone could by saying: 'The country was not governed by logic, but by Parliament.'[3] A motion to adjourn the debate was defeated by 120 votes to 47, and Cameron's amendment to make the provisions of the Act of 1867 more effective was rejected by 115 votes to 48. The second reading was then taken.

On 12 March Northcote fixed the committee stage for 15 March, but on that date, without giving any reason, he moved that the committee be deferred until the following day.[4] Monk, Liberal M.P. for Gloucester, appealed for a withdrawal of the Bill, as less than a hundred members were left in London. Lord Hartington supported the appeal. It was 'hardly decent', he said, to settle the issue in this way. Anderson pleaded with the Government not to use its 'mechanical majority'. Northcote, however, was firm. He had reminded the House when announcing the dissolution, he said, that this Bill would be proceeded

---

[1] Sir George Campbell, Liberal M.P. for Kirkcaldy. *3 Hans.* ccli (11 Mar. 1880), 866.

[2] Including Alfred Gathorne Hardy, who was to figure a few months later in the Canterbury Petition Trial.

[3] Ibid. 868.

[4] *3 Hans.* ccli (15 Mar. 1880), 1071-3.

with since 'a large number of members wished it to be settled *one way or the other*'.[1]

The committee debate on 16 March was the only long debate on the measure.[2] Two Liberal front-benchers, Hartington and Forster, led for the Opposition and the Cabinet were represented by Northcote, the Solicitor-General (Sir Hardinge Giffard), and the Attorney-General for Ireland (Gibson). Hartington and Forster argued that the Government had broken their undertaking not to introduce controversial legislation if the Opposition helped to expedite the remaining business of the session and that the bulk of the Liberal members had left for their constituencies unaware of the nature of the measure. To this, Giffard and Northcote could only offer the excuse that Northcote had on 8 March clearly foretold the change in the law and that it was a result of pressure from Dilke that the Government was introducing the Bill[3]—although all Dilke's urging had been in the opposite direction.

Despite the growing volume of Opposition protests the Government refused to concede any point except one which made the Bill look even more anomalous; in the face of pleas by Scottish and Irish members that the Bill was unnecessary in their countries, Northcote withdrew his amendments extending it to Scotland and Ireland. The Bill passed its third reading to the accompaniment of promises by the Liberals that they would repeal it as soon as they secured power.[4]

The Bill had passed through the Commons in eight days. In the Lords it took only four—a record for a piece of legislation affecting the electoral system. The only opposition came on the third reading when two Liberal amendments were moved—one on the ground of principle, the other stating that the Bill was inopportune. Replying for the Government the Prime Minister deprecated amendments for which no notice had been given. With bland disregard for the facts he said that the Government was merely obliging a large number of members of the House of

[1] *3 Hans.* ccli (15 Mar. 1880), 1072 (my italics), but see above, p. 114, n. 4.
[2] Ibid. (16 Mar.), 1100–63.
[3] Both Northcote (ibid. 1130) and Giffard (ibid. 1106) made the claim that Dilke was the instigator of the Bill. Dilke himself was absent from the House after 11 Mar.
[4] Anderson's parting shot was that the Conservatives had come in with the cry of 'Beer and the Bible' and would go out with 'Cabs and Corruption'.

Commons drawn from all parties and in any case the matter was the concern of the Commons rather than the Lords. The latter was a very unusual argument to come from the Conservative benches, but it effectively silenced the Opposition. One amendment was withdrawn, the other defeated by 39 votes to 24; the Bill passed the third stage and received the Royal Assent on the following day, 24 March.[1]

The passing of the only piece of reactionary electoral legislation of the century would at any other time have secured a great deal of attention by the press, but in the middle of the election campaign the papers could spare only a short leading article or report. The Liberal *Daily News* was quite outspoken.[2] To force the Bill through a depleted House, it said, was itself 'a corrupt practice of the most scandalous kind', and went on to conjecture that the reason why Scotland and Ireland were exempted from the scope of the Bill was that the Conservatives knew they were beaten there before the elections began. The *Spectator* was more moderate. Since payment for conveyances was legal in counties it was 'quite fair' that the practice be made legal in boroughs also. But it predicted that in London and the grouped boroughs where distances were greater the Bill might make a serious difference to the less wealthy candidates.[3] The Conservative press, for the most part, gave guarded approval. *The Times* agreed with the objection that the power of the purse would be increased, but protested that the interests of the electors must be regarded as well as those of the candidates.[4] The *Pall Mall Gazette* approved the Bill on its merits but roundly condemned the timing and manner of its passing into law as 'neither calculated to inspire respect for the present Legislature, nor consistent with the respect which the present Legislature itself owes to the decisions of a former Parliament'.[5] The prevailing sentiment among the pro-government papers appeared to be that of the *Morning Post*: that there was much to be said for the practice and

[1] 43 Vict. c. 18.   [2] *Daily News*, 18 Mar. 1880.
[3] *Spectator*, 13 Mar. 1880.
[4] The 'interest' of the voter was that he might exercise the franchise with the minimum inconvenience. *The Times*, 17 Mar. 1880.
[5] *Pall Mall Gazette*, 17 Mar. 1880. This article also pointed out the anomalous consequences of the exclusion of Scotland and Ireland. If the law is obeyed in Scotland, why not in England? If it serves no public end, why continue it in Scotland and Ireland?

much against it, and that the election would provide plenty of opportunities for seeing whether bribery would increase or not.[1] The Liberal politicians' attitude to the Bill during the remainder of the campaign was summed up in Gladstone's remarks at Gilmerton that it was 'a measure to benefit the rich candidate, and to again legalize one of the worst systems of electoral corruption'.[2] Its immediate effect on the Liberal tactics was shown by an advertisement appealing for 'private carriages' on election day for Hobhouse and Morley at Westminster, but the full extent of the benefits reaped by the cab interest was not apparent until the elections were over and the crop of petitions came up for trial.

3

The campaign in Great Britain lasted from 8 to 30 March.[3] During these three weeks the pace was set by the Liberals, taking their cue from Gladstone who excelled even his success of the previous winter. His journey from London on 16 March was another series of triumphant 'whistle-stops' with crowds numbering several thousands at all the large stations.[4] Gladstone's speeches followed the same model throughout: a number of points against the Government made clearly and succinctly, followed by a restrained commendation of the local candidates. In Scotland he made fifteen major speeches and averaged almost two every day in the fortnight before polling day. Gladstone's oratory was generally prolix—*The Times* complained that his speech at Edinburgh took up five columns of their space[5]—but whether in the train, or in the Edinburgh music hall, or in the pulpit at Gilmerton Presbyterian Church (which

---

[1] *Morning Post*, 18 Mar. 1880.

[2] *Pall Mall Gazette*, 19 Mar. 1880.

[3] The Dean of Norwich condemned the Government for selecting Passion Week and Easter Week for the election.

[4] A vivid account of the campaign is given in W. Saunders, *The New Parliament, 1880* (London, 1880). Saunders was later radical M.P. for Walworth. The book is valuable as a contemporary record on a larger scale than the *Annual Register*. It lacks insight, however, into the deeper political currents of the time and the statistics cited are sometimes inaccurate—e.g. the lists of contests (p. 37) and the estimates of the poll (pp. 380–1) are misleading—and there are several discrepancies between the final returns as given on pp. 160–3 and those on p. 176.

[5] *The Times*, 18 Mar. 1880.

he had to mount because the platform did not 'properly command' the gallery),[1] Gladstone's speeches showed unbounded confidence that the Liberals would win. This optimistic fervour was possibly the party's best electioneering asset. Triumphal arches, queues of poor workers waiting for hours to shake his hand, and loud applause whenever his name was mentioned, combined to make Gladstone (at least as far as Scotland was concerned) the first party leader with demagogic appeal. The newspapers were filled by the speeches of Gladstone, Hartington, and Bright and even the average candidate in a large constituency made two speeches every day of the week. From his unique vantage point as a peer and ex-minister who had announced in the middle of the campaign that he was leaving his party and becoming a Liberal, Lord Derby[2] reflected that it would astonish a politician of the era of Castlereagh and Canning to see ministers and ex-ministers attacking each other not only at election times but throughout the year on public platforms.[3]

The Conservatives could not hope to match the array of oratorical talent possessed by the Liberals who had the two greatest political speakers in the country. Worse still, three of the 'Inner Cabinet', Beaconsfield, Salisbury, and Cairns, were, as peers, by custom debarred from the electioneering struggle. This was not altogether a disaster as the talents of all three were more suited to the debating chamber than the stump. The government counter-attack was led by Northcote and Cross.[4] Their speeches almost invariably avoided the subject of the Government's record, and concentrated on the prospect of an unfavourable foreign reaction to a return of Gladstone and the Liberals (every country except Russia wanted Gladstone to stay

---

[1] Saunders, op. cit., p. 144. Gladstone's speeches were generally delivered in Free Churches or United Presbyterian Churches (no other suitable building could be found in small towns and the open-air meeting had not yet become general). Saunders complains that the crowds (frequently cheering and groaning) 'showed no reverence for the buildings'. In one church a blind musician (who normally was the organist) for light relief played Scottish airs on a harmonium and sang a popular tune, 'The Little Fat Man' (ibid.).

[2] *Pall Mall Gazette*, 24 Mar. 1880. Derby had been elected Patron of the National Union in 1869.

[3] Hartington made 24 set speeches to Gladstone's 15.

[4] With Sir Michael Hicks-Beach, Colonel Stanley, and Sir Hardinge Giffard as second-strings.

out of office). The Conservatives seemed to have the advantage as far as the manufacture of propaganda was concerned. The National Union circulated 178,000 copies of a speech by the 'Radical Jingo', Joseph Cowen, and even had it translated into Welsh.[1] They sold up to 750,000 placards and handbills at cheap prices with such self-explanatory titles as 'Which party makes most Wars?', 'Mr. Gladstone's Political Antecedents', 'Earl Russell's Estimate of Mr. Gladstone', 'Sir Wm. Harcourt's Opinion of Mr. Gladstone'. Of their allied pressure groups, the Church Defence Institution sold pamphlets and placards more cheaply still, and the publicans ensured that practically every public house in London was adorned with Tory slogans and colours[2] from basement to garret. Liberal propaganda by contrast seemed more decorous.

The vigour and enthusiasm of the Liberal meetings throughout the country made up for their inadequate propaganda. On the other hand, some Conservative meetings were very stormy. At a meeting in the Shoreditch Town Hall in support of G. C. T. Bartley, founder of the National Penny Bank and candidate for Hackney,[3] Northcote was interrupted throughout his speech and had to bring it to an abrupt end. Even in his own county, at Torquay, Northcote and his son, the Conservative candidate for Exeter, were mobbed by the crowd, and a bodyguard had to be formed for them. The Conservatives attempted to forestall rowdyism by printing tickets for their meetings, but tickets were somehow forged and ticket meetings at Shoreditch and the City were thrown into disorder.[4] A meeting at Barrow addressed by the Secretary for War, Colonel Stanley, became extremely uproarious and had to be abandoned, although extra police were stationed in the town to keep order. Lord John Manners was pelted at Melton Mowbray with eggs filled with 'gas-tar'.

[1] They also sent 'Election Handy Sheets' (containing statistics and general information) to all the contested constituencies. There was no successor to the *British Lion* and the *Sun* (cf. *Report of the 14th Annual Conference*, 23 July 1880), but Conservative propaganda was not confined to National Union publications.

[2] The *Saturday Review* (at this time becoming more Conservative in tone) was moved to comment that 'the danger is that they [the publicans] may have overdone a little their splendid homage to the Crown, the altar, and the tap' (*S.R.*, 27 Mar. 1880).

[3] Bartley was a member of the Council of the National Union and afterwards of the Central Committee. See below, p. 176, n. 4.

[4] *The Times*, 25 Mar. 1880.

Only at the very end of the campaign did any prominent Liberal encounter opposition of this sort.[1]

What interest there was in corrupt practices during the election centred mainly on two topics—the probable effects of the new Corrupt Practices Act and the faggot-votes of Midlothian. The creation of faggot-votes had long been a grievance among Liberal voters in Scotland,[2] and during the Midlothian campaign the 'ducal faggots' were execrated in several speeches. However, the Conservatives now claimed that the Liberals were doing the same, and *The Times* summed up the issue in a famous sentence: 'If the secret electioneering history of the country came to be written, we doubt very much if either party would be able with a good conscience to cry "shame" on the other.'[3] After the results had been announced at Northumberland North, a constituency which had returned two Conservatives without a contest since 1852, G. O. Trevelyan claimed that the Conservatives had been able to maintain the *status quo* only by unsparing landlord coercion. Tenants, he said, had been repeatedly waited upon by landlords and agents, canvassing for their votes, and warned to abstain rather than vote for the Liberal candidate.

Occasionally there were complaints made about the high cost of electioneering. Dr. Kenealy of Tichborne trial fame told the electors of Stoke that he was unable to pay the expenses of his contest and asked for their help. On the other hand Henry Campbell-Bannerman complained that the Conservative member for Buteshire, Charles Dalrymple, was promoting a Scottish Election Fund to finance Conservative candidates throughout Scotland, even in burghs where they had no chance, in order to divert the Liberals' attention from the county contests.[4]

Towards the end of the campaign the *Pall Mall Gazette* in an article on 'Bribery in the Old Time' concluded that 'comparative honesty' was the mark of elections since 1868.[5]

[1] When Hartington spoke at Ribchester, a stronghold of Conservatism, on 30 Mar., windows were broken, there were many interruptions, and Hartington himself was 'in danger of personal injury' (Saunders, op. cit., p. 55).

[2] After the election of 1868, when the counties of Peebles and Selkirk had a narrow Conservative majority, several gentlemen from Edinburgh, Fife, and even London were registered as owners of small blocks of houses at about £5 annual rental. Cf. *The Scotsman*, 19 Feb. 1869. Peebles and Selkirk remained Conservative until this election.   [3] *The Times*, 31 Mar. 1880.

[4] Ibid.   [5] *Pall Mall Gazette*, 24 Mar. 1880.

Just before polling started the Liberal leaders[1] seem to have become genuinely convinced that—to use a phrase coined after the election—the tide was flowing with them. W. P. Adam, the Chief Whip, wrote to Gladstone on 25 March: 'Things look well everywhere at present if Parnell does not spoil matters in Ireland',[2] and at the same time Bright, writing from Birmingham to a Liberal friend, said: 'From all parts of the country the tidings are encouraging. Boroughs and counties promise many changes for the Liberal party . . .'[3] On the other hand, the Conservative leaders seem to have had no inkling of disaster. By balancing the by-elections and the powerful influence of the licensed trade against the apparently successful Liberal canvass they managed to convince themselves that victory might still be theirs. How far this presumption went is shown in a remarkable speech by G. Sclater Booth, lately President of the Local Government Board, when being returned unopposed for North Hampshire. He said that, as far as he knew, not one of those taking part in the campaign had any presentiment of the sudden and unexpected change. Whereas on former occasions the by-elections had given some indication of the national trend this time they had done the reverse. Such a 'bloodless revolution' was 'a serious matter for the consideration of every thinking man'.[4] Nor was the Queen's holiday in Baden marred by any gloomy forebodings in her correspondence with the Prime Minister.[5] Polling lasted nearly a fortnight. London and the large English boroughs went to the polls on Tuesday, 31 March. By 3 April the English borough elections were concluded. The English counties and Scotland and Ireland voted on the following week and by 10 April all but 27 seats were filled.

In the 62 constituencies where the results were out on 1 April

[1] Although the leaders were convinced of victory the rank and file were afraid of a stalemate, Saunders (p. 165) says *none* of the Liberals thought they could do more than wipe out the majority against them, but this is an exaggeration.

[2] Add. MSS. 44095, Pt. I, Adam to Gladstone, 25 Mar. 1880.

[3] Bright to E. Allen of East Dereham. This letter may have been written with an eye to publication. It eventually found its way into the *Pall Mall Gazette*, 29 Mar. 1880.

[4] Quoted in Saunders, *The New Parliament, 1880*, pp. 128–9.

[5] Cf. *Letters of Queen Victoria* (ed. G. E. Buckle), 2nd ser. iii (1879–85), 68–73. In the *Life of Beaconsfield*, vi. 522, Buckle writes: 'With the exception of Gladstone and some enthusiastic Radicals, nobody expected a sweeping victory for either side.' Buckle, however, forgets Harcourt who expected a majority of 50 seats.

the Liberals had a net gain of 31 seats—their only serious reverse being in London, where the Conservatives captured three out of four seats in the City in addition to the Greenwich seat which Gladstone had deserted. The next day the Conservative majority had vanished and in the final week the question was only how large the Liberal following would be. The campaign went on in the counties right up to the various polling days, results from the boroughs being telegraphed by the 'Central News' in Fleet Street—another innovation.[1] The psychological effect[2] of the initial swing was such that one Liberal candidate, who had decided to withdraw, changed his mind at the last minute, was nominated, and returned at the head of the poll.[3] There is no means of knowing how many county voters were affected. The Central News helped the trend by forecasting, on the basis of reports from local correspondents, a Liberal majority of 80. This was so far ahead of what any newspaper had thought possible that it elated the Liberals considerably.[4]

Excitement continued right up to the end. The cab interest showed their true colours on election day in London by displaying posters ironically calling on electors to 'Vote for Gladstonkoff, Commander-in-Chief of the Russian forces in Great Britain'; afterwards many cab-drivers were prosecuted for being drunk in charge. There were also about twenty polling-day riots—all but one directed against the Conservatives.[5]

4

The campaign in Ireland deserves special mention[6] not only because the new Home Rule party was undergoing its first real electoral test but also because of the divergence of electoral

[1] The Central News advertised: 'All results telegraphed immediately and direct from each polling place—£25, five subscribers in same telegraphic delivery—£10. each. Selected results—2/- each prepaid'. *Pall Mall Gazette*, 27 Mar. 1880 (Saunders was the founder of the 'Central News').

[2] Saunders, *The New Parliament, 1880*, p. 167.

[3] Laycock at N. Lincs. Had he not stood two Conservatives would have been unopposed.

[4] Saunders, *The New Parliament, 1880*, p. 167.

[5] Only one was the subject of a petition—the Chester riot. See below, p. 138.

[6] C. Cruise O'Brien's *Parnell and his Party 1880–1890* (Oxford, 1957), a major authority for this period, is misleading, however, in suggesting that the Parnellites fought the 1880 election exclusively on the land question. O'Brien fails to mention the Beaconsfield manifesto or the double strategy described in these pages. See *Parnell and his Party*, pp. 8–9, 38–42.

tactics between the parent body, the Irish Home Rule League, and its subsidiary, the Home Rule Confederation of Great Britain.[1]

The Irish Home Rule League at the election of 1874 was a loose organization with an upper-class membership and vague aspirations towards national self-government. Discipline was very lax and during the second Disraeli administration some Home Rulers sat on the Conservative benches away from their colleagues.

Isaac Butt, the leader, and all but a handful of the Home Rulers were in favour of moderate constitutional opposition at Westminster. When Charles Stewart Parnell was elected at a by-election for Meath in 1875 he at once set about forming a nucleus of party members devoted to a more dynamic policy[2] of which the systematic obstruction of parliamentary business was the first fruits.

Parnell's militancy soon became popular with the Irish generally, both at home and in England. In 1877 he replaced Butt as President of the Home Rule Confederation and in 1879 he was elected President of the Land League, a new pressure group designed to break the power of the landlords and comprising all the physical force, anti-constitutional and republican elements, in Ireland. However, he still had to capture the Parliamentary Party, most of whom looked askance at his tactics.[3] When the dissolution was announced he was in America on a fund-raising campaign. In his absence the Home Rule Confederation of Great Britain decided to campaign on the Beaconsfield manifesto, waive all demands for Home Rule, and support the Liberals. Their manifesto proclaimed: 'Every Irishman who loves Ireland, every Irishman who seeks and appreciates the friendship of honest Englishmen and Scotchmen, will oppose to the utmost of his ability the common enemy of the peace and concord of Ireland and Great Britain[4] (Lord Beaconsfield).'

[1] The Home Rule League was formed in 1870, the Home Rule Confederation—to organize the Irish vote in Britain—in 1873.

[2] Biggar was the best known of these early obstructionists. In fact he was 'the father of obstructionism'. See below, p. 167.

[3] Out of 56 professed Home Rulers elected in 1874, 17 were landowners, 16 merchants, 21 from the higher professions, and only 2 from farming stock. Cf. *Parnell and his Party*, p. 18.

[4] Cited in Saunders, *The New Parliament, 1880*, p. 159.

Several Home Rule candidates from Ireland campaigned in England on Liberal platforms, and by 2 April the Confederation was able to report that of 43 English constituencies (almost all boroughs) where there was a significant Irish vote 37 would go to the Liberals.[1]

In so far as the aim of the Beaconsfield manifesto was to drive a wedge between Liberals and Home Rulers by making Home Rule unpopular in Britain it was foiled by the strategy of the Home Rule Confederation. For a time it looked as if the Irish Home Rule League would campaign on the same grounds, shelving the issue and stressing their affinities with the Liberals. Indeed William Shaw, who had succeeded Butt as leader of the party in 1879, issued an address on much the same lines as the manifesto of the Home Rule Confederation. Parnell, however, on his return from America flaunted the Home Rule banner very high indeed. He went round the country making speeches that displayed a complete indifference to every shade of British opinion. He supported only candidates that were uncompromisingly for Home Rule. In eight constituencies he even ran candidates of his own against the official party nominees,[2] although the outgoing members were men of standing in the area and in at least two cases the Parnellite candidates were 'carpet baggers', unknown and impecunious journalists.[3]

Parnell's campaign was not without incident. Parcels of dynamite were found under the platform at one meeting, and at another—where Parnell was opposing a local 'Whiggish' landlord—a riot[4] occurred of such violence that part of the British press decided that Parnell's popularity at home was over-rated.[5]

---

[1] Cited in Saunders, *The New Parliament, 1880*, p. 157. A. M. Sullivan made a special campaign in York, the constituency of the Chief Secretary, James Lowther. Lowther was returned at the bottom of the poll.

[2] Parnell characterized these as 'Whiggish' or 'nominal' Home Rulers.

[3] In Sligo Thomas Sexton (a poor journalist from Dublin) opposed Colonel King-Harman, whom Saunders (*The New Parliament, 1880*, p. 164) described as 'an out-and-out Home Ruler' and 'the owner of estates yielding a rental of £40,000 a year'. Sexton won.

[4] According to the reports, several of the Parnellites were beaten and pitched into the crowd with bleeding heads; a priest who was to have taken the chair was ejected from the platform with his hand cut, and another priest warded off a blow that would otherwise have split the skull of a journalist from the *New York Herald*, who was covering the campaign.

Cf. *The Times*, 29–30 Mar. 1880; *Spectator*, 3 Apr. 1880: and *contra*, *Freeman's Journal*, 31 Mar. 1880.

On that account the results when they came were even more of a surprise.

The Irish Liberals and Conservatives, lacking leadership and organization, depended on upper-class influence. The Conservative members were in the main concentrated in Ulster, the province where landlord influence was at its greatest. The Liberals fondly hoped that the effect of the Midlothian campaign and the Beaconsfield manifesto would be enough to improve their chances.

The results were a signal triumph for Parnell even without considering the very restricted state of the franchise. Parnell himself was returned for three constituencies. The 'carpet-baggers from England' were successful in Roscommon, Sligo, and Wexford, and in two constituencies only was the Parnellite nominee defeated. A direct, though unexpected, result of the Beaconsfield manifesto was the defeat by orthodox Home Rulers of four aristocrats and landowners who, though Conservative, had sat for some years for pro-Liberal or Home Rule constituencies owing to popular indulgence, since they were good landlords.[1] Thus, despite the division within the party and the double electioneering strategy; despite the propaganda value to the Conservatives in both countries of many election speeches; despite the opposition of the upper classes, the wariness of the Catholic clergy, and the narrow franchise, the Home Rule party as a whole gained five seats, and the Parnellites within it trebled their number.[2] It is not surprising that after the election Parnell jumped the last hurdle, and was elected sessional chairman of the Irish Parliamentary Party and president of the Irish Home Rule League.

Although a few petitions arising out of the Irish election came up for trial there was little mention of corrupt practices during the Irish campaign. The violent incidents, though more spectacular, were fewer than in 1874. The petitions will be treated

[1] Bruen and Kavanagh (Carlow), Lord Charles Beresford (Waterford), Marquis of Hamilton (Donegal).

[2] Before the election there were 56 Home Rulers, 31 Conservatives, and 16 Liberals. After the election 61 Home Rulers, 26 Conservatives, and 16 Liberals. Of the 61 Dr. O'Brien estimates that 24 were Parnellites (op. cit., pp. 23–26). Before the election they did not amount to more than 7 or 8. Saunders's figures for the Irish elections contradict each other in several places and are quite worthless (pp. 160–3).

separately, but although there was no petition from Galway city the election address of J. O. Lever, a London shipowner making his second attempt to be elected for the city as 'A liberal-conservative and in favour of Home Rule', is worth quoting:

> Vote for Lever—who was prevented from building extensive mills for the manufacture of flax and cotton by his non-election at his last contest. . . . Vote for Lever who has no personal interests to serve . . . who, from his extensive experience . . . influential connections and capital, is now in a better position than he ever was to secure the prosperity of GALWAY.[1]

Lever was elected.[2]

5

The results of the general election caused most newspapers considerable embarrassment. Only the *Daily News* crowed over the others, though it could not claim with any degree of conviction that it had predicted the result. The pro-government papers took several days to realize the awful truth.[3] The *Standard* tried to make a virtue out of necessity, and pressed on its readers the duty of recognizing accomplished facts. *The Times* saw the general trend clearly enough on the first day and tried to explain the swing.[4] Its first guess presumed a natural reaction away from a party that had been six years in power; moreover, the Liberals had been more 'incessant, versatile and ingenious' than any previous Opposition in mobilizing discontents that had arisen from the hardships of recent years. A few days later *The Times* warmed to that theme and expanded it: the numerous classes to which Gladstone and the Liberals had appealed were passing through the severest crisis; they did not blame the ministry for their past conduct, but they wished to see if the other side could not do better for them. This contrasted strangely with the attitude of *The Times* at the beginning of the campaign.[5] The *Saturday Review* marvelled at the universal

[1] Saunders, op. cit., pp. 249–50.
[2] A Parnellite journal, *The Nation*, described Lever as 'an arrant humbug' (13 Apr. 1880); cited in O'Brien, *Parnell and his Party*, p. 12, n. 2.
[3] Cf. *Standard*, 2–10 Apr. 1880; *Daily News*, 2–9 Apr. 1880; *Daily Telegraph*, 2–9 Apr. 1880; *Pall Mall Gazette*, 2–6 Apr. 1880.
[4] *The Times*, 2, 9, 13, 28 Apr. 1880.
[5] See above, p. 113.

Liberal triumph and the ignominious defeat of the publicans.[1]
The *Pall Mall Gazette* railed at the fickleness of the mass electorate and predicted that all future elections would be won by
the Opposition of the day.[2]

No newspaper put down the result to the Liberals' superior
organization, and when Chamberlain wrote to *The Times* pointing out that the Caucus had been successful in 60 out of 67
boroughs where it was established, the letter provoked neither
a reply nor an editorial comment.[3]

6

It has been shown that corrupt practices were hardly mentioned in Great Britain or Ireland during the election campaign.
The petition trials immediately afterwards, conducted for the
first time by two judges, brought their existence to the attention of the public again. Forty-two petitions were originally
presented, but of these only twenty-eight came up for trial,
twenty-two from England and Wales, one from Scotland, and
five from Ireland.

The Irish petitions showed that pockets of landlord influence
still existed in small boroughs in the south and throughout the
north, and that in these constituencies personal electioneering
was more important than political doctrine. The tiny borough
of Athlone[4] had been represented since 1857 by either of two
local landowners, Sir John Ennis and Edward Sheil, both professing the same moderate Liberal brand of politics—the latter a
'Liberal Home Ruler'. Once again they contested the single seat.[5]
In Irish boroughs of this size party organization did not count.
Instead the candidates had to compete in offering inducements
to the electorate. They hired hotels and large houses for purely
nominal committee rooms at very high rates, appointed a very
large number of personation agents (for a single polling station),

[1] *Saturday Review*, 3 Apr. 1880.
[2] *Pall Mall Gazette*, 5 Apr. 1880.
[3] *The Times*, 13 Apr. 1880. The *Standard* (10 Apr. 1880) attributed the defeat to
defection by the county voters but did not give any reason for it.
[4] Eight Irish boroughs, including Athlone and Dungannon, had electorates of
less than 500. All were abolished in 1885.
[5] In 1874 there had been a tie and on petition Sheil was given the seat. Cf.
above, p. 96.

and indulged in such negative bribery as not pressing for payment of debts.

On polling day Ennis defeated Sheil by one vote, and the latter petitioned on the usual grounds.[1] Baron Fitzgerald, who heard the petition, had taken a grave view twelve years before of similar practices in Cashel.[2] Here he sympathized with the candidates on the high cost of 'conveniences', such as hotels and committee rooms, without inquiring as to their necessity. The evidence of those who testified to bribery was dismissed as 'improbable', and the evidence of personation and undue influence as unproved. The junior judge, Mr. Justice Harrison, concurred and Sir John Ennis was allowed to keep his seat until the growth of the Home Rule party, and the redistribution of 1885, put an end both to his type of politics and the constituencies where it could be practised.

Another unsuccessful case, this time from County Down[3] in Ulster, was exceptionally interesting in that it provided the first and only attempt to question the secrecy of the ballot. The central figure in the petition, one Edward Finnigan, was one of the very few Conservative party organizers in Ireland during this period. He had built up the Constitutional Associations of counties Antrim and Down with skill and energy, and his aim was to retain the second seat in County Down, which had been held by a radical landlord, Sharman Crawford, until his death in 1878. At the subsequent by-election Lord Castlereagh, son of the second biggest landowner in the county,[4] had won the seat for the Conservatives.

When the campaign opened in 1880, Crawford's son determined to have a try and Finnigan in his tour of the county, canvassing support among the tenants of the Hills and Stewarts, let fall the sinister piece of information that he could prove that votes could be disclosed after the election to the landlords and that the much-vaunted secrecy of the ballot was 'a farce'.

This claim was at once taken up by the leading Liberal paper, the *Northern Whig*,[5] which bluntly denounced Finnigan

[1] See *P.P. 1880*, lvii. 71–78.
[2] See above, p. 55.
[3] *P.P. 1880*, lvii. 571–87 (Judgement); 589–829 (Minutes of Evidence).
[4] The Marquis of Londonderry. The other county member (Lord Arthur Hill) was the son of the biggest landowner, the Marquis of Downshire.
[5] Cf. *Northern Whig*, 20–26 Feb. 1880.

as a fraud. Nevertheless he insisted, in a letter to the paper, that 'it is not only possible, but easy, to ascertain, if desirable, how each individual voter has recorded his vote'. This letter, as might be expected, caused quite a stir in the province. An ex-(Liberal) M.P. for Belfast wrote to Forster asking him to restore public faith in the secrecy of the ballot. Forster replied that Finnigan's claim was absurd, an 'electioneering manœuvre meant to alarm ignorant voters', and grimly reminded him that the Ballot Act prescribed six months' imprisonment for any official, including an election agent, who attempted to violate secrecy, and that returning officers who were remiss in their duties were liable to a fine of £100.[1]

Forster's letter forced Finnigan to attempt to vindicate his claim. He advertised a meeting at a Belfast hotel to which journalists from almost all the Belfast papers were invited to see him demonstrate his 'invention'.[2] The first report of the meeting, which was sent in by a strong Conservative, appeared in the *Belfast News-Letter* and was to the effect that 'every gentleman present admitted that he [Finnigan] had fully substantiated his statement'.[3]

Two days later two of the Liberal journalists present at the meeting indignantly wrote to the *News-Letter* denying that they were at all convinced by the demonstration. But it was too late. Finnigan's organization had ordered 16,000 copies of the *News-Letter* issue (at Castlereagh's expense) for distribution throughout the province, and also had the article inserted as an advertisement in the other Ulster newspapers. On polling day the electors of Down were confronted by the unusual sight of the largest landowners in the county acting as Conservative personation agents, and at least one presiding officer allowed a landlord to stand between him and the voters despite the objections of Crawford's agents. The subsequent explanation of this singular move was that it was motivated by a desire 'to keep down expense'.[4]

[1] *Northern Whig*, 11 Mar, 1880. The relevant sections of the Ballot Act were sections 4 and 11.
[2] The *Northern Whig* was not asked to send a representative.
[3] *Belfast News-Letter*, 24 Mar. 1880. This report, the first on Finnigan's meeting, did not appear until *four days* after the event. The Liberal journalists might have written their accounts sooner.
[4] *P.P. 1880*, lvii. 744–5, 590–1.

When the results came in and Castlereagh was seen to have won the second seat by a mere 20 votes, a petition was at once lodged. At the hearing it was proved that both sides had remunerated their canvassers, who professed to serve 'without pay', and paid travelling expenses for voters. The chief interest, however, lay in the exposure of Finnigan's 'invention'. Under a searching examination by Mr. Justice Barry, Finnigan was forced to admit that it would only be possible to break the secrecy of the ballot if a personation agent managed to see the number printed on the back when the paper was issued to a voter, memorized the number and afterwards at the county capital identified that particular paper among thousands of others. This combination of circumstances, Mr. Justice Barry said, could only arise if the presiding officers were criminally ignorant of their duties and the polling booths beset by an organized gang of conspirators.

Mr. Justice Barry found that Finnigan's fraudulent but widely-publicized claim must have affected many of the voters, but it was impossible to assess the number. In his opinion a corrupt practice (undue influence) had clearly been committed and the election might be set aside. Baron Fitzgerald,[1] however, in a judgement which for confused thinking and ignorance of the law would be hard to beat, decided otherwise, and since the judges disagreed the petition was dismissed.

7

Of 22 English petitions, 6 were unsuccessful and 16 succeeded. Eight of the latter led to the appointment of Royal Commissions and will be considered separately. Most of the others showed in some way the impact of the new party machinery on electioneering. In Harwich it was discovered that the Liberal Association had received a circular dated 20 March 1880 from the Central Office, pointing out that to pay travelling expenses in boroughs would not affect the seat, unless a conditional promise

---

[1] He made no effort to establish the truth or falsity of Finnigan's claim; he based his judgement on the erroneous assumption that what the Ballot Act was intended to eliminate was not knowledge of how the votes were cast but retaliatory action based on that knowledge; he made the derisory remark that the coalition between Hill and Castlereagh must be considered a failure because Castlereagh (although elected) got 300 votes less than Hill! Cf. *P.P. 1880*, lvii. 577–8.

were involved. This advice was obviously designed to take advantage of the Corrupt Practices Act of 1880 and might have been given to all the Liberal Associations in the country.[1] In two cases where individual electioneering was still the rule, in Plymouth and Evesham,[2] and the members were accustomed to give indiscriminately to charity, they were unseated not on account of the charity (although the judges disapproved of it) but because of individual acts of bribery by their agents.[3]

The findings of the Royal Commissions set up in the case of the eight English boroughs led ultimately to the passing of the Corrupt and Illegal Practices Act of 1883. These boroughs may be considered as falling into three classes—those with electorates of 5,000 and more (Oxford, Chester, Gloucester, and Macclesfield); those with electorates between 2,000 and 5,000 (Boston, Canterbury, Sandwich); and lastly the ancient one-seat borough of Knaresborough with a mere 651 registered voters.

The Gloucester petition forged the first link in the chain.[4] When Baron Pollock and Sir Henry Hawkins came to hear the allegations of bribery against the two successful Liberal candidates, Charles James Monk and Thomas Robinson,[5] they found that Robinson was unwilling to defend his seat. After hearing enough evidence to prove that Robinson's agents had bribed they declared his seat vacant, and Monk duly elected, but their suspicions had been aroused by the fact that the petitioners, although they did not withdraw the charges against Monk, made no effort to press them and that Monk's counsel at the end of the hearing said he was not instructed to ask for costs— although the judges intimated that he was entitled to them. Accordingly, they reported to the Speaker that they were not satisfied with the manner in which the petition against Monk was conducted and also that they believed corrupt practices had extensively prevailed at Gloucester.

[1] *P.P. 1880*, lviii. 70, 172. *The Times* (14 June 1880) denounced the 'exceptional shamelessness' of the circular in view of the Liberal opposition to the Act.
[2] *P.P. 1880*, lvii. 134–6; lviii. 20. The member at Plymouth was a Conservative, at Evesham a Liberal.
[3] All the English petitions except one (West Worcestershire) were from boroughs.
[4] In this section the findings of the election courts and Royal Commissions are considered together, excepting Gloucester where because of some peculiar features they are taken separately.
[5] See below, p. 143, n. 1.

As soon as the judges' report was laid on the table of the Commons early in June, Lord Randolph Churchill tabled a motion asking for a Select Committee to inquire into the abandonment of the petition against Monk. After several postponements the motion came up for discussion on 25 June.[1] Churchill pointed out that there was a serious reflection on a member of the House which merited further investigation. Monk in reply offered no objection to the motion but insisted on the propriety of his conduct; he was 'surprised', he said, that his counsel had not asked for costs. The motion was passed without a division and a Select Committee was set up.[2] After several long sessions during which they interviewed Monk and witnesses from both sides several times, the Select Committee reported[3] that they had discovered that during the fortnight before the petition came up for trial the Conservatives had proposed several times to drop the charges against Monk, that on the morning of the trial an agreement had been drawn up but never signed, and that Monk had paid Robinson's costs. In spite of all these suspicious circumstances they concluded that the petitioners, having attained their chief object of proving their case against one of the sitting members were not worried about the other, and that there was no corrupt bargain between them to withdraw the petition. The report passed completely unnoticed, since at this time the question of the Royal Commissions was absorbing the attention of the House.

When the judges' certificates were presented to the House of Commons between 2 June and 11 August 1880, eight, including Gloucester, had recommended the setting up of Royal Commissions. The first move by the Government was in the form of a resolution on 15 June by the Chief Whip, Lord Robert Grosvenor, to the effect that no new writ could be issued for the constituencies whose members had been unseated without two days' notice. This effectively prevented a snap resolution. Although on six separate occasions members asked when the Government would move the implementation of the judges' reports, the Attorney-General, Sir Henry James, invariably

[1] *3 Hans.* ccliii (18, 21, 24, 25 June 1880), 299, 432–3, 725–7, 938–48.
[2] Consisting of Sir E. Colebrooke, Viscount Galway, Sir Henry Jackson, the Solicitor-General for Ireland, Messrs. Stanhope and Whitbread.
[3] *P.P. 1880*, ix. 203–4 (Report); 211–80 (Minutes of Evidence).

pleaded pressure of public business.[1] At last, on 1 September, James[2] moved for an address to the Queen praying for Royal Commissions for Gloucester, Boston, Canterbury, Chester, Knaresborough, Macclesfield, Oxford, and Sandwich, and giving the House at the same time the names of the proposed Commissioners. His speech was very summary; he reviewed the legislation of the past quarter of a century, refreshed the members' memories with statistics of election petitions, and concluded that there was no reason for supposing that corrupt practices were more extensive than formerly; it just happened that constituencies were larger and required greater organization. In reply to questions why the Government did not prosecute the offenders scheduled by the judges, James said that there was a practical objection: the smaller offender would be caught, while the greater escaped, and the effect on the public mind 'would unquestionably be demoralizing'. For the Conservatives, Beresford Hope made a long rambling speech in which he laid all the blame for electoral malpractices on the ballot: 'I opposed the Ballot at its rise; I oppose it now in the day of its disgrace and its exposure.'[3] But the most significant speech was made by Gorst. The former Conservative Principal Agent, speaking, as he said, for the general run of Conservatives as well as for his newly founded Fourth Party, challenged the optimism of the Attorney-General. He believed very strongly that the recent general election was far more corrupt than the preceding one, for in 1874 there was not a single judge's report of extensive corrupt practices.[4] If the House refused to issue a Commission for Gloucester, as some Conservatives had suggested, the country would not believe they were seriously trying to put down electoral corruption.

The Royal Commissions were duly appointed, heard evidence in the boroughs concerned throughout the autumn and winter of 1880, and presented their reports in February and March of 1881. The Blue Books contain the most careful and elaborate indictment of electoral malpractices in seven of the boroughs. The Knaresborough report, which was favourable, was quite

[1] *3 Hans.* ccliii (25 June), 842–3; ccliv (22 July), 1103–4; cclv. 323, 1215, 1841–2; cclvi (5, 16, 23, 30 Aug. 1880), 655.
[2] *3 Hans.* cclvi (1 Sept. 1880), 969–73.
[3] Ibid. 982.
[4] Ibid. 988–90. He forgot Norwich and Boston.

brief. Some of the reports were enormous: the Macclesfield Commission examined over 3,000 witnesses, asked over 80,000 questions and its proceedings cover over 1,600 pages. The investigations in every case extended as far back as 1858, and in some cases farther.

Chester[1] was represented entirely by Liberals between 1832 and 1868, when H. C. Raikes[2] was elected. Raikes held the seat in 1874; his genius for organization had ensured the establishment in 1873 of a 'Constitutional Friendly Society', run virtually on a non-profit-making basis and organizing trips and entertainments for its members. The Liberals did not try to make up the leeway until 1879, when a Liberal Association[3] was formed, with the unsuccessful candidate of 1874 (Sir Thomas Frost) as President, and an ex-M.P. of 1857–9 (E. G. Salisbury) as Vice-President.

Under Salisbury's guidance the association quickly chose two candidates[4] and determined that the next election would not be 'starved'.[5] Salisbury told the candidates that £3,000 would be needed for the contest, twice what had been spent in 1874.

As the election approached, the main question was whether the Conservatives would run a second candidate as the Liberals dared them to do. Eventually the president of the Constitutional Friendly Society, Maysmor Williams, a tobacco manufacturer and the chief Conservative agent, went to London, armed with 2,000 promises of support that had been given at mass meetings, and inquired at the Carlton for a man who would be prepared to provide as much as possible of the £3,000 that the Conservatives too considered necessary for the election. Eventually they found a suitable candidate in Major Sandys, a retired officer living on his own estate in North Lancashire. He had no previous political experience and was a perfect stranger to Chester, but was willing to pay two-thirds of the amount required.

[1] See *P.P. 1881*, xl. 1–25 (Report); 33–825 (Minutes of Evidence).
[2] See above, p. 110.
[3] The first Liberal Association at Chester was founded in 1868, but did not last beyond 1874. A former member described it as 'a sort of dead-alive thing' *P.P. 1881*, xl. 109.
[4] The sitting Liberal member, J. G. Dodson (until 1874 M.P. for East Sussex), and the Hon. Benjamin Lawley. Salisbury had been beaten in 1859 and 1868, so he was out of the running.
[5] As far as the Commissioners could ascertain corrupt practices in 1874 were limited to treating (ibid. 17). See below, p. 139.

This £3,000 by no means exhausted the Conservative expenditure. The Commissioners calculated that in all £9,000 was spent on the election, coming from the most diverse sources—small contributions by clerks and shopkeepers and at least £1,500 from the mysterious 'Conservative Central Fund'. A fascinating glimpse of the way in which Conservative election finances were managed is afforded by the evidence before the Commission of Colonel Wellington Talbot, who had been appointed 'treasurer of the Conservative fund' in 1880 although he too had no previous experience of electioneering.[1]

During the campaign he sent large sums to agents and chairmen of associations throughout the country without asking or receiving any account as to how the money was spent. He could not remember how Maysmor Williams got into contact with him nor his standing in the Chester Society. Colonel Talbot admitted that he gave £1,000 as 'caution money' for the petition without asking any questions ('it is a constant thing: irrespective of who the petitioners are').[2] Under considerable pressure he handed in a document stating the complete sum distributed on the Conservative side, but asked that it should not be published as that would be 'very unfair to the Party'. The Commissioners refused to give any assurance and the paper formed the basis of their estimate of £9,000.

On the Conservative side no effort was made to separate the candidates from the party, but the Liberals hit upon an ingenious plan to divest their candidates of responsibility. Early in 1880 (before the dissolution) the candidates, agents, chairmen of committees, and clerks all resigned from the association. The election campaign was to be managed by Salisbury, and his vice-president Walker was 'sole committee' for the candidates. When March came the 'sole committee' was in Spain, so Salisbury, who was also responsible for the Liberal campaign in West Cheshire, was left in charge, with Moss, the official agent. When the campaign started both parties were 'arrayed in

---

[1] *P.P. 1881*, xl. 792–3. Colonel Talbot did not explain how he had got his position, except that he had been 'well known to the Central Office'.

[2] Cf. ibid. Q. 45,218: 'That is why I want to know—why you sent down £500 to a man you do not seem to know much about?'

Talbot: 'I am afraid if that is the case, I sent it all over the country to people I did not know. It is the recognized plan—the recognized system, to send it to the agents and chairmen of the different committees and responsible people.'

bitter hostility'.[1] The tradition in the borough had been that the party which controlled the public houses would control the election.[2] A large proportion of the money on both sides went on treating, partly dispensed by a class of professional treaters indigenous to the borough, partly given on credit by the publicans and afterwards recouped from the organizations. Some attempts to restrict the expenditure were made (e.g. by asking the publicans to give credit only to recognized treaters or the people with vouchers) but they were unavailing, and in each district the parties had to foot the entire bill. Colourable employment was the other principal offence. Demands for jobs were so numerous and persistent, and the competition between the parties so keen, that the number eventually employed at high wages for nominal work was far beyond the original estimate. Salisbury was approached so often that in the end he wrote out a list of 88 clerks and messengers, which he thought would be sufficient for the Liberals, but 130 had already been appointed unknown to him, and the final number was 480.

A diversion was caused by the nomination of Frederick Lewis Malgarini, a Londoner who had been connected with some unsuccessful business ventures and had already been bankrupt. He introduced a touch of the young Disraeli to his campaign by appearing at meetings in evening dress. A rumour with no foundation arose that he was a Tory decoy to take the Irish vote away from the Liberals and, like others on whom the same suspicion fell, he got very rough treatment. At one of Malgarini's meetings the platform was stormed, he was knocked to the ground and kicked, and barely escaped with his life.[3] He did not return to Chester and polled a mere 16 votes. Apart from

---

[1] *P.P. 1881*, xl. 6.

[2] One witness said: 'the great weapon of Parliamentary warfare at Chester is beer.' Hickey, a butcher (who in 1874 had been a Conservative), was so well known to the publicans that he was supplied with beer to the value of £80 without any questions asked. This time he was treating for the Liberals (ibid. 252–6). There was a smaller number of professional bribers, including one Mottershead of whom a former Mayor told the Commissioners that he was 'as straight as the North Pole'. When asked: 'You mean that he bribes straight?' he replied: 'What I mean to say is that he does not pocket anything' (ibid. 265).

[3] See Saunders, *The New Parliament, 1880*, pp. 231–2. Malgarini's total expenses were £524. 12s. 2d., which meant on average £32. 15s. 9d. per vote—the highest of the election! The published expenses of the other four candidates were approximately £6,460, the real expenses nearly £13,000 (see *P.P. 1880*, lvii. 3 ff.).

this incident, however, violence was not noticeable during the campaign.

When the results came in, Dodson and Lawley led by over a thousand votes and Raikes lost his seat. A petition was quickly lodged by the Conservatives.

After his electioneering triumph, Salisbury had to face bills amounting to £4,448 covering sums not in the published accounts of the Liberals. At first he refused to pay, but on being told that they had been 'eliminated from the accounts' in order to save the members embarrassment at the petition trial, he authorized the treasurer of the Liberal Association to pay £725, on the understanding that the members would afterwards reimburse him. In July Salisbury wrote to the Liberal Chief Whip, Lord Richard Grosvenor, asking for help to meet the debt—he himself was willing to contribute £600—but Grosvenor replied: 'It is not safe to write about these matters and I am really sorry that I ever knew anything about them.'[1] Dodson and Lawley also refused to pay, so the Liberal treasurer was out of pocket to the extent of £725.

The verdict of the Commissioners was that the constituency as a whole was not corrupt, but about 2,000 (approximately 30 per cent.) were venal; that the professional treaters were mainly employed at the municipal elections, which were very corrupt. They found treating and colourable employment extensive at the elections of 1874 and 1880 and scheduled 401 people for bribery and 512 for treating.[2]

Like the city of Chester the borough of Macclesfield had managed to keep out of the petition lists before 1880 although with the exception of the 1865 election it had been contested since 1832, when it first secured the parliamentary franchise.[3] The town was mainly dependent on the silk industry and its wealth was increasing, although the population was declining slightly.[4] From 1832 to 1865 the representation was shared

[1] Grosvenor to Salisbury (21 July 1880) cited in *P.P. 1881*, xl. 9-11. This letter was written five weeks after Grosvenor had moved a resolution in the House of Commons to delay the writs for constituencies whose members had been unseated through corrupt practices. See above, p. 134.

[2] Among those scheduled were Salisbury, Maysmor Williams, Moss (the official Liberal agent), and another Liberal who was elected Mayor of Chester for 1881 while the Commission was sitting.

[3] It had been a municipal borough since 1261.

[4] *P.P. 1881*, xliii. 5-21 (Report); 69-1631 (Minutes of Evidence).

between the two parties ('the one and one' arrangement, as it was locally called). John Coare Brocklehurst, the largest silk manufacturer, was the Liberal member throughout that period. After his retirement his son was elected. David Chadwick, an accountant, a native of Macclesfield, wished to stand as the second Liberal, but the Liberals of the town were satisfied with the 'one and one' arrangement and would not adopt him. He therefore stood as an independent—and used strong language about his former fellow Liberal, Brocklehurst. Chadwick was popular in the town since he had started new silk mills at a time when trade was declining. During the campaign he ran up a bill of several hundred pounds at his hotel, much of which went in 'open and undisguised treating'.[1] But many Conservatives, feeling a certain loyalty to the old arrangement, split their votes between their candidate, Egerton, and Brocklehurst, and Chadwick was defeated. Each side had two sets of agents, one for legal, the other for illegal expenses, and the actual expenditure though not large by 1880 standards was far greater than the published accounts.[2]

By 1868 the character of elections in the borough had changed considerably. The electorate had been increased by more than five times in 1867;[3] and both parties finally abandoned their policy of co-existence. They developed organizations of similar pattern. The Conservatives followed the caucus model (a nexus of ward committees with three 'gentlemen' and three 'working men' selected from each to form an executive committee for the entire borough) more closely than the Liberals. The latter had a 'Central Liberal Association', independent of the ward committees and composed of the Liberal members of the corporation, who were expected to join immediately after election. Both parties expected their candidates to pay for canvassers.[4]

These developments were gradual between 1868 and 1880, but the trend was unmistakable. Both organizations were highly efficient. Each ward committee at the start of the campaign

---

[1] *P.P. 1881*, xliii. 6.

[2] Brocklehurst: (published) £336; additional (unpublished) £820. 10s. Chadwick: (published) £820; (unpublished) £717. Egerton: (published) £600. His unpublished expenses could not be assessed, since by 1880 both he and his agent were dead.

[3] From 964 to 4,925.

[4] Paid canvassers at municipal elections were long established at Macclesfield together with payment of rates for poorer voters and travelling expenses, where needed.

divided up its area into districts and appointed a member of
the committee, who was called the 'Captain of the Book', to
go around canvassing with his helpers ('bookmen'). All those
whose names were entered in the canvassing books were understood to receive payment later—at the recognized rates. The
custom arose of putting the names of doubtful voters on the
books as a means of purchasing their votes. At the election of
1868, when Brocklehurst and Chadwick collaborated to the
extent of sharing the ward expenses and were both successful,
the bookmen were paid by Conservatives and expected to be
paid by the Liberals, but were not. The unpublished expenses
of Brocklehurst were again greater than his published accounts,
and Chadwick's were two-thirds as much again.

In 1874 there were two Conservative candidates and for the
first time the Liberals openly collaborated. Bookmen were paid
by both parties, and the other practices were continued, but the
expenses, both real and acknowledged, were lower than in 1868.[1]

Direct bribery was still comparatively rare in Macclesfield,
but this changed in 1879 when an energetic young solicitor was
made secretary of the Conservative Association. During the
municipal elections in November he bought a piece of waste
land and set up a tent where money was distributed to willing
voters. The Liberals followed suit in an empty warehouse. From
that time onwards, to quote one Alderman Wright, they 'were
going to fight the Conservatives with their own weapons'.

The organizers on both sides convinced the candidates—
Chadwick agreeing very reluctantly—that at least £1,000 per
candidate would be needed, and when the campaign began in
February 1880 the captains of the books surpassed themselves—
870 names were entered on the Liberal and 950 on the Conservative books. In addition there were new electioneering
officials called 'money captains', of higher social standing (town
councillors and rate collectors) whose function was to give direct
bribes at their own discretion. Votes were purchased individually, except at a copper works where two labourers bargained
on behalf of their fellows and got a promise of 10s. per man and
50s. commission from the Conservatives. These two, though
illiterate, showed considerable political acumen by then going

[1] An unsuccessful attempt to start a Conservative newspaper (the *Macclesfield
Advertiser*) accounted for £1,000 of the Conservative outlay.

to the Liberals and securing the same terms on condition that the men be left to vote as they pleased. The men received £1 each and plenty of refreshment, and the entrepreneurs pocketed £5 apiece! As to the total number bribed, the Chairman of the Conservative Association candidly told the Commissioners that he thought 4,000 people (or 80 per cent. of the electorate) were paid in one way or another.

The Commissioners saw no reason to differ from that estimate,[1] but through lack of proof they had to leave many suspects out of the schedules. They were impeded by many witnesses first denying flatly they had received any money and afterwards, when that was proved, pretending that it was not offered for their votes. Once when the Commissioners tried the experiment of summoning fifteen people whose names had not yet been mentioned but who lived in a corrupt area, all admitted to having been bribed. The schedule contained 2,872 names, the largest number ever reported for corrupt practices.[2]

Gloucester resembled Macclesfield in having a large number of voters reported at the end of the Royal Commission's sittings. Unlike Macclesfield it had two petitions between 1832 and 1880 and one Royal Commission in 1859,[3] which found that bribery had prevailed over a long period.

The petition of 1873[4] was dismissed and though it then appeared that leaders of both parties sincerely desired to avoid corrupt practices its sequel brought back bribery with a rush to the city. Shortly after the petition was heard the successful Conservative paid out nearly £500 for 'payments incidental to the petition'. Between the by-election and the general election in 1874 the Liberals founded a 'Liberal Registration Association', ostensibly a body of canvassers. In the election campaign, however, it was used as a channel for various kinds of illegal expenditure—payment for committee rooms, refreshments, and conveyances in addition to straightforward bribery. It was

---

[1] P.P. 1881, xliii. 16, 145.

[2] Ibid. 23–43. 2,766 were voters and 106 non-voters.

[3] Cf. P.P. 1859 (Sess. 2), iii (Minutes of Evidence on Petition); P.P. 1860, xxvii (Report of Royal Commission); P.P. 1860, lv (Names of Persons to whom Certificates of Indemnity granted); P.P. 1880, ix (Minutes of Evidence and Report of Select Committee); P.P. 1881, xli. 5–20 (Report of Royal Commission), 59–1066 (Minutes of Evidence).

[4] For the petition following the by-election in 1873 see above, p. 93.

William Price,[1] whose appointment as a Railway Commissioner
had occasioned the by-election in 1873, who persuaded the
Liberal candidates to indulge in illegal expenditure. The Conservatives also bribed heavily, largely through friendly publicans. The amounts spent by both parties were far in excess not
only of the published accounts but of the agents' estimates.

The result was one Conservative and one Liberal elected.
Both parties considered petitioning but were able to convince
each other that the bribery had been so notorious that both seats
would probably be lost. After some negotiations the agents of
both parties signed an agreement not to lodge a petition against
each other.[2]

In 1875 a Liberal Hundred[3]—one of the first fifty in the
country—was established in Gloucester, and in 1877 an attempt
was made to prevent the defeated candidate Powell[4] and his
predecessor Robinson from being nominated again on the
ground that their reputation after the last election was likely
to prejudice the party's chances, but it was defeated in the
Executive Committee by a majority of one. From that time the
sitting member, Monk, and Robinson (who had decided to
stand again) were regarded as the prospective candidates.

Conservative organization in Gloucester was very imperfect
compared with the Liberal. Just before the 1880 election a 'Sick
Benefit Society' was formed, but there was no central, or even
ward committee, and the party entered the campaign with the
barest semblance of a machine.

However deficient they may have been in organization the

[1] In 1859 the sitting Liberal members, Price and Charles James Monk, were
unseated for bribery and disqualified during the lifetime of that Parliament. They
were both re-elected in 1865. In 1873 Price was made a Railway Commissioner and
had to resign his seat, but kept up his interest in the borough. The unsuccessful
Liberal candidate at the 1873 by-election, Thomas Robinson, a former Mayor, did
not stand in 1874, but was nominated again in 1880. The unsuccessful Liberal in
1874 was John James Powell, Recorder of Wolverhampton, who had been one of
the stop-gap M.P.s between 1862 and 1865. Monk remained Liberal member for
the city until 1880.
[2] The signatories to the agreement were Price, Robinson, and the Conservative
and Liberal chief agents. Price and Robinson were, after the members, easily the
most important Liberals in the city.
[3] There were 130 in the representative body which elected the Executive Committee.
[4] Powell had not only connived at illegal expenditure in 1874, but (with Monk)
he had refused to pay £1,604 outstanding after the election. Powell fades out after
1874.

Conservatives had no lack of the 'sinews of war'. The chief agent told the two candidates[1] that £1,500 would be required; they later agreed to double the amount in order 'to get the people to the poll'. The total sum spent by the Conservatives was £3,600, which the agent who kept the funds cunningly arranged should not appear in full on the books of his bank. Most of this went in straightforward bribes by publicans, who curiously enough got very little out of it for there was scarcely any drunkenness on polling day.

The Liberal campaign methods were equally brazen. Shortly before the election a meeting of the party leaders in the house of a town councillor named Mousell decided that bribery would be necessary; the councillor offered £1,000 to start with. The party hired twelve public houses as 'committee rooms', four of which were centres of bribery, where voters were invited in by canvassers, identified on a copy of the register, handed a ticket signifying the amount of the bribe they were to receive (ranging from 5s. to £2) and then conducted under escort to the polling station, after which the tickets were cashed. Councillor Mousell visited most of the 'committee rooms' and personally distributed £1,382. All this time Monk had misgivings about standing again with Robinson and about the committee arrangements, although Price had told him that though a small committee of personal friends might have been able to manage an election in the old days, it could only create jealousy in 1880.[2]

When the elections were over the Liberals had regained the second seat,[3] and the Conservatives as a matter of course lodged a petition. Negotiations were opened for another compromise. After a time Robinson withdrew and the Conservatives agreed not to press the case against Monk, but it was too late: already the petition trial had begun and the judges' suspicions were aroused.

The Royal Commission found that both municipal and

[1] William Killigrew Wait, who had won the by-election of 1873 and held the seat in 1874, and Benjamin St. John Ackers, landlord of Prinknash Park, who had twice before been pressed by the local Conservatives to stand for the city.
[2] On 12 Mar. 1880 Price wrote to Monk: 'Of course, the weak point is, that we cannot be sure that we can protect the seat, all we can protect is the candidate from all personal consequences' (cited in *P.P. 1881*, xli. 1044–5).
[3] The figures were Robinson (Lib.) 2,797; Monk (Lib.) 2,690; Wait (Cons.) 2,304; Ackers (Cons.) 1,898.

parliamentary elections were very corrupt in Gloucester; for many of the poorer voters would not come to the polls unless bribed. They scheduled 2,185 out of a total electorate of 5,767.

The city of Oxford[1] had been considered a Liberal stronghold since the Reform Act[2] although Cardwell, who sat for the city from 1852 to 1874, was officially listed as 'Liberal-Conservative', and was regarded by the Conservatives as 'in a certain measure representing their opinions', even when he was a minister in Gladstone's Cabinet. He lost his seat in 1857, but the successful candidate, Charles Neate (Liberal), was unseated, because he had employed 198 clerks and messengers of whom 152 had voted for him afterwards. At the by-election Cardwell stood again and defeated the novelist Thackeray, who stood as a radical. Between them they spent £1,600, of which roughly half was for clerks and messengers; so the lesson of the previous petition had scarcely been learned.[3] There was no contest between 1857 and 1865.[4]

In 1868 a Conservative candidate, Dr. James Parker Deane, Q.C., appeared at the same time as the young William Harcourt stood as junior colleague to Cardwell. The electorate had been increased to 5,033 in 1867. The Conservative was soundly beaten but his expenses were proportionately equal to Harcourt's and Cardwell's combined, or approximately £1 per vote. On both sides the money was mainly spent on colourable employment.

In 1874 Alexander Hall, the brewer, stood in the Conservative interest. He was about the most popular candidate they could find, the largest employer in the city, with a great reputation for charity. Although Harcourt headed the poll, Hall cut Cardwell's majority to 73 votes. Shortly after the election Cardwell went to the Lords and at the by-election Hall won by 462 votes over the Liberal candidate J. D. Lewis, who was a stranger to the city.[5]

When the election of 1880 came up the Liberals had estab-

---

[1] *P.P. 1881*, xliv. 3–20 (Report); 21–23 (Schedules); 31–1085 (Minutes of Evidence).

[2] After the Reform Act the electorate was 2,312 (the total poll at the 1832 general election was 1,770). Thomas Stonor (Liberal), elected in 1832, was unseated on petition, but replaced by another Liberal. In 1833 two Conservatives were elected; from 1837 one Liberal and one Conservative, and, from 1847 onwards, two Liberals, were returned.

[3] Cf. *P.P. 1857* (Sess. 2), viii. 11–141 (Minutes of Evidence before Select Committee).   [4] Neate was re-elected in 1863 and sat till 1868.

[5] The combined expenses of the two elections were £5,690 for the Conservatives

lished an association, but the Conservative organization was virtually restricted to Hall, John Parsons of the Old Bank, and a few dons. Once again colourable employment was the chief feature of the election, but the amounts spent were not excessive compared with 1874.[1]

After the election Harcourt was given a seat in the Cabinet by Gladstone and had to seek re-election. The Conservatives were short of funds[2] and at first decided not to contest the by-election, but after an interview with Hall, a prominent supporter named Evetts went to London to see the Chief Whip (Hart Dyke) and Colonel Talbot at the Carlton, and told them that £3,500 would be needed unless they were to let the seat go by default. After some hesitation, the Central Office advanced £3,000, which was afterwards admitted to be an unusually large sum for one election.[3] Evetts telegraphed the good news, and a meeting was held that evening to try to raise the additional £500. Montagu Burrows, Chichele Professor of History, impressed on the party supporters present that a crisis had come in their fortunes and that some sacrifice would be necessary. He would guarantee £50 on condition that three others would guarantee £300. Parsons offered £100, the Rev. Washburne West of Lincoln, another £100, and the third £100 came from a gentleman in Headington. Burrows, however, wished to make up the balance as quickly as possible, so he wrote that evening to the Public Orator (Rev. T. F. Dallin) asking for £10. It is not clear whether Mr. Dallin gave the required subscription, but he lost Burrows' letter in the High and the letter, containing the tell-tale phrase that the fight must collapse unless £500 could be provided 'over the Carlton £3,000', was found by a small boy who gave it to his father, a tradesman, and eventually it found its way to the Mayor, Thomas Galpin, a strong Liberal.[4] He sent it back with a very polite note to Dallin and later refused to answer Dallin's angry demands as to how he had got hold of it.[5]

and £4,779 for the Liberals, but the amounts officially returned were £2,536 and £1,748. The registered electorate was 5,680.
[1] The electorate was now 6,166. Harcourt got 2,771, Chitty 2,669, Hall 2,659 votes.
[2] Hall had spent as much as he could afford at the general election.
[3] See above, p. 137, also *P.P. 1881*, xliv. 557.
[4] The Liberals had a majority of 32–8 on the Town Council.
[5] *P.P. 1881*, xliv. 36–37.

'The Carlton £3,000' was brought to Oxford in the form of gold and was lodged in two banking accounts, so that, if a petition followed, it could be pretended that only £1,500 came from the Carlton and that Hall had supplied the rest. The pretence would probably have been successful but for Mr. Dallin's carelessness. All except £300 was distributed by one agent, Perceval Walsh.[1]

The by-election campaign lasted a mere ten days, but in that time the Liberals spent £3,275 and the Conservatives £3,611. Although there were only 9 polling districts in the city, the Liberals hired 24 committee rooms and 389 helpers of various kinds; the Conservatives 26 committee rooms and 355 helpers. That this expenditure was mainly colourable seemed clear; one feature of the election was the employment of poor men at 5s. a day to deliver circulars. But although they held that a 'residuum' of the constituency was always open to the influence of money the Commissioners did not have evidence to convict more than 180 people of giving or receiving bribes;[2] and they believed that the money or employment offered was generally not intended to induce them to transfer their allegiance, but to confirm it.[3]

Like Boston, Canterbury had a long history of corrupt electioneering. It was always a poor constituency, and since 1867 a large proportion of its electors came from the labouring classes. In 1832 two Liberals were returned, and again in 1835, but one was unseated on petition (on a scrutiny). From 1835 until 1852, with the exception of a Conservative victory in 1841, the seats were shared. In 1853 the Royal Commission discovered that votes were purchased at prices ranging from £5 to £20 apiece:[4] the writ was suspended until 1854, when the same balance resulted.[5] The Conservative then elected was one of a

---

[1] *P.P. 1881*, xliv. 9–11.

[2] Forty-one in respect of the general election in April, 139 of the by-election in May.

[3] For the election petition trial (before Mr. Justice Lush and Mr. Justice Manisty) see *P.P. 1880*, lviii. 563–609 (Minutes of Evidence); *P.P. 1880*, lvii. 127–9 (Judgement).

[4] See above, p. 28, n. 3.

[5] Cf. *P.P. 1852–3*, ix (Minutes of Evidence on Election Petition); *P.P. 1852–3*, xlvii (Report of Royal Commission); *P.P. 1854*, l (Canterbury Bribery Prevention Bill); *P.P. 1880*, lvii. 447–8 (Judgement on Petition); *P.P. 1881*, xxxix (Report and Minutes of Evidence of Royal Commission).

family that was to dominate the electoral history of the borough for the next thirty years—Henry Butler-Johnstone. In 1862 he retired and was succeeded by his son, Henry Alexander Butler-Johnstone who had a majority of 3 votes. He was then a very young man and his father paid his expenses, including £400 on illegal expenditure. From that year onwards, like Bates at Plymouth and Ratcliff at Evesham, Butler-Johnstone played the fairy godfather. He not only gave hundreds of pounds to charity every year, but even gave sovereigns regularly ('out of weak good nature' as he pleaded before the Commission) to casual passers-by in the streets of Canterbury.[1]

Butler-Johnstone's largesse paid off in 1865 when two Conservatives were elected, but in 1868 he quarrelled with his party over the Irish Church Bill, and stood as an independent in alliance with Captain Brinckman (Liberal). Butler-Johnstone and Brinckman won. Huddleston,[2] the defeated Conservative member, urged the formation of a party association so that the fortunes of the party would not be at the whim of a single man. Thus the Canterbury Conservative Association was founded. The ill-feeling generated by Butler-Johnstone's secession in 1868 was removed when he rejoined the party in 1874; he and another Conservative were returned, his erstwhile colleague, Captain Brinckman, being defeated by some 500 votes. Never a typical party man Butler-Johnstone pursued an individual course to the end. In 1878 his chief supporter in the party, Harry George Austin,[3] objected to the appointment of Frederick Mudford[4] as secretary and resigned from the council of the association. Butler-Johnstone reacted to the slight on his friend by applying for the Chiltern Hundreds, and in the by-election Alfred Gathorne Hardy, the son of Lord Cranbrook, was returned unopposed.

In 1879 Majendie, the other Conservative M.P., resigned for private reasons. At the by-election the Conservatives nominated Colonel R. P. Laurie, a member of the London Stock Exchange, and the Liberals, Charles Edwards. Neither had any previous connexion with the city, but it is worth noting that while Laurie

[1] The Butler-Johnstones never lived in Canterbury.
[2] See above, pp. 102 ff.
[3] The architect of Canterbury Cathedral.
[4] The proprietor of the *Kentish Observer*.

lived in Mystole near Canterbury Edwards came from Dolgelly. In the elections since 1852 the Liberals had avoided corrupt practices, but Edwards had no such inhibitions. His agent spent about £140 in bribery and treating (at a few shillings a head) and Edwards frankly admitted to the Commission that he had repaid the agent with full knowledge of the illegality of the transaction. On the other side Laurie gave his agent, Mudford, £125 which was distributed in 'gratuities' to members of the Conservative Association. In spite of this precaution the Conservative majority was reduced from 572 to 56.[1]

In March 1880 the egregious Butler-Johnstone stood again in opposition to the sitting Conservatives, Gathorne Hardy and Laurie, and in alliance with Edwards. The Conservative Association, faced by this second treachery of their former member and by the drop in their majority at the by-election, came to the conclusion that bribery would be necessary. The amount was not large—£250 provided by Mudford and another £150 mainly subscribed by a Canterbury brewer. Once again the agents distributed it in very small sums (the largest bribe being £1) to labourers and small tradesmen under the guise of 'loss of time' money or travelling expenses. Mudford anticipated that the association would eventually fix a fee for his services that would indemnify him.

This time the Liberals did not organize any bribery, but treating and colourable employment were employed extensively by both sides. Hardy and Laurie again headed the poll, and Butler-Johnstone immediately lodged a petition. He was obsessed with the idea that the money provided for bribery by the Conservatives had come from Gathorne Hardy's family and was determined to find out which member of the family was responsible and then prosecute him. The Conservative solicitor made frantic efforts to dissuade him, even offering to surrender one seat and pay his costs, but all to no avail.[2]

The Royal Commission decided that out of 3,000 voters about 500 to 600 were at all times accessible to bribery, but that the

---

[1] Laurie 1,159, Edwards 1,103. The published expenses were Laurie £487, Edwards £522.

[2] *P.P. 1881*, xxxix. 92–93, 121–5, 418. It must be noted that Edwards was also a party to the petition. The Conservatives tried to buy him off with £1,000, but he refused; he wanted £2,500 so that he could fight the by-election and cover his expenses for 1879 and 1880.

form and scale of the bribery in the two previous elections resembled local election practice rather than the open corruption of 1852.[1] They scheduled 241 voters for bribery in 1880 (61 for offering and 180 for accepting) and 132 for bribery in 1879. The schedules included the names of Edwards for both elections, Laurie for 1880, two J.P.s and two members of the corporation. Butler-Johnstone's 'annual and occasional distributions' had, they said, debased public morality in the city but they acquitted him of any complicity. Hardy was entirely exonerated.

The previous electoral history of Boston was chequered; a petition in 1866, a petition in 1874, a Royal Commission in 1875, followed by the Norwich and Boston Corrupt Voters' Act, and the suspension of the writ until 1880.[2] The Liberals again put up William Ingram and selected as his colleague a rising young journalist, Sydney Charles Buxton. The Conservative candidates were Thomas Garfitt and William Rowley—whose merits in the eyes of the prominent party member, who introduced him at two public meetings, were that he was a bachelor and had lots of money. The Liberals had one 'Liberal Club-room', but no association. The Conservatives relied heavily on their Workmen's Club and the entertainments provided there.

At the beginning of the campaign there was a very general impression in the borough that the Conservatives were going to bribe, accordingly the Liberals determined to outdo them. As before, the main feature of Boston electioneering was colourable employment. The borough was divided into districts, each with a 'captain' (like Macclesfield) and the captains were authorized to hire as many helpers as they pleased—who were paid at rates of from 2s. 6d. to 10s. a day. The total number employed by the Liberals was 368 and by the Conservatives 506. At least 600 of these (20 per cent. of the constituency) were voters.

The result of the election was to maintain the even balance that had persisted since 1832: Ingram and Garfitt were elected. Immediately the Conservatives petitioned against Ingram and

[1] In Canterbury up to 1872 the annual municipal elections fostered bribery at general elections. A reliable witness said the price of a municipal vote ranged from 2s. 6d. to 7s. 6d. But from 1872 both parties agreed to share the civic offices without contests (ibid. 210–11).

[2] See above, pp. 105, 108, n. 4.

the Liberals against Garfitt. On the second day both respondents withdrew their defence, since the evidence against them was conclusive; but Garfitt flatly denied that he or his friends had spent a single shilling on the election. He claimed that he had campaigned independently of Rowley, whose money was spent profusely, and that he did not know of the Workmen's Club until shortly before the election, when he attended an entertainment there and 'did not like exactly what he saw', but since he did not like to offend the others, he came away quietly.[1]

The Commissioners found 326 men guilty of accepting bribes (at rates of from 10s. to 30s.), 95 guilty of giving them, and one man guilty of personation. The bribers were men of good position (the chief Conservative briber was a maltster) and had no qualms about the number they had corrupted—one admitted bribing 70 others.

Knaresborough[2] was the one constituency where the election judges' suspicions proved unfounded. A small but ancient borough with a population in 1871 of 5,205, it had in pre-Reform days been a burgage borough with both members nominated by the Duke of Devonshire. In 1852 there was a petition, as three candidates tied for the two seats with 43 votes each. The Election Committee of the House struck one vote off one candidate (a Liberal) and the other two (a Liberal and a Conservative) were returned. The successful Conservative, Basil Thomas Woodd, sat for the borough until 1868 when one seat was abolished by the Redistribution Act,[3] and he was defeated by a Conservative. Woodd was successful in 1874 and in 1880 was opposed by Sir H. M. Thompson.[4] In Knaresborough, as in so many other boroughs, the public houses were used as committee rooms and after the election the candidates used to pay back sums that they knew must have been spent illegally. After the 1874 election the publicans were annoyed that their claims had not been met in full and threatened not to vote Conservative next time. On hearing this, a wealthy lady, the widow of a former Conservative candidate, hastened to pay the bills.

---

[1] *P.P. 1881*, xxxviii. 5–9; *P.P. 1880*, lvii. 387–90.

[2] Cf. *P.P. 1852–3*, xiv (Report from Select Committee); *P.P. 1880*, lvii. 121–3 (Judgement on Petition); *P.P. 1880*, lviii. 189–235 (Minutes of Evidence of Petition); *P.P. 1881*, xlii. 5–628 (Report and Minutes of Evidence of Royal Commission).

[3] In 1832 the registered electorate was 278; in 1865, 279; in 1880, 762.

[4] Both Woodd and Thompson were landowners.

In 1880 the same thing occurred and treating as well. The
judges, Mr. Justice Lush and Mr. Justice Manisty, were misled
by the inflated language of some witnesses into believing that
corrupt practices were extensive, but the Commissioners found
no evidence of systematic malpractices: the acts of direct
bribery were few and isolated and the acts of treating not so
serious as the witnesses at the original trial had pretended; the
total illegal expenditure did not exceed £120. The Commissioners found neither Woodd nor Thompson implicated in any
corrupt practice.[1]

The Royal Commission at Sandwich unearthed the strangest
story of all—that of a borough of the Beverley type surviving
until 1880 unscathed by petition trials.[2] The constituency comprised three small towns (Sandwich, Deal, and Walmer) with
about 2,000 voters. Most of them were rural workers, boatmen
or fishermen, but one-tenth of the electorate were publicans.
There were very few resident gentry in the borough, no manufacturers, and no special trades.

Every general election since 1832 had been contested, but
although the strength of the parties had fluctuated until 1857,
since then with the sole exception of a by-election in 1866, two
Liberals had been returned. E. H. Knatchbull-Hugessen, a
member of a family long associated with Kentish constituencies,
had sat for the borough since 1857. He and his colleague, Henry
Brassey, had in spite of the strong licensed interest defeated the
Conservatives in 1864. In order to keep in with the constituency
Brassey had subscribed almost £500 to charities every year since
1877. Consequently, when a wealthy Londoner, C. H. Crompton Roberts, wished to contest the borough in 1880, he was told
by the small Conservative Association that it would be a hopeless venture. Therefore Sandwich became one of the minority
of uncontested constituencies at the general election.

After the Liberal victory Knatchbull-Hugessen was raised to
the peerage and immediately Crompton Roberts entered the

[1] They scheduled 5 for giving bribes, 4 for receiving bribes, and 36 for corrupt
treating. *P.P. 1881*, xlii. 13–15.
[2] *P.P. 1880*, lvii. 137–41 (Judgement on Petition Trial); *P.P 1880*, lviii. 615–77
(Minutes of Evidence); *P.P. 1881*, xlv. 5–16 (Report of Royal Commission),
17–28 (Schedules), 39–434 (Minutes of Evidence). Knatchbull-Hugessen had been
a member of the Select Committee of 1867 and had strongly opposed the ballot.
See above, p. 35, n. 3. In the 1840's Sandwich had been a government borough.

field. He engaged as election agent Edwin Hughes, a London solicitor who had managed the elections in the City of London and Greenwich for the Conservatives. Hughes had the reputation of spending money lavishly in order to get the licensed trade on the side of his candidates—at Greenwich he had hired 350 public houses as 'committee rooms'. His first act on reaching Sandwich on 5 May (before the writ had been moved) was to engage eighty-eight public houses as committee rooms at £5 apiece. Only seventeen of these were ever used, and then for small meetings only; all that most of the innkeepers did for their money was to post a few bills on their windows or bars. By his prompt action Hughes stole a march on the Liberals who found the pick of the public houses taken when the writ was moved and the campaign had officially begun a week after Hughes's visit to Sandwich. The Liberal candidate, Sir Julian Goldsmid, was advised by his friends that £2,000 would probably be necessary. They spent it partly on direct bribery, partly on the forbidden attractions of flags and banners, partly on colourable employment. Sir Julian Goldsmid later admitted that he consented after some hesitation to this 'monstrous expenditure'.[1]

Goldsmid's campaign suffered from lack of skilled helpers. His agent was not a professional and seemed quite ignorant of his duties. Crompton Roberts, however, had the inestimable advantage of Hughes, the last of the genre of brilliant election manipulators. Hughes dominated the election completely.[2] Although he had hired so many 'committee rooms', he took care not to have a committee. Instead, he divided the constituency into districts and appointed forty-two 'canvassers' at £6 a day; their main argument was that if the Conservatives did not win it would be the last time that they would contest the borough. Hughes had a number of ingenious ideas. He spent nearly £350 on rosettes for the wives and children of voters, thousands of yards of bunting and ribbon were purchased from traders (all of whom were voters), and on the day before polling cards were sent printed in Conservative colours to all the inhabitants allowing them the use of the Deal pier free of charge on that

[1] An enormous flagstaff was put up in front of his house with twenty flags, and 'no end of men to watch it'. *P.P. 1881*, xlv. 146.
[2] He said that he 'never had a more obedient set to deal with than the Conservatives at Sandwich' (ibid. 6).

day. Hughes was also fortunate in his employer. Crompton Roberts admitted afterwards that he 'was under the impression . . . that elections cost something like £10,000'.[1] Hughes asked him for £6,500, but spent only £5,600 of that and could not account for the rest. The Liberals spent £2,668.[2]

The result gave Crompton Roberts 1,145 votes and Goldsmid 705, Hughes's virtuosity having reversed the 1874 result. The Liberals thereupon lodged a petition from which they could hope to gain no advantage at all, not being able to claim the seat because they knew their own activities could not bear investigation.

The election judges found that both shared in the guilt. Giving judgement Mr. Justice Lush said: 'The conduct of the election . . . is distinguished from all others which we have had to deal with, in that both the requirements and the prohibitions of the Corrupt Practices Prevention Acts seem to have been totally disregarded from first to last.'[3] This assessment corresponded closely with the judgement of the Commissioners:

But observing the nature and the manner of the bribery committed . . . the general expectation that money would be distributed in bribery, the almost universal willingness and even avidity to accept bribes, the great proportion of the population implicated, the ease with which the most extensive bribery was carried out, the organization for the purposes of bribery, which was far too facile and complete to be inexperienced, the readiness on the part of many to accept bribes from both sides, and the total absence of a voice to warn, condemn, or denounce, we cannot doubt that electoral corruption had long and extensively prevailed in the borough of Sandwich.[4]

The Commissioners scheduled 1,005 people for accepting bribes (127 from both sides),[5] 128 for bribing, and 48 for treating. They were 'unable to avoid the conclusion' that both candidates were implicated.

[1] *P.P. 1881*, xlv. 362.
[2] The official returns were Liberals £883. 13s. 1d., Conservatives £3,153. At the petition trial Hughes said that Crompton Roberts had given him £4,000; to the Commissioners he revealed the full total.
[3] *P.P. 1880*, lvii. 137.
[4] *P.P. 1881*, xlv. 15.
[5] The Master of the Sandwich Hospital testified that at every election for 60 years he had given one vote to one side and one to the other. His son was bribed by both sides. Ibid. 302.

8

The reports of the Royal Commissions taken together disclosed that bribery and treating still persisted in the eight boroughs to a greater or lesser degree, despite over a quarter of a century of remedial legislation. The Ballot Act on which so many hopes had been pinned had demonstrably failed to prevent bribery; in the most venal boroughs it had even helped to promote it because of the facility with which money could be taken from both sides. The reports also showed that the law regarding election expenses could be flouted with the greatest ease since a strict audit was never required, and that the law preventing the withdrawal of petitions could also be evaded. Even when petitions were tried it depended on the judges whether a Royal Commission would be appointed or not, and while one pair of judges[1] were quite strict in their approach to corrupt practices the others were more lenient.

The degree of electoral corruption in the eight boroughs may be gauged from the proportion of voters scheduled, though it must be remembered that through lack of complete proof the Commissioners scheduled a smaller number than they actually believed guilty:

Name	Registered electorate[2]	% of electorate reported
Boston	2,935	14
Canterbury . . .	2,880	8
Chester	6,227	15
Gloucester . . .	5,767	38
Knaresborough . .	651	11
Macclesfield . . .	5,221	55
Oxford	6,495	2
Sandwich . . .	2,225	53

Before considering the impact of these revelations on an astonished House of Commons it is necessary to sum up the points discussed in such detail above. Undoubtedly in the small number of constituencies where exhaustive investigations took place all the old forms of corrupt practice still continued, aggravated by the new evil of bribery mixed with fraud. Some of

[1] Mr. Justice Lush and Mr. Justice Manisty reported on four of the eight boroughs, Boston, Knaresborough, Oxford, and Sandwich. The Irish judges are left out of this comparison as they form a class by themselves.

[2] These totals include voters registered under two qualifications.

these constituencies were ancient cathedral cities with remnants of the venal pre-reform electorate still alive and the tradition they had created still persisting, but the borough with the highest proportion of corrupt voters (Macclesfield) was a new town enfranchised in 1832, where bribery had increased enormously in the period between 1874 and 1880.[1]

If the expenses returned in the corrupt boroughs were invariably lower than the actual outlay, how may the official returns be assessed for constituencies where no Royal Commission had been appointed or no petition presented?

It may safely be assumed that the official returns did not exaggerate the expenditure. Twenty-five candidates returned an average expenditure of over £2 per vote in constituencies where no petitions were presented;[2] while the corresponding number in constituencies where petitions were presented was three.[3] Among the twenty-five were three candidates whose total outlay exceeded £10,000.[4] The highest individual total officially returned was £13,053. 19s. 1d. by C. W. W. Wynn, a descendant and namesake of the last of the Grenvillites, who sat for Montgomeryshire.[5] It is impossible to see how these levels of expenditure could be legitimately reached. Furthermore, no less than eleven constituencies, including the Cities of London and Westminster, submitted incomplete returns. There was no return at all from Radnorshire, and at Derbyshire and Shropshire the returning officers saw to it that the relevant papers were destroyed by fire. The figures from Ireland were more unsatisfactory still—no return at all from eighteen constituencies and only partial returns from eleven! At the other end of the scale, among the leaders of the parties the highest average expenditure

[1] See above, p. 141. The petitions for 1880 came from 12 shires (3 each from Glos., Worcs., and Kent; 2 each from Yorks., Wilts., Cheshire, 1 each from Devon, Berks., Essex, Lincs., Oxon., Staffs.). In 1874 12 shires were also concerned (4 from Glos., 3 from Durham, 2 from Devon, Lincs., and Worcs.; 1 from Lancs., Berks., Dorset, Cornwall, London, Hants, Yorks.).

[2] This estimate covers those candidates only who polled more than 200 votes. Cf. *P.P. 1880*, lvii. 3–49.

[3] R. E. Webster (Bewdley) averaged £2. 11s. per vote; John Fowler (Tewkesbury), £3. 9s. 6d.; Colonel George Tomline (Harwich), £2. 18s. 2d.

[4] Sir George Elliot (Durham N.), C. F. Surtees (Durham S.), C. W. W. Wynn (Montgomeryshire).

[5] Wynn's return listed £5,828. 4s. 10d. for conveyances alone. His opponent averaged £2. 19s. 7d. per vote to Wynn's £6. 11s. 10d., and beat him by 2,232 votes to 2,041.

per vote was 19s. 1d. for Selwin Ibbetson at West Essex, and the lowest 1s. 4d. for Gladstone at Leeds. Lowest of all were the four candidates at Oldham who between them averaged 1s. 2d. a vote.

The excessive cost of the general election of 1880 cannot be accounted for by any simple explanation. It was not confined to any part of the country: Welsh and Scottish elections cost as much per vote as English; nor to any party: the Liberal totals were as high as the Conservative.[1] It does not appear to have been the result of a deliberate policy by either party. The exposures of the petition courts and Royal Commissions roused an immediate reaction from the newspapers and members on both sides of the House of Commons and that reaction more than any other factor was responsible for the carrying through in 1883 of a draconian limitation of expenses which ensured that the next general election would be just over one-quarter as expensive as the election[2] of 1880.

The most likely explanation is that the increased nationalization of politics, of which the mass party organizations and the public campaigns of the leaders were obvious signs; the exceptional keenness of the party struggle; the absence of a legal ceiling on election expenditure; and, most important of all, the fact that bribery and treating were only theoretically discreditable, all combined to make of the election an unparalleled orgy of extravagance. Without detailed knowledge of the lives and circumstances of local M.P.s throughout the country one cannot apportion the blame with any degree of precision between the parties. The Parliamentary Elections and Corrupt Practices Act of 1880 undoubtedly gave a fresh impetus to corrupt expenditure, but although it was engineered by the Conservatives in face of strong Liberal opposition, the Liberal mass organization, as well as the local groups, did not scruple to derive the maximum advantage from it. The scornful remark of *The Times* that when the secret electioneering history of the country came to be written little difference would be found between the practices of Conservatives and Liberals contains a good deal of the truth.[3]

[1] *P.P. 1880*, lvii. 3–49.
[2] *P.P. 1886*, lii. 483; see below, Chap. VI.
[3] See next chapter for newspaper reactions to the Reports of the Royal Commissions. No newspaper predicted in the summer of 1880 that their revelations

The party associations and agents may have decided that whenever necessary they would use corrupt means to defeat their opponents, but they were not enamoured of them. Parkes had spoken strongly in 1835 and 1860 in favour of abolishing paid agency;[1] likewise Gorst, before the Royal Commissions were set up, expressed his conviction that the election of 1880 was far more corrupt than that of 1874 and urged the House to treat the problem seriously.[2]

During the debates on the 1883 Bill, Gorst was to press strongly for the same reforms as Parkes had urged. Thus the two machine leaders showed a desire to reduce organization to a minimum because of the close connexion between machine politics and malpractices.[3]

In the previous chapter it was said that the election of 1874 was the last of the old-style elections. The election of 1880 was in some respects, but not all, the first of the new: it was the first with national campaigns by the leaders, it was also the first with two mass organizations.

This resemblance to modern practice is, however, superficial. The fundamental rules of the game were unchanged. The belief that the wealthy classes had a right to maintain their influence even by means that the legislature had condemned was still implicitly held by a large number of practising politicians. It was, however, an instinctive, not a rational belief, and when they were forced to consider it during the prolonged self-examination of the years 1881, 1882, and 1883 the politicians had to admit to a strong sense of shame.

In conclusion, the general election of 1880 marked the transition: it was the first general election fought on the national level; it was the last to be disgraced by widespread corrupt practices.

---

would be so unsavoury. *The Times* at the beginning of the petition trials smugly remarked: 'The ballot is an institution which has made good its footing in the country. Its efficacy in discouraging bribery may be trusted . . . Law and public opinion have pretty well eradicated the vice of personal and individual corruption' (*The Times*, 26 Apr. 1880).

[1] See Chap. I.

[2] *3 Hans.* cclvi (1 Sept. 1880), 988–90. See above, p. 135.

[3] Of course in Gorst's day the machine was far more important than in Parkes's. The comparison is made here to show the similar state of mind of the two men.

CHAPTER VI

The Corrupt and Illegal Practices Act (1883)

I

THE judgements on the crop of petitions following on the general election of 1880 were published between 2 June and 11 August 1880. The eight Royal Commisssions were appointed on 1 September and heard evidence throughout the winter of 1880–1.

The reaction to the petition disclosures by the newspapers[1] and on both sides of the House of Commons was immediate and spectacular. Anger and shame at the extent of the malpractices were blended with surprise at their persistence in spite of thirty years of remedial legislation. During the winter, while the Commissioners were still taking evidence, many questions were asked in the Commons about the intentions of the Liberal Government.

The Government did not wait for the reports of the Royal Commissions. When Parliament reassembled on 6 January 1881 the Queen's Speech announced a Bill 'for repressing the corrupt practices of which, in a limited number of towns, there were lamentable examples at the last General Election'. On the following day the Attorney-General, Sir Henry James, introduced the Parliamentary Elections (Corrupt and Illegal Practices) Bill of 1881.[2]

In his speech[3] James assumed that after the disclosures already

---

[1] See below, p. 161, n. 4.

[2] It seems strange that Gladstone should have entrusted all the Corrupt and Illegal Practices Bills to the Attorney-General. James had some experience of election legislation—he had sponsored two private members' bills (one on election expenses) during the Parliament of 1874–80—but he did not have a seat in the Cabinet and three of the other four names inscribed on the Bill belonged to Cabinet ministers, viz.: Harcourt, Chamberlain, and Dilke. Forster (now Chief Secretary for Ireland), Hartington, and Bright rarely made an appearance during these debates; Gladstone, merely to announce the course of business.

[3] *3 Hans.* cclvii (7 Jan. 1881), 265–71.

made at petition trials there would be general agreement that it was the duty of the Government to try to mitigate, if not to stop, corrupt practices, particularly lavish and extravagant expenditure—if for no other reason than that they restricted the parliamentary arena to those whose only virtue was wealth and kept out men of ability. The Bill had two main objects—to lessen election expenditure and to make the penalties for corrupt practices much more severe. The first was to be realized by restricting every candidate to one election agent, one personation agent for every polling station, one clerk and messenger for every polling district (in counties) or every 500 voters (in boroughs) and by fixing a ceiling to legitimate expenditure. The ceiling was determined by the size of the electorate, though this standard was applied more flexibly in the counties. Broadly speaking, no candidate could spend more than £1,000 per 5,000 voters—apart from his own personal expenditure, which in any case might not exceed £100.[1] The effect of this ceiling would be to reduce the expenditure in many constituencies by two-thirds or more of their 1880 totals.[2]

To place responsibilities of candidates and agents on a more equal basis the Bill provided that all electoral payments be made only by the election agent, to whom a statement of claim had to be made within 30 days of polling; the bills to be paid by him within 40 days and a full return of every expense sent in within 50 days, together with a declaration in a form laid down by the Bill.[3]

The second aim was implemented by drawing a distinction between offences that were merely 'illegal' and those that were 'corrupt', and by visiting the latter with much heavier penalties than before. The practices classified as corrupt were bribery, treating, intimidation, abduction of voters, undue influence, personation, and making a false statement in the official return of expenses. Those found guilty by an election court or Royal Commission were liable to a sentence of two years' imprisonment, with or without hard labour, a fine of £500, and the loss of voting rights for ten years. In addition, a candidate found

---

[1] The Bill of 1881 differed in some details from the Bill that passed into law in 1883. See below, pp. 174-5.
[2] See below, pp. 206-7.
[3] For the text of the Bill see *P.P. 1881*, iv. 233-72.

guilty of corrupt practices was banned for life from representing
the constituency concerned. Illegal practices were colourable
employment, payment of travelling expenses, and any infringe-
ment of the very detailed rules for making the official return of
expenses, and were punishable with a fine of £100.

Other important changes made in the Bill were the prohibition of public houses as committee-rooms and the repeal of the
Act of 1879 prescribing two judges instead of one for election
trials.[1] The Bill was applicable to the entire United Kingdom.

After the Attorney-General's speech, Sir Richard Assheton
Cross, who led for the Opposition throughout the debates on the
Bills of 1881, 1882, and 1883, as he had done in the Ballot Bill
debates, simply asked when the reports of the Royal Commissions would be published.[2] The Attorney-General promised
them within the next fortnight. The Bill was then brought in
without a division and given a first reading.

The importance of the Bill was immediately recognized by
the newspapers. *The Times* wrote: 'If passed in its present form,
it can scarcely fail to effect something like a revolution in the
mode of conducting Parliamentary elections.' The Government
were clearly acting under a strong sense of shame at the recent
election scandals and had realized that no gentle measures
would succeed in rooting up the 'foul and noisome weed' of
electoral corruption.[3] The defect of the existing laws was that
they could not be applied with sufficient promptness and because of their complexity very few of the guilty were ever
punished. As far as the small venal constituencies were concerned the only way to make them pure was to remove the very
possibility of sinning.

The leading article in *The Times* summed up the reactions of
most of the press, both national and provincial, at first sight of
the Bill.[4] The consensus of opinion seemed to be that the Bill's

[1] The Bill also prescribed that polling places should be more numerous; that (as
the Select Committee of 1875 had suggested) a representative of the Attorney-
General should attend at every petition trial and prosecute those found guilty of
corrupt practices before the election judges; that the judge might throw the cost of
the petitions on the constituencies. It repealed most of the Acts of 1863 and 1880,
the whole Act of 1879, and several sections of the Acts of 1854 and 1867.
[2] 3 *Hans.* cclvii (7 Jan. 1881), 271.
[3] *The Times*, 8 Jan. 1881; cf. also 10 Jan.
[4] The *Daily Telegraph* (8–9 Jan. 1881) wrote that candidates would rejoice at the
statutory limitation of expenditure; the *Standard*, that the appearance of so drastic

provisions, though severe, were necessary if the new mass electorate were not to be further corrupted. There were, of course, some misgivings—but mainly among politicians. The National Liberal Federation sent a deputation to the Attorney-General suggesting various amendments to the Bill, including a definition of agency and a provision that qualified voters might be legally employed during an election campaign as long as they did not vote, because in some constituencies it might be difficult to find non-voters who would make suitable election officials. James refused and the *Pall Mall Gazette* rejoiced that he had not mitigated the 'chief safeguard against indirect bribery'.[1]

Supported by the large Liberal majority and not actively opposed by the Conservatives the Bill ought to have passed speedily through the Commons, but the Government's time-schedule was ruined by the obstruction of the large, compact Home Rule party which in the session of 1881 reached its peak of efficiency.[2] The obstruction was directed chiefly against the Coercion Bill for Ireland which the Queen's Speech had promised as a make-weight for a new Land Bill. As a result, the debate on the Address lasted eleven nights, the sitting of 25 January, twenty-two hours; and after the unique forty-one hour sitting of 31 January–2 February, which was brought to an end by the intervention of the Speaker, the 'new rules' were framed (comprising the closure) and presented to the House on 9 February.

The 'new rules' spelt the ultimate defeat of obstructionism

a law was the best possible commentary on the change that had come over public opinion; the *Scotsman* thought some clauses even needed to be strengthened; the *Leeds Mercury* believed that the bill would be accepted by all save bribers and bribees, despite some 'small inconvenience' to innocent candidates. See also the *Contemporary Review*, xxxix (May 1881), 758–79. Only the *Saturday Review* (see especially 27 Aug., 31 Dec. 1881) held out, claiming that the standard set by the Bill was too high for public opinion to tolerate. By 1880 the *Saturday Review* had become very tinged with Conservatism, many of its radical writers having left to join the *Pall Mall Gazette*—which was very strongly for the Bill (see 10–11 Jan. 1881).

[1] *The Pall Mall Gazette*, 18 Feb. 1881.

[2] The obstruction generally lacked finesse, consisting in the main of endless motions for the adjournment and 'that the Speaker do now leave the Chair'. T. M. Healy, however (recently elected in a by-election at Longford), showed considerable ingenuity by making 'a series of short, dogged, savagely insulting speeches, which could be relied on to stimulate some government supporter to reply indignantly and thus waste his own time'. C. Cruise O'Brien, *Parnell and his Party 1880–1890*, p. 58.

but it had already upset the ministerial order of business for the entire session. The second reading of the Corrupt and Illegal Practices Bill had been fixed for 17 February; but on that day James had to ask that it be deferred until 3 March.[1] Nothing more was heard until 11 July, when James moved that the order for the second reading be discharged as by then it was obviously too late in that session to carry a complicated measure of 59 clauses.[2] Cross agreed that it was necessary to withdraw the Bill at that stage. He wanted, however, to extract a pledge from the Government that it would be brought in again as early as possible; to that James replied that 'so far as he was aware' the Government intended to reintroduce the Bill early in the following session. Cross went on to give the official Conservative view —that the Bill was intended to remove a great scandal and therefore would receive a good deal of support, but that parts of it would really constitute traps for honest candidates, and ought to be modified.[3]

The Government did manage, however, to carry the Corrupt Practices (Suspension of Elections) Bill which suspended until eight days after the beginning of the 1882 session the issue of writs for the seven venal boroughs.[4] Other private Bills forced aside by the pressure of Irish business would have thrown the necessary expenses of elections on the local rates[5] and consolidated the anti-corruption laws. Just before the end of the session the Government suffered an unexpected reverse. A petition was tried at Wigan (after a by-election) and the judges reported that corrupt practices prevailed extensively there. According to custom, the Attorney-General moved for a Royal Commission but his motion was rejected. The clannishness of Lancashire

[1] On the same day T. P. O'Connor gave the first indication of Home Rule opinion on the Bill by saying that he would withdraw a negativing amendment if he were encouraged to believe that the Government would meet his objections, but he did not think it likely. Home Rule opposition to the Bill was clear from the very start. Cf. *3 Hans.* cclviii (17 Feb. 1881), 1194.

[2] The Irish Land Bill (which provided judicially fixed rents and was the greatest concession yet to agrarian feeling) stayed in the Commons from 7 Apr. to 27 July. During this time some Home Rulers were in prison and the rest gave Gladstone little help in getting the Bill through the House.

[3] *3 Hans.* cclxiii (11 July 1881), 621.

[4] 44 & 45 Vict., c. 42. It passed through the Commons in three days.

[5] Sponsored by Thomas Burt and Ashton Dilke. This point was to come up again in 1882 and 1883. See below, pp. 168, 172. Essentially the argument was the same as Fawcett's in 1870-2. See above, p. 70.

members, the obstruction of Home Rulers, and a sudden whip of the Conservatives in a very small House combined to bring about the only occasion on which the House of Commons refused to act on the report of an election court.[1] The *Saturday Review*, indulging in some wishful thinking, professed to see a reaction away from 'the somewhat inquisitatorial proceedings of the Election Commissioners and from their ineffectual results',[2] but this defeat had no more significance than the result of any other snap division.

2

Thus, although the interest of Parliament had been keenly aroused by the petition trial disclosures and the reports of the Commissioners the intention of the Government to pass their Bill in 1881 was frustrated. When the Bill was reintroduced at the beginning of the session of 1882 it contained three extra clauses, but was otherwise the same as before.[3] It was ordered without a discussion on 9 February, given a first reading the next day, and the second reading was fixed for 24 April.[4]

The second reading debate lasted three days, from 24 to 26 April. It immediately encountered opposition from a small but important group. The Conservative front bench, represented by Cross, approved in principle, but desired some modification of the penalties, which they thought too severe, and of the schedules which they considered too rigid. Cross also said that he was 'absolutely and entirely' opposed to reverting to the practice of a single judge. No one man ought to have the power to exclude another from public life without any possibility of an appeal. These points might be thrashed out in committee; the real opposition came from Conservative back-benchers who loudly protested the impossibility of conducting an election within the narrow expense margins allowed.[5] R. N. Fowler,

[1] The Government were defeated by 43 votes to 37. See *3 Hans.* cclxv (20 Aug. 1881), 504-9.　　　　[2] *Saturday Review*, 27 Aug. 1881.
[3] One of these extra clauses invalidated any election in which the electoral employees (agents, poll clerks, clerks, or messengers) had been found guilty of corrupt practices less than seven years before. For the text of the Bill see *P.P. 1882*, v. 33-80.
[4] The budget debate was dispatched in time to allow the second reading debate to start on 24 Apr.; see *The Times*, 25 Apr. 1881.
[5] For the debate on the second reading see *3 Hans.* cclxviii (24 Apr. 1882), 1327-65; (25 Apr.), 1421-46; (26 Apr.), 1581-1630.

C. N. Warton, D. R. Onslow, and the young A. J. Balfour[1] spoke against the Bill. Fowler and Warton moved an amendment stating that since no corrupt practices had been associated with the larger boroughs it was 'inexpedient to adopt such uniform restrictions as would render the fair conduct of an election in a great constituency perilous and penal'. The egregious Colonel (now Sir William) Barttelot[2] complained that the Ballot Act had promoted that 'most un-English' practice of taking bribes from both sides, or voting against the side from which a bribe had been accepted; he also feared that the passing of the Corrupt and Illegal Practices Bill would mean that if people were sent down to 'disturb and debauch' a constituency, then those who spent 'large sums of money' in 'resisting' them might be found guilty of corrupt practices. Sir Gabriel Goldney said that he had never before been so frightened by a parliamentary Bill; the scales allowed were so low that it would be extremely difficult to employ any reputable agent.

The Conservative leaders tried to dispel these fears. Gorst, speaking with the authority of a former Principal Agent, said that many members had extravagant ideas of what expenditure was really necessary to conduct an election: 'All that was really required was that the constituencies should have the means of amply being informed, or informing themselves, of the character, qualifications and political views of the candidates.'[3]

The Bill, Gorst said, would be of no use at all without the maximum schedule. He suggested (and James agreed) that a similar Bill be introduced for municipal elections, as otherwise the lavish expenditure might be diverted into them. Gorst also suggested—a sly dig at the Caucus—that the expenditure by national party organizations, allegedly on registration, would in time reach enormous proportions and ought to be curbed.[4] The ex-Attorney-General, Sir Hardinge Giffard, perhaps with his

[1] Fowler (not to be confused with H. H. Fowler, Liberal M.P. for Wolverhampton, who was in favour of the Bills) was Conservative M.P. for the City of London; Warton was M.P. for Bridport; Onslow, M.P. for Guildford; and Balfour (first elected in 1874), M.P. for Hertford. See below, p. 172, n. 2.

[2] See above, p. 75.

[3] 3 Hans. cclxviii (27 Apr. 1882), 1609–11. Despite his membership of the Fourth Party, Gorst remained Vice-Chairman of the National Union (1882–4).

[4] Gorst added that what was necessary was not severe but speedy penalties; he would be in favour of invoking summary jurisdiction for electoral offences (ibid.).

own experiences at Horsham in mind,[1] said bluntly that a class had grown up with no political convictions, but the firm purpose of extorting as much money as possible from candidates at election times, and that the principle of a limit to expenditure was of the highest importance to both sides.

None of these arguments had any effect on C. E. Lewis, the Conservative member for Londonderry, who had taken an active interest in electoral questions since 1868 and had sat on some Select Committees. Lewis opposed the Bill on two fundamental grounds: that it introduced a new class of offences with penal consequences, and that it would deter worthy men from contesting elections. Both of these results he considered would be 'highly inexpedient, if not unjust'. Lewis mockingly suggested that the title of the bill should read: 'A Bill for the purpose of frightening persons from becoming Candidates for a seat in Parliament, and for imprisoning and disqualifying all those who do'. He called it 'the most reckless and vital invasion of the rights of members' to confer these powers on one judge, and as a proof of judicial fallibility cited a number of recent decisions that had been reversed on appeal, as well as alluding to the peculiarities of some election judgements.[2]

Orange and Green for once came together. The Home Rule party as a whole agreed with Lewis as to the imprudence of reverting to one judge, indeed on conferring so much power on the judges at all. Healy, who never minced his words, said that since the last judge of the 'old school . . . who administered justice according to the abstract principles of justice'[3] had died a short time before he would not trust a single member of the existing Irish bench with an election petition. Philip Callan[4]

---

[1] See above, p. 56, n. 4.

[2] *3 Hans.* cclxviii (25 Apr. 1882), 1442–5. Throughout the debates on the Bills of 1881, 1882, and 1883 Lewis showed himself the most implacable opponent of the Government. In the 1883 debates he contrasted the actual expenditure in 1880 of himself and three Liberal ministers with what the schedules would allow, viz.:

Gladstone (1880) £2,495; (schedule) £580.
Harcourt (1880) £3,200; (schedule) £500.
Dilke (1880) £3,200; (schedule) £1,150.
Lewis (1880) £850; (schedule) £380.

See *3 Hans.* cclxxix (4 June 1883), 1656–8.

[3] Mr. Justice O'Brien, an unusual Irish judge in that he had never been active in politics. His judgements on election petitions were far more detached and impersonal than those of Baron Fitzgerald, Mr. Justice Lawson, or Mr. Justice Keogh.

[4] Home Rule M.P. for Louth; cf. *3 Hans.* cclxviii (27 Apr. 1882), 1586.

asked whether the Attorney-General had sought the advice of
the judges before deciding to return to the one-judge practice.
Charles Dawson[1] reminded the House of the notorious Keogh
judgement and also of the remarks of Mr. Justice Harrison at
the Louth petition in 1880—that it was a great advantage to
have a second judicial opinion. But there was one prominent
Irish member, Joseph G. Biggar, the Ulster ex-Presbyterian,
Home Ruler, and 'father of obstructionism', who openly supported the Bill, not only on account of its restrictions on expenditure but also because of the severer penalties for treating,
a very common feature of Irish elections.

At the close of the debate, which ended without a division,
Dilke for the Government complimented Gorst and Giffard on
their 'valuable' speeches, and Cross thanked the Attorney-
General for meeting his objections in an 'extremely fair and
candid spirit'. The harmony between the front benches was in
striking contrast with the wrangling and bitterness over the
Ballot Act and the still more contentious Parliamentary Elections and Corrupt Practices Act of 1880;[2] it was to remain unbroken up to the passing of the Act in 1883.

The Government were determined to get the complicated
Bill through both Houses by the end of the session. The Opposition leadership facilitated this by allowing the committee stage
to be formally moved on 9 May so that the Bill could be brought
in again without notice.[3] The debate in committee began on
15 May.

The cleavage between the front and back opposition benches[4]
was even more noticeable than during the debate on the second
reading. Warton, Fowler, and Onslow put down several amendments which Cross and Gorst opposed: amendments to restrict
the penalties for treating to candidates and agents alone; to incorporate a definition of agency in the Bill (Gorst said this was
both impossible and unnecessary);[5] to reduce the penalties for

---

[1] 'Moderate' Home Rule M.P. for Carlow. Ibid. 1603.

[2] See above, pp. 114 ff.

[3] The technical procedure was to report progress immediately after moving for
a committee.

[4] The conduct of the Conservative front bench belied the prophecies of the
Saturday Review (27 Aug. 1881) that there would be a reaction against the 'inquisitorial proceedings' of the Election Commissioners and a 'lively fight' on the issue
of the Bill. See above, p. 164.

[5] James told the House that when the Ballot Bill was going through Forster had

treating (Gorst's opposition to this greatly annoyed Fowler);
and to indicate precisely the time-base of an election campaign.[1]
In return for this very substantial help James accepted a suggestion by Cross to insert the word 'corruptly' into the definitions
of bribery and treating to agree with the Act of 1854, although
he thought it unnecessary. He also agreed to reduce the fine
on those found guilty of corrupt practices from £500 to
£200, and the prison term to one year from two years. By the
end of the evening the House had got to the fifth clause of the
Bill.[2]

They were to get no further. The Irish party[3] had been
quiescent and disorganized since the arrest of Parnell and his
chief lieutenants over the 'No Rent manifesto' in October 1881.
They had largely absented themselves from the Commons until
his release on 2 May, which was followed within a few days by
the totally unexpected assassination of the new Chief Secretary,
Lord Frederick Cavendish, and his under-secretary, T. H.
Burke, in the Phoenix Park. British public opinion forced the
Government to introduce a new 'coercionist' Crimes Bill, which
came up for its second reading on 18 May, three days after the
opening of the committee debate on the Corrupt and Illegal
Practices Bill. This brought back the Home Rulers in force and
by a spirited, but not recklessly obstructive, opposition they
succeeded in prolonging the committee stage of the Crimes Bill
for over a month (1 June–4 July). Thus they ruined all hopes of
getting through the remaining 57 clauses of the Corrupt and
Illegal Practices Bill.

Once again the Attorney-General had to move that the order
for a committee be discharged (28 July), and again Cross re-
quested the Government to introduce a similar Bill in the next
session. Both made more cordial speeches than in 1881, Cross
thanking the Attorney-General for the way he had conducted
the measure and James assuring the House that he had learnt

---

promised to draft a definition of agency but that he had to give it up as 'utterly
impossible'. See *3 Hans.* cclxix (15 May 1882), 722.

[1] Ibid. 680–767.

[2] An amendment that James did not welcome was one by Broadhurst and Ashton
Dilke on the lines of the latter's Bill of the previous year (see above, p. 163), which
threw the expenses of returning officers on the constituency rates. It was carried by
a majority of 2 votes. See also below, p. 172.

[3] Cf. C. Cruise O'Brien, *Parnell and his Party*, pp. 71–83.

much from the opposition amendments and would consider during the coming months how the Bill might be improved.[1]

The debates on the abortive Bill of 1882 got little attention from the press because of more exciting public events—the imprisonment and release of Parnell, the Phoenix Park murders, and the Bradlaugh episode, now in its second year. *The Times* noted that the public knew much less about the measure than it deserved, but, apart from renewing its attack on those who argued that legislative severity unsupported by the general sense of the people must be ineffective, *The Times* itself paid little attention to the measure.[2]

3

On 4 December 1882 Gladstone wrote to James outlining the ministerial programme until the following Easter. Three technical Bills were to be referred to Standing Committees of the House of Commons and the Corrupt and Illegal Practices Bill was to take every other available evening,[3] taking priority over all other legislation. The Bill was introduced, ordered, and given a first reading on 16 February. It contained 67 clauses, 5 more than the Bill of 1882, but the schedules were simplified so that the classification of legitimate employment and the rules for limiting expenditure all appeared on the same schedule. The first five clauses of the Bill were a reprint of the previous year's Bill as it had left the committee, except that the amendment to throw the expenses of returning officers on the rates was omitted. Otherwise the only significant change in the draft was that the two judges provision of the Act of 1879 was restored. That was the sole result of the reconsideration that James had promised at the end of the 1882 debates.[4]

[1] *3 Hans.* cclxxiii (28 July 1882), 83–84.

[2] Cf. *The Times*, 25 Apr. 1882, in which the disclosures before the Royal Commissions were stigmatized as the 'unclean survivals' of another age. The only other leading articles on the 1882 Bill appeared on 28 Apr. and 16 May. See below, p. 177.

[3] Lord Askwith, *Lord James of Hereford* (London, 1930), p. 119. The three Bills were the Criminal Code Bill, the Bankruptcy Bill, and the Patents Bill.

[4] For the draft Bill see *P.P. 1883*, viii. 91–146. It is not generally known that Asquith (then aged 30) had a hand in drafting the Bill. He joined the staff of the Junior Counsel to the Treasury in that year, and his biographers write that 'Asquith, at the request of James, practically drafted the Act'. J. A. Spender and C. Asquith, *Life of Herbert Henry Asquith, Lord Oxford and Asquith* (London, 1932), i. 47, n. 1. Presumably Spender and Asquith mean the bill of 1883. But the texts of all three Bills are very similar.

Despite all Gladstone's good intentions the second reading could not be taken before Easter, and then the Agricultural Holdings Bill, which the Conservatives welcomed, was introduced and given a second reading. It was not until 4 June that the House could give its attention again to corrupt practices and by then it was clear that only through the closest co-operation between Government and Opposition would the Bill get to the Statute Book by the end of the session.

That this co-operation would again be forthcoming became evident at the opening of the debate, when Warton and Lewis moved a hostile amendment, on the familiar ground that it was inexpedient to legislate in advance of public opinion and iniquitous to create a new category of crimes. Both made no secret of the coldness between themselves and their leaders.[1] Lewis complained that there was 'not the slightest concerted party action' on his side of the House, and frankly admitted that he expected his amendment would be defeated. Nevertheless he persisted in his obstructive tactics. On the other hand, Cross pointedly offered James his hearty support and that of those 'who sat near him'.

At the same time Cross found room for further improvement: the penalties for illegal practices were too high, some limit ought to be put to the 'terrible stretch' of agency, and the expense schedules ought to be revised so that two candidates in coalition might not spend twice as much as a single opponent.[2]

Baron de Ferrieres said that no real moral improvement could be expected until large-scale redistribution and extension of the franchise had first taken place; he had no faith in legislative prohibitions. The remaining speeches were an enlargement on Lewis's theme—that the expense levels were too low for the proper running of elections. Raikes asked why the case of the 'peccant boroughs' had been allowed to lapse, and paid an unconscious tribute to the efficiency of the National Liberal Federation by saying that the real danger came from agents of central organizations who could go where they liked.[3]

[1] For the second reading debate see *3 Hans.* cclxxix (4 June 1883), 1651–1707.

[2] This was later conceded. See below, p. 175, n. 1.

[3] The Corrupt Practices (Suspension of Elections) Bill expired eight days after the opening of the 1882 session. A Bill was then brought in to disfranchise the seven boroughs, but James refused to speed it up (pleading the necessity of full discussion) and it lapsed. No Bill was introduced in 1883, so the writs for the boroughs were

In reply James denied that the expense levels were too low. In Hackney (19,000 voters) the candidates spent only £914 in 1880, while in Southwark (9,000 voters) £8,000 was spent. James asked the Conservative member for East Surrey, who had complained that he could not possibly conduct an election on the £1,380 allowed by the Bill, whether he did not see anything wrong in the fact that he and his colleague had to spend £13,000 in 1880, and whether he would not prefer to be rid of this enormous burden.[1] James also reproached Raikes for asking the Government to disfranchise a constituency that he had represented for so long,[2] and he would not promise another disfranchising bill.

Again the second reading was taken without a division. The Home Rulers had not been present in force but for the committee stage their opposition was assured. Their hostility to the Irish judges had been deepened (16 Aug. 1882) when Mr. Justice Lawson committed one of their number, E. D. Gray, editor of the *Freeman's Journal*, to prison for three months for contempt of court, because the *Freeman* had criticized his handling of some criminal cases. Gray's outraged colleagues claimed that the freedom of the press was being challenged and under pressure from them Gladstone set up a Select Committee of Privileges on which he himself, Northcote (the leader of the Opposition), and Parnell sat. Immediately after the setting up of the committee Mr. Justice Lawson released Gray,[3] and no further action was taken.

The Bill went to committee on 7 June 1883, where it remained for twenty-three nights. Much of the delay was due to the Irish party who again joined forces with Lewis, Warton, and Onslow in fruitless, though troublesome, opposition. The Irish members' fear of a possible abuse of the new powers by Mr. Justice Lawson

allowed to lapse until the Redistribution of Seats Act (1885), which abolished Sandwich and Macclesfield.

[1] James had made the same point on the second reading debate in 1882. There were at least thirty-five cases (including Chamberlain's and Bright's) where the expenditure of 1880 was well within the scheduled limits. Compare an expenditure of 2s. 1d. per vote by a successful candidate at Hereford with the record £6. 5s. per vote by an unsuccessful candidate at Montgomery, almost adjoining. Cf. *3 Hans.* cclxviii (24 Apr. 1882), 1341–5; see also above, p. 156.

[2] Chester.

[3] Lawson had also imposed a fine of £500, which had to be paid before Gray's release.

and his like was justified, but when an amendment by Parnell asking for special consideration for Ireland had been defeated by an enormous majority, and another amendment suggesting a more precise definition of spiritual influence had been accepted, further verbal amendments served only to irritate the Government and the section of the press that supported them.[1]

In addition to open opposition from the Parnellites and back-bench Conservatives some Liberal back-benchers showed a veiled hostility, especially to the early sections that defined and prescribed penalties for corrupt practices. Both the draconian punishments and the increased accountability of candidates weighed heavily on them. Sometimes the ordinary party lines became tangled. An amendment by H. H. Fowler[2] that the election should not be invalidated if the candidate had taken all reasonable precautions against corrupt practices, or if the corrupt practices were trivial and did not affect the result, was defeated by the narrow margin of 29 votes; among those voting for it were Northcote and Gorst, while Cross sided with the Liberals against it and spoke sarcastically of his leader's speech.

Broadhurst's amendment[3] came up again, but was defeated by a very large majority drawn from both sides of the House. Gladstone, making one of his rare appearances in these debates, explained why the Government had rejected this alone among the amendments carried in 1882. He admitted that he agreed with the principle that candidates ought not to be saddled with these expenses, but to have introduced it then would have made the Bill a controversial measure—which was what he wanted to avoid. Speaking soon afterwards, Northcote said that the Government would have been guilty of a breach of faith if they had accepted the amendment.[4] The hint was not lost on the Irish party: Healy, taunting Gladstone with going back on his own principles, ironically suggested that he had introduced the Agricultural Holdings Bill to please the Conservatives and was jettisoning the Broadhurst Amendment because they did not like it.

Whatever his original intentions may have been Gladstone

[1] See below, p. 177.
[2] Fowler (M.P. for Wolverhampton) professed strong agreement with the principles of the Bill, but doubted whether the penalties would be effective.
[3] See above, pp. 163, 168.
[4] 3 Hans. cclxxix (7 June 1883), 1935.

was able to use the Agricultural Holdings Bill as a bargaining counter. After some days of pressure by the Conservatives to bring it on he made it quite clear that the Corrupt and Illegal Practices Bill would take precedence over it.[1] That was on the fifth night in committee, when they were still on the first clause. The Bill made greater progress after that; the fifth clause was reached on the eighth night (22 June) and in spite of many pages of amendments the debate in committee was finished by 13 July.

The report stage was to be taken on 8 August, but on that day the Attorney-General moved for recommital to allow increased expenditure in the counties, a sop to the worried backbenchers. On 10 August he moved another recommittal to allow an appeal from the decisions on summary prosecutions to the election judges. Lewis and Healy then made a last unavailing effort to get the schedules reopened, although Healy's 'astute vigilance'—to quote *The Times*[2]—had been rewarded on the previous day by James's acceptance, despite the misgivings of the Irish Attorney-General, of an amendment providing that no electoral offences in Ireland might be the subject of proceedings under the Crimes Acts.

After a final exchange of compliments between James and Cross the Bill was given a third reading.[3] It passed through all stages in the Lords between 13 and 22 August, where several amendments, mainly verbal, were made,[4] and received the royal assent on 25 August 1883.

4

The Corrupt and Illegal Practices Act (1883)[5] was such a landmark in the struggle for electoral purity that a summary of its main provisions will not be out of place.

[1] *3 Hans.* cclxxx (18 June 1883), 838. [2] *The Times*, 9 Aug. 1883.

[3] James: Sir, I have to congratulate honourable Members on having reached this stage of the Bill . . .

Cross: Sir, I concur with the remarks of the honourable and learned Attorney-General . . .

(*3 Hans.* cclxxxiii (10 Aug. 1883), 138.)

[4] For the Lords' amendments see *P.P. 1883*, viii. 205–10. The most important was the provision that a Royal Commission should not have the power to upset an election result allowed by the election judges.

[5] 46 & 47 Vict. c. 51. Its full title was: The Corrupt and Illegal Practices Prevention Act (1883).

A. PENALTIES

I. *Corrupt Practices*[1]

(i) For all found guilty by an election court a punishment of one year's imprisonment[2] (with the option of hard labour) and a fine of £200.

(ii) In addition, candidates found personally guilty were to suffer perpetual exclusion from the constituency concerned, withdrawal of voting rights, and exclusion from the House of Commons and all public and judicial offices for seven years. Where candidates were found guilty through their agents the punishment was merely exclusion from the constituency for seven years.[3]

II. *Illegal Practices*

(i) All found guilty were liable to a fine of £100 and exclusion from voting rights and public and judicial offices for five years.

(ii) In addition, candidates found personally guilty were to suffer seven years' exclusion from their constituency, but where the agents were guilty and the candidates innocent the exclusion was to be for the lifetime of the existing Parliament.

B. CLASSIFICATION OF ILLEGAL PRACTICES

Illegal practices were spending in excess of the expense maxima, payment for conveyances, employment of voters, wearing party favours or marks of distinction, and any violation of the following rules:

(i) All contracts and payments to be made through the single election agent who should be appointed at the beginning of the campaign.

(ii) All accounts to be paid within four weeks of the election.

(iii) The personal expenses of the candidate not to exceed £100.

(iv) Every item in the return of expenses to be listed separately.

(v) The return to be made within thirty-five days of the election and to be accompanied by a declaration of the agent verifying the statement; a similar declaration to be made by the candidate within a week afterwards.

(vi) A successful candidate who does not comply with (v) to be

---

[1] Bribery, treating, undue influence, assaulting or abducting a voter, personation, perjury and a false statement in the return of expenses.

[2] Except that personation was punished by *two* years in prison with hard labour.

[3] See below, pp. 181, 193, n. 4.

liable to a fine of £100 for every day that he sits in the House of Commons until the declarations and returns are sent in.

(vii) In boroughs one clerk and one messenger (non-voters) to every 500 electors: in counties one clerk and one messenger to every 500 voters in a polling district, plus the same (in the central committee room) to every 5,000 voters.

(viii) One committee room to every 5,000 voters.

(ix) Paid agents, &c., may not vote.

C. EXPENSE MAXIMA[1]

(i) *English, Welsh, and Scottish boroughs*
With less than 2,000 voters—£350
With over 2,000 voters—£380 (plus £30 for every additional 1,000)

(ii) *Irish boroughs*
With less than 500 voters—£200
With 500–1,000 voters—£250
With 1,000–1,500 voters—£275 (plus £30 for every additional 1,000)

(iii) *English, Welsh, and Scottish counties*
With less than 2,000 voters—£650
With over 2,000 voters—£710 (plus £60 for every additional 1,000)

(iv) *Irish counties*
With less than 2,000 voters—£500
With over 2,000 voters—£540 (plus £40 for every additional 1,000)

The Act was by far the most stringent ever passed in Britain against electoral malpractices; its effect was to transform the whole character of British electioneering within a generation. The motives which prompted the Liberal Government seem clear enough: a sense of shame at the unpleasant facts unearthed by the election judges and commissioners of 1880—perhaps made keener by the knowledge that the worst boroughs tended to be Liberal rather than Conservative;[2] a realization that the Acts of 1854, 1868, and 1872 for all their good points were but

---

[1] Where two candidates stood together the amounts were reduced by one-quarter; and where more than two, by one-third.

[2] See above Chap. V.

palliatives for a still raging disease, and that an effective remedy must be a very strong one. Nor was self-interest absent. Gladstone had written in 1877 that he feared lest the good effects of the vast increase in the electorate might be neutralized by a corresponding increase in the cost of electioneering, which would keep out of Parliament all but the very rich.[1] Though the restrictions on expenditure would serve to lighten the load on the pockets of all candidates, they would especially make lower middle-class candidatures easier and working-class candidatures possible; and both types were more likely to be Liberal. In the ministerial long-term programme the Act of 1883 may be envisaged as the logical counterpart not only of the Ballot Act but also of the Representation of the People Act of 1884 and the Redistribution of Seats Act of 1885.[2]

The Conservative leaders might very easily have opposed these Bills by magnifying the points of difference that even those most amicably disposed could find. That they not only refrained from doing so but facilitated their passage in every way, and even seemed genuinely disappointed at the withdrawal of the Bills of 1881 and 1882, is not so easy to explain. The *Saturday Review*, which was prejudiced from the start against the Bills, saw in Gorst's suggestion that paid canvassing be prohibited altogether an attempt to make the Government look ridiculous.[3] But Gorst's speeches are all of a piece. With his vast knowledge of electioneering he cannot have been unaware that the maximum expense levels were far lower than what most of his party had spent in 1880.[4] Yet he said the expense scales were essential to the Bill; and so did Cross. Even though they knew that many of their plutocratic supporters would be inconvenienced during

[1] W. E. Gladstone, 'The County Franchise and Mr. Lowe thereon', *The Nineteenth Century*, ii (Nov. 1877), 554–7.

[2] For the development of Liberal ideology see above, pp. 72–73. Although the Ballot Bills almost provoked a crisis within the Cabinet the principles of the Corrupt and Illegal Practices Bills were so clearly unexceptionable that they could be entrusted to a law officer who did not sit in the Cabinet.

[3] *Saturday Review*, 7 July 1883.

[4] At the 1883 Conference of the National Union at Birmingham (2 Oct. 1883) G. C. T. Bartley, now Principal Agent of the Conservative Party (see above, Chap. V), analysed the cost of contesting fifty-five seats in the Midlands in 1880 and found that the total expenditure was £100,000—under the Act the expenses could not exceed £37,000. Cf. *Minutes of the 17th Annual Conference of the National Union of Conservative and Constitutional Associations*, p. 55. Bartley's paper is headed 'Private'.

the next few elections the Conservative leaders must have seen that in the long run the extirpation of the class of electioneering parasites, which ate up most of the large sums spent on campaigns, would benefit all candidates, and that enthusiastic voluntary supporters of the sort that kept down Chamberlain's and Bright's expenses were far more desirable. As far as the grosser forms of corrupt practice were concerned Conservative repugnance and regret seem quite sincere.

The debates show that the leaders of both parties were keenly aware of a 'strong public feeling' that some remedy must be found for electoral malpractices. James made no secret of the Government's intention that the Bills should satisfy this feeling, but it is difficult to assess the quality and extent of this public opinion without making a far more careful examination which would be outside the scope of this work. There was no great popular movement for the reform of electioneering methods, no impact of outside forces on the parliamentary machine. One may cite a pamphlet here, a speech there,[1] but apart from such scraps of evidence the newspapers must be relied on for guidance on the public reaction to these reforms. Not that the newspapers[2] spoke with one voice: the *Saturday Review* and the *Standard* believed the Act to be too far ahead of public opinion and so likely to be deliberately defied; the *Spectator* and *The Economist* quarrelled with points of detail and also pleaded public opinion; the Liberal organs, on the other hand, were consistently for the Bills—the *Daily News*, *Pall Mall Gazette*, and *Scotsman* had been very impatient with the tortuous delays in committee in 1883.

The Times changed its line in 1883, as in 1871. Up to February it still thought the Bill to be in the candidates' interest and that until a further remedy could be devised, it would 'make corruption, if not impossible, so difficult and dangerous that it will be very much less frequently tried'.[3] In the middle of June, however, *The Times* expressed the fear that the penalties were so

[1] e.g. Spencer Walpole, *The Electorate and the Legislature* (London, 1881), and 'Sixty Years' Liberal Work', an address to the Hampstead Liberal Club by E. K. Blyth (London, 1881). Both predicted the appearance of a stringent government measure.

[2] Cf. p. 161, n. 4; also *Spectator*, 9 June 1883; *Standard*, 22 June 1883; *Saturday Review*, 7 July 1883.

[3] *The Times*, 23 Feb. 1883. See above, p. 161.

exact and draconian that the Bill might not be supported by public opinion, and persisted in this attitude to the end.[1]

The public opinion of which the newspapers were interpreters was in the last analysis merely the gradual change in ethical standards that characterized the later Victorian age. Bribery, like drunkenness, was coming to be looked on as a social evil. Previously, whatever the official front-bench view in the House of Commons might have been, candidates, agents, and voters alike had refused to believe that there was any moral evil in using money and other influences for political ends.[2] But the almost imperceptible tightening-up of personal moral standards and social conscience that went with increased prosperity and more widely diffused education must inevitably have driven the old-fashioned malpractices out of existence. The years after 1880 provided the opportunity for measuring the extent of his change. It was not enough to pass the Act of 1883: it had also to be made to work.

[1] *The Times*, 20 June, 13 July, 9 Aug. 1883.
[2] *Blackwood's Edinburgh Magazine*, cxxxiv (Dec. 1883), 728.

CHAPTER VII

1885–1900

I

BY 1885 the British electoral system had assumed much the same form as it has today. The three great reformist measures of Gladstone's second administration had exhausted the energies of members and also their interest in the structure and working of the system. Although universal suffrage would obviously be the last stage in the long process of development, it was 1891 before a resolution was moved to alter the qualification of voters and 1904 before a government promised a further measure—a longer interval than at any time since 1832.[1]

Similarly, as far as purity of elections was concerned it was generally felt that the Act of 1883 marked the limit of interference and control by legislation over electioneering habits. Apart from an occasional question about a particular judgement few suggestions were made in the Commons for modifying the Act. One alteration, however, was made to the law during these years,[2] by way of a private member's Bill which created a new illegal practice.

On 8 February 1895 T. H. Bolton, Liberal-Unionist member for St. Pancras North,[3] introduced a Bill to make false statements of fact calculated to prejudice a candidate's chances at a parliamentary election subject to the same penalties as illegal practices. The appearance of the Bill was undoubtedly due to

---

[1] The main concerns of the reformist element in Parliament (when they did succeed in reviving interest in the subject) were the abolition of plural voting, women's suffrage, and the simplifying of registration procedure, rather than universal suffrage *per se*. See H. L. Morris, *Parliamentary Franchise Reform in England from 1885 to 1918* (New York, 1921), pp. 10–15.

[2] Among the few Bills introduced during this period (apart from the Act of 1895) were two Bills to enable employers to pay full wages on polling days in spite of absence at the polls. Cf. *P.P. 1884–5*, iv. 73; *P.P. 1887*, v. 159; 48 & 49 Vict. c. 56.

[3] Bolton had been a Gladstonian Liberal until the second reading of the Home Rule Bill of 1893.

the passions engendered by the Home Rule split and the Parnell divorce case during the campaigns of 1886 and 1892.

On the second reading Bolton[1] pointed out that until then
this 'flagrant offence' left the injured party no remedy except to
file a libel action, and before the action was heard considerable
damage might have been done to his reputation. He pointed out
that after twelve years in operation the general opinion of the
1883 Act was that it was 'an excellent measure', but also that
many members in 1883 had wished to make it stronger.[2]

The Bill found support on both sides of the House, members
regaling each other with tales of their own unhappy experiences.
Most amusing were stories by the veteran Conservative, Sir
William Hart Dyke, about a circular which had been sent to
each of about 10,000 voters in Dartford in 1865 by his (Liberal)
opponents proclaiming his withdrawal from the contest; and,
as a counterweight, Sir Donald Macfarlane's[3] account of the
damage done to his reputation by a claim in a local (Conservative) newspaper—two days before the 1886 election—that
he had been seen poaching for salmon on a Sunday: this charge,
he assured the House, would be considered more serious in
Scotland than abducting half a dozen lairds' wives.[4] The only
opposition came from Labouchere and a few Liberal back-
benchers, who claimed that legislative remedies for abuses of
this kind would do more harm than good,[5] but they withdrew
their opposition at Asquith's request, and the Corrupt and
Illegal Practices Prevention Act (1883) Amendment Bill speedily passed through both Houses in good time for the general
election of 1895.[6]

[1] Among the cases cited by Bolton were two where the Conservative members
were falsely accused of underpaying their labourers; one where the *Daily News* (in
1893) accused a (Conservative) candidate who was also a magistrate of imposing
a savage sentence on a poor man for a trivial act of larceny. The Liberal Attorney-
General (Sir Robert Reid) had also been accused of bribery but had taken a libel
action and won an apology in good time. Cf. *4 Hans.* xxxiii (1 May 1895), 217–26.

[2] An amendment very similar to Bolton's Bill had been ruled out of order by the
Speaker during the debates in 1883.

[3] Hart Dyke was a former Conservative Chief Whip; Macfarlane, Liberal
member for Argyll.

[4] *4 Hans.* xxxiii (1 May 1895), 249–50.

[5] Commenting on the Bill *The Times* wrote that while approving its principle:
'The dangers of attempting to circumscribe statements as to the opinions and the
political action of public men are great and obvious' (2 May 1895).

[6] For its effect on the petition trials see below, pp. 200–1.

In 1897 the Conservative Government set up a Select Committee to examine the working of the Act of 1883 from the aspects of increased expense in petitioning and inadequate recovery of costs. With these limited terms of reference, as might be expected, its witnesses, apart from three judges, were experts with little practical experience of electioneering.[1] Even the judges were not asked for their general opinion on the Act of 1883 although they did manage to express broad satisfaction with it. All agreed that the £1,000 security for costs was too high—£100 should be sufficient; various suggestions were made for reducing the vast number of particulars that were becoming more and more frequent in petitions. The Director of Public Prosecutions testified that great and unnecessary expense was being caused by the section in the Act requiring his representative to sit through every day of every trial. In one petition his representative had attended for thirty days and made three observations—which could have been done by someone fetched at short notice by a hansom-cab.[2]

The committee had not finished its work by the end of 1897 and was duly reappointed in 1898. The report[3] recommended an increase in the number of judges on the rota; that relief under section 22 of the 1883 Act[4] be extended to every class of corrupt practice; that before a petition was heard in open court the particulars be examined and whittled down by a Master.[5] They refused, however, to recommend a reduction in the deposit which they considered a good safeguard against vexatious petitions.

The report was quietly shelved and no one seemed to mind. It appeared that the House had lost interest in this aspect of the electoral system, but it is hardly surprising to find a piece of routine domestic legislation put on one side during the early months of the Boer War.

[1] Two Masters of the Supreme Court, an official from the Parliamentary Petitions Office and the Director of Public Prosecutions (Hamilton Cuffe).

[2] *P.P. 1897*, xiii. 82–83.   [3] *P.P. 1898*, ix. 558–62.

[4] Section 22 allowed a discretion to the judge to relieve a candidate of responsibility for any corrupt or illegal practice, with the exception of bribery, committed by an agent.

[5] E. C. Cooke (of the Parliamentary Petitions Office) submitted a schedule to the committee showing the costs incurred by the successful parties in the post-1880 petitions and the net amounts they received after taxation; these ranged from half to one-third of the total costs. Cf. *P.P. 1897*, xiii. 92–94.

2

The general election of 1885 fell in a year when an election
was not at first expected. The Gladstone Government, weakened
by internal dissensions on foreign policy and violently assailed
by the Parnellites, resigned in favour of the first Salisbury administration, which was in a minority in the Commons.[1] A
general election was then considered reasonably imminent.

Parliament was not formally dissolved until 18 November,
but the campaign may be considered to have begun with the
Queen's Speech at the prorogation on 14 August, which announced that an election would be held 'before long'. Thus the
campaign lasted over four months—a far longer period than at
any election since 1868. The constitutional changes preceding
the election resembled those of 1867–8. The Representation of
the People Act (1884)[2] had increased the electorate of the United
Kingdom by two-thirds. The Redistribution of Seats Act (1885),
which passed into law just before the fall of Gladstone's Government, had thrown ninety-nine borough electorates into the
counties, taken one seat from thirty-nine other boroughs, and
disfranchised Macclesfield and Sandwich. The county areas
had also been rearranged.[3]

The chief effect of the Redistribution Act was to abolish the
electoral advantage of the south of England (two-thirds of the
entire House of Commons being elected by one-quarter of
the voters) and came closer to the ideal of equal electoral districts, although the theoretical distinction between boroughs
and counties was preserved.

The country had been so convulsed by the four-week election
campaign of 1880 that it could think of nothing else. The same
ordeal was experienced in 1885, but this time it lasted for over
three months: public meetings were held almost every day from
August to November; addresses were written; speeches were
delivered, a record number of candidates[4] was nominated, and

[1] Gladstone resigned on 12 June after a hostile amendment had been carried in
the Budget debate. Salisbury became Prime Minister on 15 June.
[2] The Act increased the county electorate of England and Wales by 162 per cent.
the Irish electorate by over 200 per cent., and the total U.K. electorate by 67 per
cent. Five 'counties of towns' were also thrown into the counties.
[3] This Act increased the total membership of the Commons from 658 to 670.
[4] The number of candidates nominated in Great Britain and Ireland was 1,061.

the number of unopposed returns was lower than ever before.[1]
The issues covered a very wide area—Irish Home Rule, Egypt,
and the famous 'unauthorized programme' by means of which
Chamberlain and the radicals sought to woo the working-
classes. This programme was succinctly explained by Morley
when he said that the working-class had then attained full
political power but practically no property, and 'three acres
and a cow' was intended to redress the balance. Corrupt
practices were scarcely mentioned during the campaign, except
that some Conservatives indignantly claimed that radical
promises of houses, lands, and other property ought to be con-
strued as bribery. Lord Radnor wrote: 'It seems to me to be
greater bribery and worse corruption to promise portions of
land which are not your own than to offer a sum of money out
of your own pocket.'[2] But Chamberlain's group continued to
make their expansive promises, undeterred by threats that the
great penal law would be invoked against them.[3]

Although in their speeches the politicians avoided the subject
of the Act of 1883 the party headquarters kept it very much in
mind. They carefully supplied their local associations with
abstracts and copies of the Act and made sure that local agents
understood its provisions.[4] As far as the expenses maxima were
concerned they achieved what many M.P.s two years before had
roundly declared was impossible: the total published expenditure in Great Britain was lower, and in Ireland far lower, than
the limits fixed by the Act. Moreover, not a single petition was
afterwards able to prove that these limits had been exceeded.

The election of 1885 was the first to be more or less dominated by the party associations. In 1880 many candidates had
stood on their own initiative; in 1885 very few were not
nominated or actively supported by their local party groups.
The caucus system was little short of perfect. *The Times* predicted that in future the new mass electorate must 'educate

---

[1] There were 37 uncontested constituencies, comprising 40 seats which went as
follows: Liberals 13; Parnellites 17; Conservatives (including Irish Conservatives)
10; 22 of the uncontested constituencies were in Ireland.

[2] *The Times*, 7 Oct. 1885; see also 21 Aug., 16 Oct. 1885.

[3] The *Pall Mall Gazette* commented (23 Nov. 1885) that the leaders of the
democracy were studying not what was needed, but what was popular.

[4] Cf. J. E. Gorst, *An Election Manual, containing the Parliamentary Elections Corrupt
and Illegal Practices Act, 1883* (London, 1883).

their volition to dance in chains', and hoped that the organizations would not abuse their power by pulling the reins tightly too often.[1] Robert Hudson,[2] in the Central Association, and Captain Middleton, the new Conservative principal agent, in the Central Office, showed a professionalism that Bonham and Coppock would have marvelled at. It was not, however, until the split of 1886 that the discipline and loyalty of the Liberal local associations became fully apparent.

The results left the Liberals equal to the combined force of Conservatives and Home Rulers. Parnell reaped a rich harvest from the very considerable extension of the franchise in Ireland in 1884 and despite strong opposition from Irish Conservatives, Moderate Home Rulers, and Liberals claiming gratitude for the Act of 1884, he[3] secured 86 out of 103 seats. He was thus placed in a strong position to bargain with either party; and so began the chain of events that led up to the conversion of the Liberal leadership to Home Rule and the split within the party.[4]

Within four months of taking office Gladstone had lost 107 out of 333 followers elected in the previous November, including practically every important member of the party who had been actively for electoral reform—Hartington, Bright, Chamberlain, Trevelyan, James, and Leatham. The main question was what would be the attitude of the local associations throughout the country. Some immediate guidance was given at a meeting on 5 May in London when, by an overwhelming majority, the National Liberal Federation voted in favour of Home Rule. On 4 June the Scottish branch[5] issued an address urging all the associations to follow their 'great and venerable leader'. In the event the local associations did not withdraw from the federation—in fact fifty new ones were formed within the first month

---

[1] *The Times*, 19 Oct. 1885.

[2] Hudson had joined the staff of the L.C.A. in May 1882. During the election he ran a comic sheet called *The Cracker*. Cf. J. A. Spender, *Sir Robert Hudson, A Memoir* (London, 1930), p. 10.

[3] The Home Rulers won every seat in Munster, Connaught, and Leinster (except Dublin University) and a majority of seats in Ulster. The Moderate Home Rulers and Irish Liberals were wiped out. See C. Cruise O'Brien, *Parnell and his Party*, pp. 159–66.

[4] Gladstone became Prime Minister on 1 Feb.; the Irish Home Rule Bill was introduced on 8 Apr. and defeated on the second reading on 8 June; Parliament was dissolved on 10 June.

[5] The Scottish Associations were separately organized in the National Liberal Federation of Scotland.

after the split.[1] Chamberlain, as was expected, carried his
machine with him into the Liberal-Unionist camp, and many
areas in the midland counties followed suit. Elsewhere Liberal-
Unionists found themselves deserted by their local associations.
A good example was E. A. Leatham: his own organization was
in ruins; the local Conservatives promised their votes but could
not bring themselves to canvass for him or attend his meetings;
so he gave up the contest.[2]

The 1886 election was more acrimonious than that of the
previous year because personal issues were inextricably bound
up with the schism; but the area of discussion was much smaller
and the speeches and articles more repetitive and uninteresting
than in former years. The sharp rise in the number of uncontested constituencies (219, almost one-third of the House) was
due partly to pacts between the Conservatives and their former
allies, the Liberal-Unionists. But the Gladstonian Liberals also
found great difficulty in getting suitable men with sufficient
means to stand not only the expenses of election but the other
responsibilities of unpaid legislators. Gladstone appreciated the
difficulty, and would have liked to introduce a Bill, as Labouchere suggested, to relieve candidates of *all* electoral expenditure and so thereby facilitate working-class candidatures,
but he saw no hope of carrying it.[3]

The elections of 1892 and 1895 show much the same features
as that of 1886 except that the personalities have become muted.
The two national organizations had managed to enforce rigid
discipline on their followers: Captain Middleton kept the
National Union in tow behind Lord Salisbury, ignoring the
Tory democrats, and during these years the Conservative
machine reached technical perfection;[4] at Parliament Street
Hudson succeeded the prematurely aged Schnadhorst in 1893,
but even before then he was practically running the organization. He tried to revive Liberal fortunes by having prospective
candidates chosen well in advance, by intensifying the ordinary
modes of propaganda, and by lecture tours of the country in the
off-years, not only by party leaders but also by paid public

[1] Spender, *Sir Robert Hudson, A Memoir*, pp. 10–11.
[2] *The Times*, 6 July 1886.
[3] Cf. Add. MSS. 44647, ff. 110–18. For a letter from the Chief Whip lamenting
the dearth of candidates see Add. MSS. 44253, f. 15.
[4] R. T. McKenzie, *British Political Parties*, pp. 266–7.

speakers. One of these was Chadwick the Chartist who did a lecture tour with a van for the N.L.F. in 1891.[1]

The result of the general election of 1892, which converted a Conservative majority over Liberals and Home Rulers combined into a minority of 40, was far from satisfactory, and the dissensions within the party over the leadership, after Gladstone's retirement in 1894, paved the way for an electoral defeat in the following year.

In 1895 the Liberals did not think it worth while to contest 110 Conservative and Liberal-Unionist seats in England and the number of uncontested English constituencies rose from 40 to 122. Hence the Unionist Group was considerably over-represented.[2] The fault of this, however, cannot be laid at the door of Hudson and the N.L.F.—or the young active men whom he was pressing the leaders to advance in the party hierarchy. Rather it seems that even the best organization will not be of any use without inspiration and direction from above.

3

The most remarkable fact about the post-1883 petitions is the falling off in their number in spite of the keener competition between the parties and the increased opportunities of challenging an election afforded by the Corrupt and Illegal Practices Act.

Year	No. of contests	Petitions presented	Petitions successful	% successful
1874	299	22	14	64
1880	348	28	16	57
1885	606	8	4	50
1886	424	3	1[3]	33
1892	558	12	6	50
1895	458	7	2[4]	28

[1] T. P. Newbould, *Pages from a Life of Strife* (London, 1910), pp. 2–18, gives a lively account of the adventures of 'Liberal Van No. 21'.

[2] For a statistical analysis, one of the first of its kind in England, of the elections of 1892 and 1895 see J. A. Baines, 'Parliamentary Representation in England illustrated by the Elections of 1892 and 1895', in *Journal of the Royal Statistical Society*, lix (Mar. 1896), 38–118. Baines tried to prove that in 1892 the Unionists secured 27 seats more than their votes entitled them to, and in 1895, 92 seats more.

[3] The Buckrose petition, where the votes were exactly equal and the returning officer on his own initiative declared one candidate elected in order to state a case for the election court, is not classed here as a successful petition.

[4] One in this group (Southampton) must be regarded as only partially successful, since one of the two members challenged kept his seat and the petitioners were obliged to pay the costs of all but two charges. See below, p. 196.

The petitions may conveniently be divided into two groups comprising the eleven tried in 1886,[1] and the nineteen tried in 1892 and 1895.

In the first group the traditional offences of bribery and treating were pleaded successfully in three boroughs only, and these three were of very diverse types—Norwich with its long history of election trials, Ipswich, a much smaller industrial town which had not appeared in an election case for thirty years, and the prosperous manufacturing town of Barrow-in-Furness, long a municipal borough but without parliamentary representation until 1885.

The petition from Norwich[2] was remarkable in showing how far old electioneering habits had already been changed for the better. The Conservative candidate (Henry Bullard) was extremely concerned about the unsavoury history of the town and his agent took care to post up copies and abstracts of the Act of 1883 for all to see. Nevertheless, the Liberals were able to point to three canvassers who gave beer to voters and drove to the polling station people who otherwise would not have voted. There was a strong suspicion that one or two public houses had been centres of treating—but that was as nothing compared to the Norwich of old.[3]

By the 1883 Act[4] the judges were empowered to relieve the candidate of responsibility for illegal and even corrupt practices committed by their supporters, if they were satisfied that the candidates had taken all reasonable precautions. Justices Denman and Cave were willing to allow Bullard this relief. Bribery, however, was specifically excepted from the judges' discretionary power and there was one trivial case of bribery—a member of a Conservative ward committee who was seen giving half a crown to a poor voter and immediately reported to the police. The election was therefore annulled, but the judges refused to award the petitioners any costs, because they had put the respondents to the trouble of preparing a defence against twenty-three charges of almost every kind of corrupt and illegal practice, of which only four were established. Years afterwards, Mr.

[1] Since the 1885 general election took place in Nov. and that of 1886 in July, it happened that the petitions after both elections were tried in the same year 1886; the first judgement was given on 4 Mar., and the last on 11 Dec.

[2] *P.P. 1886*, lii. 359–83.   [3] See above, pp. 55, 102–5.

[4] Section 22. See above, p. 181, n. 5.

Justice Cave referred to this as a 'very cruel case' and said that
he and Denman would have liked to be able to give Bullard
relief, but were forced by the law to upset the election. Nevertheless it is difficult to recognize in this case-report the venal
borough of 1868 and 1874.

The Ipswich petition[1] was its first since 1857: the return of the
well-known radical Jesse Collings and his colleague H. W.
West was impugned after a very close contest on a wide variety
of grounds, including general bribery. Only three cases, however, were material. One arose from the unpopularity of some
Liberal workmen. Brawls had occurred at meetings addressed
by Collings and West until a member of a ward committee[2]
hired several men at a small wage to keep order at further meetings. The same partisan had marked 'can be had' against the
names of several doubtful voters in his canvassing books, and
was also proved to have bribed straightforwardly. Another
member of a ward committee wrote to an outvoter living in
Colchester urging him to vote Liberal and conveying a broad
hint that he would be rewarded. Apart from these cases, and a
few others that were not proved, there was no evidence in
support of the charge of general bribery, although the judges
were satisfied that some voters would not give a decided answer
to the canvassers because they were holding out for money. The
proportion of the electorate so affected could not have been
large.

The judges annulled the election on account of bribery by the
ward committee member, illegal payments to the 'chuckers-out',
and the offer of travelling expenses. At the same time they paid
tribute to the 'perfect propriety' with which the official Liberal
agent had performed his duties.[3]

Barrow-in-Furness[4] was a thriving manufacturing town with
an outlying agricultural population, making 6,000 voters in all.

[1] *P.P. 1886*, lii. 339–53.
[2] The Liberal machinery followed the usual caucus model: in each of five wards
there was a ward council consisting of a chairman, secretary, and thirty members.
[3] Ibid. Although both the *offer* and payment of travelling expenses were clearly
made illegal practices by the Act of 1883 the judges found it necessary to review
the history of earlier judgements from *Cooper v. Slade* (1854)—which classified as
bribery the offering or payment of travelling expenses as an inducement to vote
—through Willes's decision at Coventry (1869) to Quain's at Horsham (1875).
See above, pp. 51–56.
[4] *P.P. 1886*, lii. 309–21.

It was created a parliamentary borough by the Redistribution of Seats Act (1885) and almost immediately afterwards a Liberal Four Hundred was set up. Their first intention was to invite a local worthy, Sir James Ramsden, to stand, but he declined; instead David Duncan, 'a gentleman of position' at Liverpool, was nominated. The Four Hundred thought best to efface themselves and leave their secretary as election agent, to be helped by a number of ward committees. A complication arose. At municipal elections in Barrow there had long been a tradition of giving refreshments; and since those elections were not fought on a political basis that did not matter much. However, after the passing of the Act,[1] it was generally agreed to put a stop to the practice, and at the beginning of the campaign the Conservative agent assured his opposite number, one Garnett, that he was perfectly willing to abide by the Act. Shortly afterwards in several Liberal ward committees the question was asked whether refreshments might be provided on polling day for canvassers and helpers. To settle the question, Garnett informed a large meeting attended by the candidate and some 400 party supporters that on polling day the helpers would be employed continuously for twelve hours, but refreshments would be provided for them and to this end a special 'refreshment committee' would be set up.

On election day no real effort was made at the committee rooms to ascertain whether the people who were served refreshments were in fact entitled to them. The Conservatives then lodged a petition pleading bribery, treating, intimidation, and illegal practices. The judges found all the charges unproved, except that concerning refreshments. This, however, was quite enough to invalidate the election: one judge, Mr. Justice Field, suspected that it was a corrupt practice in that no check was made on the number of people entitled to resfreshment, but he was not certain. The judges rejected the agent's plea that 'human nature could not stand a fast of twelve hours' duration': many of the helpers, they said, lived quite near the polling stations and committee rooms and could easily have gone home for their meals.[2]

[1] Although the 1883 Act did not apply to municipal elections James had promised that he would bring in a similar Act to deal with them. 47 & 48 Vict. c. 70.
[2] *P.P. 1886*, lii. 309–21.

The fourth success in this batch of petitions was lodged against C. E. Lewis,[1] the implacable opponent of the 1883 Act, after his election at Londonderry City in 1886. Lewis had defeated a Home Rule candidate, Justin McCarthy, by two votes. On a scrutiny two votes were struck off Lewis's total: one belonging to an undoubted agent of Lewis's who made an illegal payment, the other, to the man who received it. The judges were satisfied that neither of the candidates had committed or condoned any corrupt or illegal practice, but they could not allow Lewis to keep the seat and therefore they awarded it to McCarthy.[2] Ironically enough Lewis saw his parliamentary career terminated by the very power in the Act of 1883 that he had most feared—the power to unseat a candidate on account of some malpractice of which he was quite ignorant.

Another successful petition, from St. Andrew's Burghs, involved a scrutiny as a result of which fourteen votes were rejected because of inadequate marking.[3]

The unsuccessful petitions of 1885 and 1886 were mainly lodged on technical grounds. The old offences loomed large, however, in three.

In Aylesbury[4] Baron Ferdinand de Rothschild had increased his majority from 900 to 2,850. Baron Ferdinand and his sister owned estates of several thousand acres in Buckinghamshire. The gravamen of the petition was that some 400 of the Baron's workers were paid full wages for a half day's work on polling day and that a school treat annually given on the Baron's estates in the month of August was this year expanded until nearly 10,000 people were present and it therefore constituted treating.

---

[1] In the general election of 1885 Lewis actively helped the Loyal and Patriotic Union—an organization of extreme Conservatives which ran 'Loyalist' candidates (all unsuccessful) against the Parnellites throughout Ireland. In 1886 the Parnellites carried the war into Lewis's constituency, where the Orange and Green factions were almost of equal strength. Lewis's victory—by two votes—was followed by a premature celebration held in a part of the city bordering on the nationalist quarter, and a thin line of soldiers had to keep the two parties separate. Lewis later wrote to *The Times* (10 July 1886) complaining that the 'joyful tunes' of his victory band had been upset by 'savage attacks' from soldiers and police.

[2] *P.P. 1887*, lxvi. 249.

[3] *P.P. 1886*, lii. 385–7. One case of intimidation had also been made in the particulars, but since the vote of the alleged intimidator had already been struck off and he had not been called as a witness the judges decided, with some misgivings, to let the matter rest.   [4] Ibid. 303–8.

Mr. Justice Field and Mr. Justice Day (trying their first petition) agreed that the foremen who authorized the payment of a full day's wages were not agents of de Rothschild. They also accepted the explanation by the defence that the main reason for the enormous crowd at the school treat was that a relative of the Baron who, for some unspecified reason, 'found herself unable' that year to hold a temperance society outing separately had amalgamated it with the school treat. The petition was rejected. It is hard, however, to see Baron Bramwell or Sir Henry Hawkins allowing the return to stand even under the pre-1883 state of the law.

A petition from the Thornbury division of Gloucestershire combined technical charges with those of corrupt practices. The latter arose out of rioting at several places on polling day (23 November 1885). All the riots were directed against the Conservatives: voters were hooted, windows broken, and a house that displayed Conservative posters was badly damaged. This was the only case of rioting alleged in a petition in 1885 or 1886. The judges found no connexion between the riots and the successful Liberal candidate, Stafford Howard, and the outbreaks were too isolated to constitute general intimidation. On the second question, the validity of 273 ballots (240 of which were cast for Howard) that had not been stamped on the face, though duly marked on the back, the petition judges stated a case for the full Queen's Bench division, which by a majority judgement decided that the Ballot Act did not require the presiding officer to look at the *face* of the ballot papers. Thus the votes were allowed, and the result stood.[1]

The general election of 1886 also produced a petition from West Belfast. Until 1885 that city, like Dublin, returned two members only, but since its population had greatly increased it was given two more—all in single-seat divisions. After the Gladstone-Parnell alliance on Home Rule the Protestant Liberals, who were quite numerous in Belfast, voted for a Home Ruler, Thomas Sexton,[2] one of Parnell's lieutenants, and put him in a

---

[1] *P.P. 1886*, lii. 323–37. The first judgement by Mr. Justice Field and Mr. Justice Day was given on 10 Mar., the decision of the divisional court on 5 Apr., and the final judgement by Day and Field, allowing the election, on 13 Apr. 1886. The majority judgement was that of Lord Chief Justice Bovill, Mr. Justice Grove, and Sir Henry Hawkins; Mr. Justice Brett and Mr. Justice Keating disagreeing (ibid. 332–5).   [2] See above, p. 126, n. 3.

majority of 103, as against a minority of 35 in 1885.[1] The defeated candidate, J. H. Haslett, claimed that a number of Sexton's supporters had committed personation. Thirteen cases were proved, but only five of these on Sexton's side, and the judges had no difficulty in refuting the claim that general personation, sufficient to invalidate the election at common law, had prevailed.

Another charge involved one Mullins, a supporter of Sexton, who was alleged to have connived at personation. Mullins, surprisingly enough, had been a personation agent at the November election, but Sexton did not reappoint him in July 1886. The judges, while considering him 'too zealous perhaps in his activities on [Sexton's] behalf', did not find him guilty of any corrupt practice. One judge, Baron Dowse, was unfavourably impressed by some prosecution witnesses whom he described as 'not very attractive sights as human beings'. The personated votes were all struck off, but Sexton was still in the lead and so kept his seat.[2]

A very unusual case occurred at Tower Hamlets (Stepney Division).[3] The original result gave J. C. Durant (Liberal) 2,141 votes and F. Wootton Isaacson (Conservative) 2,119. Stepney was possibly the most cosmopolitan borough in London and the judges were able to strike off over 140 votes on account of nationality, leaving Isaacson with 2,054 votes to Durant's 2,053. They reserved for the full court, however, the question of 23 votes of people either born in Hanover before Queen Victoria's accession, or after 1837, of parents born before her accession and never subsequently naturalized.[4] The full court decided that these Hanoverian voters were aliens: the effect of this was to reduce Isaacson's total by sixteen and Durant's by seven, so that Durant remained in the lead.[5]

---

[1] The total poll was 7,561 (out of a total electorate of 8,131); Haslett secured 3,729, Sexton 3,832 votes. The total number of charges of personation on which evidence was offered was 28.

[2] *P.P. 1887*, lxvi. 239–48.   [3] *P.P. 1886*, lii. 389–99.

[4] One voter was born in Prussia of Hanoverian parents born before 1837.

[5] The final totals were Durant 2,045; Isaacson 2,035. While waiting for the Queen's Bench decision on the Hanoverian voters, the election court heard a recriminatory case, claiming that Isaacson was guilty of the illegal practice of paying for the distribution of handbills similar in shape and appearance to ballot papers with Isaacson's name in very large print and Durant's squeezed into a corner. Mr. Justice Field strongly condemned the giving of 'bastard directions' of this kind. Ibid. 399.

The petitions of 1885-6 showed a marked falling off in the incidence of the customary offences of bribery, treating, and undue influence, and very little of the new corrupt practice, personation. They concentrated more on the class of illegal practices created by the Act of 1883, and so gave a pointer to the electioneering habits of the future. This showed that the Act had succeeded beyond the hopes of its promoters,[1] but there was also evidence that some of the fears of its opponents were being realized, especially the fear that honest candidates would be trapped in its labyrinthine meshes. Most petitions took advantage of the intricacies of the Act to hurl at the respondents' heads far more charges than they could answer—the Norwich and Thornbury petitions were examples of this 'war of particulars'. The most extreme cases were those of the Kennington division of Lambeth (1885) and the Buckrose division of Yorkshire East Riding (1886). At Kennington[2] the Conservative candidate, R. Gent-Davis, a resident in the borough who had recently bought the *South London Standard*, was forced to answer sixty charges of illegal practices—including the absurd charge that his registration expenses and the cost of the *South London Standard* ought to have been returned as election expenses. Virtually no evidence was offered; there was only one witness in chief, the others were the respondent and a friend of his, who was bullied into admitting that he owed to Gent-Davis his escape from bankruptcy in a matter that had nothing whatever to do with the election. The judges strongly condemned the abuse of the powers of the Act,[3] and not only dismissed the petition with costs but also awarded the Public Prosecutor costs against the petitioner.[4]

The Buckrose petition arose out of a tie between the Liberal W. A. McArthur and the Conservative, Christopher Sykes.[5]

[1] See below, pp. 202 ff.

[2] Kennington was one of the few English constituencies in which Irish Home Rulers stood for election in 1885 or 1886.

[3] *P.P. 1886*, lii. 355–8.

[4] The election judges were empowered under section 43 (sub-section 8) of the Act of 1883 to award costs to the Public Prosecutor for sending a representative to attend the trial. This was the only case in which they exercised this discretion: elsewhere the Public Prosecutor had to bear his own costs—which meant the tax-payer had to foot the bill.

[5] 'The last of the dandies', as his appreciative great-nephew calls him—and friend of the Prince of Wales—entered Parliament as member for the notorious

The sheriff declared McArthur elected and left it to the election court to decide between them. Sykes in a petition demanded a scrutiny of some of McArthur's votes, and on the scrutiny the court awarded him eleven votes, which would have given him the seat. McArthur's side, however, had prepared a recriminatory case in which the only material charge was that Sykes's agent had not complied with section 33 of the 1883 Act (which prescribed a *complete* return of all election expenses) in that he had written down as committee-rooms, 'Temperance Hall, Driffield' and 'Schoolroom, Langtoft', without specifying *which* temperance hall and schoolroom had been hired. Sykes's counsel admitted the charge but claimed the benefit of section 22. The judges concurred and Sykes was awarded the seat; he did not, however, get the costs of the recriminatory case.[1]

The nineteen petitions after the elections of 1892 and 1895[2] may be divided into four classes:

  (i)   *Four* petitions in which bribery or treating were successfully pleaded.
  (ii) *Seven* petitions which offered evidence of bribery or treating but not enough to unseat the respondent.
  (iii) *Six* petitions which involved illegal practices.
  (iv) *Two* (Irish) petitions in which spiritual intimidation was successfully pleaded.

(i) The four constituencies where bribery or treating was successfully pleaded (Hexham, Pontefract, Rochester, Southampton) were populous English boroughs where the party organizations were in keen competition and indulged in treating in as covert a manner as possible.

In Hexham, during the election year 1892, the Conservative agent spent three times the usual annual outlay of the Hexham Divisional Association, not only to make up losses in the

borough of Beverley in 1865, left it before the storm broke and sat for Yorkshire county seats from 1868 to 1892. During this period 'he made in all six speeches and asked three questions'. Cf. C. Sykes, *Four Studies in Loyalty* (London, 1946), p. 19.
  [1] *P.P. 1887*, lxiv. 251–3.
  [2] The petitions heard in 1892 were from Hexham, Pontefract, East Manchester, Walsall, Worcester City, Rochester, Stepney, Cirencester, Montgomery Boroughs, North Meath, South Meath, and East Clare.
  The petitions heard in 1895–6 were from Lancaster, Lichfield, Shoreditch (Haggerston), Southampton, Sunderland, Elgin and Nairn, and Tower Hamlets (St. George's).

accounts of impecunious local associations which was legitimate, but also to carry on the Primrose League tradition of lavish entertainment, especially at the time of the contest. He also confused the accounts of the divisional association, which did not sponsor such activities, with those of local associations, which did. The judges unseated the member, N. G. Clayton, because he had given £326 to the agent without laying down any conditions as to its use, and warned local associations of the consequences of the 'pernicious practice of picnics and treats'.[1]

The Rochester case was very similar. There the Constitutional Club for several years spent far more than its revenue from subscriptions on socials, conversazioni and entertainments of various kinds, and the member (Alderman H. Davies) always made up the deficit.[2] The Birthright Club (a sister institution) also spent the surplus money 'in giving additional drink by means of double tickets to persons to whom such additional drink may be taken to be not at all unwelcome';[3] and even individual agents, when in public houses, did their best to prove the superior liberality of the Conservatives, especially when the Liberals were holding meetings. The official agent, a humbly paid clerk, was incompetent and did nothing to stop the illegal expenditure.[4]

The petition from Pontefract[5] contained 109 allegations, but no evidence at all was offered in 75 cases. The judges, censuring this 'scandalous recklessness', wistfully recalled the days when petitions were very short and merely listed the heads of the charges. They considered that there was some suspicion attached to the free gift of ten gallons of beer at two public houses but they could not prove that it was given to influence votes. Various charges of illegal practices failed. Nevertheless Reckitt was unseated because his agents allowed his subordinates to run the election in the outlying part of the borough much as they liked, and one of them bribed a worker with 10s., 5s. of which were

[1] *P.P. 1893–4*, lxx. 807–17. The activities of the Primrose League (founded 1884) at this period duplicated those of the Conservative Associations.

[2] Ibid. 883–92. In 1890 Davies subscribed £250 out of a total income of £299; in 1891 £300 out of £315.

[3] Ibid. 885.

[4] This appointment bore out to some extent Goldney's prediction in 1883 that candidates would not be able to pay well-qualified agents on the expense limits allowed by the Act. See above, p. 165.

[5] Against the Liberal candidate, H. J. Reckitt.

for travelling expenses. A plea that a pamphlet circulated by
Reckitt promising to build a library in Pontefract constituted
general bribery was rejected; Reckitt had sent it out because he
was sensitive to charges that he was a carpet-bagger.[1]

In Southampton[2] the return of the Conservatives, Tanker-
ville Chamberlayne and Sir Barrington Simeon in 1895, was
linked with the Local Veto Bill of which they were both strong
opponents. Some drinking unknown to the police had taken
place at public meetings at the docks, but there was no evidence,
although the charge was made, to connect it with the candidates
and their agents. Indeed, a good deal of drinking took place
throughout the town during the campaign to show the feeling
of the people on Local Option. Simeon took every precaution
against treating and no charge was brought against him, except
the one about the docks. Chamberlayne was much less discreet.
He made one speech which might have been interpreted as containing a corrupt promise. Even more rash was a procession
through Southampton headed by the candidate's carriage,
which was immediately followed by costermongers' carts bearing
'symbols of drink', and including, for the sake of realism, several
people who were obviously drunk—including three on the box
of the carriage. The procession took two hours to complete its
journey since it stopped at several public houses on the way.

The judges found no difficulty in exonerating Simeon, but
they unseated Chamberlayne,[3] mainly because of the procession.

(ii) The seven[4] petitions which did not offer sufficient
evidence to unseat the respondent for corrupt practices resulted
in one candidate being unseated for illegal practices in Walsall;
the other petitions were dismissed. The Walsall judgement was
afterwards cited by an Irish judge as 'considered to have gone
to the extreme verge of the law and of common sense'.[5] The

[1] *P.P. 1893–4*, lxx. 915–23. The judges imposed on the petitioners the costs of
all the charges on which they had offered no evidence.

[2] This petition was brief and in common form, alleging simply corrupt and
illegal practices and general treating. Chamberlayne was a Conservative, Simeon
a Liberal-Unionist.

[3] *P.P. 1896*, lxvii. 443–50. The judges were able, under section 22, to relieve
Simeon of responsibility for payment of 2s. travelling expenses to a voter by an
undoubted agent.

[4] Manchester East, Walsall, Worcester City, Montgomery Boroughs (1892);
Lancaster, Shoreditch (Haggerston), Tower Hamlets (1895).

[5] Mr. Justice O'Brien in the East Clare case. *P.P. 1893–4*, lxx. 822.

court decided that the candidates were not guilty of treating—
although here too the Conservative Association had worked
hand in hand with the licensed trade—but they were unseated
for the illegal practice of printing 6,000 'hat cards', distributing
them to voters, and including them in their accounts, on the
grounds that hat cards were 'marks of distinction' within the
meaning of the Act of 1883, and even within the Act of 1854.
The original prohibition of the Act of 1854 which was carried
over into the Act of 1883[1] was not intended to prevent people
from wearing party favours, but rather to avoid the clashes
which at that time used to take place between the Blues and the
Buffs. A card with the portrait of the candidate to be worn on
a hat in 1892 was, in the narrow legalistic view, equivalent to a
cockade as worn in 1854, but its real significance was far different.[2]

Walsall was one of the extreme examples of judicial stringency. At the other end of the scale came Montgomery Boroughs,[3]
where the wife of the outgoing Conservative, Sir Pryce Pryce-
Jones, promised employment to the daughter of a bitter political
opponent; a public-house landlord, 'an undoubted agent of the
sitting M.P.', treated on a considerable scale before the election;
and a notorious drunk was made vice-chairman of the candidate's election committee and tendered small bribes in public
houses. The judges disagreed, so the result was not affected. It is
interesting, however, to note that the judge who placed the most
charitable construction on all these very dubious transactions,
even believing the story that the vice-chairman was so drunk
that he did not know what he was doing, was Baron Pollock,
who was also one of the judges on the Walsall petition.[4] The
judgements of Baron Pollock never make for easy reading, but
it seems likely that when, as at Walsall, he sat with so stringent
a colleague as Sir Henry Hawkins,[5] for the sake of peace he sup-
pressed his more charitable instincts.

Baron Pollock with Mr. Justice Wills also dismissed a petition from Worcester City, largely because there were so many
allegations of corrupt practices (chiefly bribery and treating)

[1] The Act of 1883 (sec. 13) prohibited 'bands, torches, flags, banners, cockades
or other marks of distinction'.
[2] *P.P. 1893–4*, lxx. 866–72.
[3] Ibid. 851–64.
[4] At Walsall Hawkins read the main judgement and Pollock concurred.
[5] Hawkins was never styled 'Mr. Justice'—at his own request.

that they could not all be true; and the respondents were allowed
only ten days to prepare a defence against more than three
hundred different charges.[1] They frowned on the regular treating by a Pickwickian character at the Conservative Club, but
for the rest censured the petitioners for inflicting upon the
respondents the intolerable hardship of answering 'every piece
of idle gossip floating about the city'. Nevertheless, Mr. Justice
Wills, though not Baron Pollock, found cause for concern in the
appointment of a 'thoroughly unscrupulous' man as election
agent, who was suspected of bribing voters in a house with a
back entrance through which they could conveniently slip.
The allegation was not proved and the petition failed. But the
very same sort of charge was spectacularly proved at Worcester
by the Royal Commission of 1906. Had the petitioners presented their case better, cleared away the dead wood of uncon-
vincing charges and concentrated on one or two, they might not
have antagonized the judges and so lost their case.[2]

The petition at Manchester East (1892) is interesting, merely
because it was the only one in this period involving a front-
bencher, Arthur Balfour, who was defended by his young
cousin, Lord Robert Cecil. Once again there was a great variety
of peculiarly vague charges and the judges had to give another
homily on this growing practice. For example, there were forty-
two charges of treating, but no evidence was offered in thirty-
seven of them. In one case only was any proof of agency given
and there the evidence was too confused to lead to any conclusion, except that the agent was much given to treating in
public houses, independently of elections.[3]

The Shoreditch (Haggerston) case provided another addition
to the list of judicial determinations of the doctrine of agency.
During distress in Shoreditch in the winter of 1894–5 John
Lowles, the Unionist candidate, arranged for the distribution of
500 food cards to the value of 6d. per head to the most necessi-
tous people in the borough. This gesture was duly advertised in
the local press by Protheroe, Lowles's agent. Mr. Justice Wright
held that this was done to influence votes, otherwise why

[1] There were 147 charges of bribery, 156 of treating, and 28 of illegal practices
alleged in the particulars; less than one-sixth of these were pursued during the trial.
P.P. 1893–4, lxx. 873–81.
[2] See below, pp. 220–1.
[3] *P.P. 1893–4*, lxx. 905–8

advertise the fact that 'the Unionist candidate' was responsible, and that 'preference would be given to residents of Haggerston'? Mr. Justice Bruce, however, in a well-thought-out judgement, refused to come to this conclusion, first because he could not carry the constructive doctrine of agency back to February 1895 —when there was no reason to expect an election later in the year—and also because the act of Lowles, if in itself innocent, was not converted into a guilty one by Protheroe's announcement, which apparently was made without Lowles's authority. If the act was innocent, which Mr. Justice Bruce believed, there was no obligation on Lowles to repudiate a statement that he had never authorized.[1]

The petition from St. George's-in-the East (1895)[2] was the most celebrated heard between 1883 and 1900. St. George's with some 3,000 voters was the smallest borough in London. It comprised a well-knit merchant class served by the ships and docks and a mainly Irish proletariat. The candidates were John Williams Benn,[3] a thriving business man and Whip of the Progressive Party in the London County Council, and Harry Marks, proprietor of the *Financial Times*, who was backed by the Irish Unionist Alliance, a pressure group trying to kill Home Rule by kindness through organizing concerts, lectures with refreshments, and other entertainments for the London-Irish. Marks was also helped by a philanthropic society of which he was the founder and chairman. In the bad winter of 1893–4 the society distributed tickets for food and fuel to the poor of the borough and out of 13,600 tickets distributed nearly one-fifth were held by Marks and another Conservative. In addition, a considerable number of drinks were stood at public houses, Oddfellows' meetings, and at the Constitutional Club.

When Marks won the election the Liberals unearthed all these facts for their petition. However, the judges, Baron Pollock and Mr. Justice Bruce, found nothing intrinsically corrupt in providing refreshments at a political meeting held with

[1] *P.P. 1896*, lxvii. 436–7.
[2] Ibid. 461–87. The constituency was the St. George's-in-the-East division of Tower Hamlets borough.
[3] Sir Ernest Benn in *Happier Days, Recollections and Reflections* (London, 1949), pp. 31–35, gives a racy account of his experiences as election agent for his father. He does not, however, mention the petition. John Benn had first won the St. George's seat in 1892 from Ritchie, the Unionist President of the Local Government Board.

no election in the offing.[1] Baron Pollock recalled that the Anti-Corn Law League used to do the same and the distribution of tickets would be corrupt only if coupled with a request for a vote, or made without due consideration of people's needs, or on a large scale.

A charge under the recent Act of 1895 claimed that Marks was responsible for a report by the *Eastern Post* that Benn had a 'skeleton in his cupboard', 'a very dark passage in his own life',[2] but neither Marks nor his agent was responsible for this statement, and as soon as he heard of it Marks swore an affidavit denying any previous knowledge. Before the petition trial Benn had sued the proprietor of the *Eastern Post* for libel, and extracted an apology and an admission that the statement was quite untrue. Undoubtedly, however, the report was made by way of retaliation for Benn's numerous posters containing 'Oh Marks!' in large letters and some handbills alleging that Marks had misbehaved himself many years before.

Benn had put the Conservatives to the trouble of preparing a defence against 352 charges of every description of corrupt and illegal practice, but during the trial 200 were withdrawn and in some of the remainder no evidence was offered. The judges dismissed the petition after a hearing lasting twenty-five days. They still had to hear a recriminatory case to show that Benn would be ineligible for the seat even if Marks had lost the first petition.[3]

The Conservatives now got their own back by proving Benn to have been guilty of illegal practices; he had paid for banners which were displayed in the windows and hung across the streets of the borough, and schoolchildren had taken part in processions carrying Benn's portrait and shouting 'Vote for Benn'. Other charges of illegal practice were dismissed, but the judges held that the Walsall judgement gave Benn no excuse. His counsel gave no notice of intention to ask for relief under

---

[1] This meeting took place on 4 May 1895—seven weeks before the Cordite Vote.

[2] *Eastern Post*, 13 July 1895. Its proprietor was one of Marks's supporters.

[3] As the recriminatory case had (under the Act of 1868) the status of an independent petition the judges were obliged to hear it. They refused to make any order as to the costs of the first petition until they should have heard the recriminatory case—despite an impassioned plea by counsel for Marks that Benn should give additional security for costs to the 'perfectly puerile' £1,000 demanded by the Act of 1868 (*P.P. 1896*, lxvii. 471–6).

section 22. So Benn was saddled with the costs not only of the
first petition (except the *Eastern Post* charge), but also of the
recriminatory case. The entire hearing lasted forty days[1]—a
record for petition trials. The costs were enormous, but they did
not prevent Benn from standing for Bermondsey a few years
later.[2]

(iii) One of the six petitions[3] that involved illegal practices
was the Sunderland petition of 1895, which was based solely on
the charge that the Liberal election agent had printed as a
circular an extract from *The Labour Leader* denouncing the
Unionist candidate[4] as an employer of sweated labour in his
factory. Baron Pollock was not sure whether the statements
came within the meaning of the Act of 1895, or whether, if they
did, the candidate was responsible. In spite of his confusion,
however, he agreed that the Act did not go against the spirit of
the existing law of libel which allowed even malicious statements where reasonable grounds of credibility existed. The
election agent clearly believed in them and the petition was
dismissed. Mr. Isaacson of Stepney was again hauled into court
because of voters employed for reward who afterwards in ignorance of the Act voted, because of payment of expenses by other
than election agents, payment for banners, and confusion of
election expenses and registration expenses. He admitted all
the charges and asked for relief under section 22, which
the judges, though doubtful about his agent's bona fides,
granted.

The only successful petitions in this category occurred at
Cirencester[5] in 1892 and Lichfield in 1895.[6] In the former
eleven votes were struck off on account of inadequate marking,

---

[1] See *Pall Mall Gazette*, 14 Mar. 1896.

[2] See Benn, *Happier Days, Recollections and Reflections*, p. 31. Benn's younger son,
William Wedgwood Benn (later Lord Stansgate), was elected for St. George's in
1906.

[3] Stepney, East Clare, Cirencester (1892), Sunderland, Elgin and Nairn, Lichfield (1895). The judges at Elgin and Nairn refused to unseat the Unionist candidate, J. E. Gordon, because of treating on his behalf some ten months before the
election, on the ground that an election was not expected for several years—
although he was even then a prospective candidate.

[4] W. T. Doxford.

[5] *P.P. 1893–4*, lxx. 909–11. Sir Henry Hawkins said that although corrupt and
illegal practices were vaguely alleged in the particulars 'not a syllable of evidence
was breathed on either side'.

[6] *P.P. 1896*, lxvii. 421–8.

which was a violation of the Ballot Act, and the constituency changed hands; in the latter, the candidate kept his accounts in a very loose manner, drawing cheques of upwards of £300 without any record, and the judges were quite convinced that this was not a technical error but deliberate. There was also a suspicion of canvassing and voting by a paid agent.

(iv) The two Irish cases of spiritual intimidation were among the few in which this peculiarly Irish practice was successfully pleaded since the famous Keogh judgement at Galway County in 1872.[1] They were rather eccentric cases. The Bishop of Meath, who had been a strong supporter of Parnell, turned violently against him after the divorce case, and his aversion was extended to all the Parnellites. During the election campaign of 1892, when (although Parnell had died in October of the previous year) the Home Rulers fought under Parnellite and Anti-Parnellite labels, the Bishop issued a pastoral letter condemning 'Parnellism'. Two Parnellites were defeated and pleaded spiritual intimidation successfully in the courts. But these two cases seemed rather anachronistic, even for 1892.

4

The remarkable falling-off in the number of election petitions after 1885 and their changed character—the predominance of treating and illegal practices over bribery and undue influence—might lead to the conclusion that the Act of 1883 was entirely responsible for the improvement and, as a consequence, that it was completely successful. There were, however, certain important points not covered by the Act.

Ironically enough, the most obvious difficulty left by the Act that aimed to reduce the cost of electioneering was the cost of presenting a petition. At the very outset a deposit of £1,000 had to be paid down as security for costs, and even when costs were awarded they very rarely covered more than half the actual expenditure. *The Times*, citing the *Law Journal*, wrote (18 December 1885) that the remedy of a petition was in practice 'denied to all but very rich persons or to political associations, whose aims are seldom single'. The Select Committee of 1897 discovered that in the petitions heard since 1880 the successful

[1] See above, p. 57. There was another successful case in Galway, in 1874.

party did not recover on average more than from one-third to one-half of the costs. Thus the practice of overloading petitions with particulars—against which the judges vainly protested—served merely to line the lawyers' pockets, and owed more to cut-throat rivalry between the parties than to any consideration of self-interest.

Another loophole left in the Act of 1883 was the imprecision of the law of agency and kindred issues, such as the time-base of an election. The framers of the Act deliberately avoided a legal definition of agency. James admitted that so great an expert as Forster had given up the attempt as impossible, and the pile of judicial decisions since 1868 did not clear up the confusion. Again, the judges refused to extend the period during which a candidate was responsible for the acts of his supporters beyond that in which the election was reasonably imminent; ten months was considered outside this limit by the judges in the Elgin and Nairn case.[1]

The political associations undoubtedly took advantage of these loopholes. They were able in the first place to use the registration acts of 1878 and 1885[2] as a shield for expenditure that was designed to make the candidate popular in the inter-election periods, while at the same time severing all apparent connexion with him. The socials, tea-parties, and conversazioni of Rochester, Haggerston, and Hexham all came into this category of 'vast influence . . . which during the election would certainly be considered corrupt [but] can [at other times] be exercised without danger'.[3] It was extremely difficult to furnish legal proof of the candidate's responsibility for policies and actions of associations that were not directly connected with the elections. Did that mean that while the expense levels of the Act of 1883 were not exceeded, and the grosser forms of corrupt practice passed into abeyance, the political associations were able to canalize the bulk of their expenditure into the period between elections, and in fact to increase it? A sophisticated foreign observer, Ostrogorski,[4] expressed surprise that the judges should have been so indulgent of new forms of treating and

[1] See above, p. 201, n. 3.
[2] Seymour, *Electoral Reform in England and Wales*, pp. 375-6.   [3] Ibid. 451.
[4] M. Ostrogorski, *Democracy and the Organization of Political Parties* (London, 1902), i. 437-9.

hinted that the associations were able to make the Act of 1883 nugatory. On the other hand, the dilemma of the judges was adequately expressed by Mr. Justice Bruce[1] in the Haggerston judgement and by Baron Pollock[2] in his evidence before the Select Committee of 1897. Tea-parties, conversazioni, and such functions were part of the social pattern of middle-class English life just as gatherings in public houses were part of working-class life. The most that a democratic legislature could do would be to try to eliminate abuses in both during election campaigns; to attempt to control them at other times would mean an unheard-of restriction of individual freedom, which public opinion would be highly unlikely to tolerate. If even very learned societies found it necessary to use this social bait to attract people to their meetings, as one judge said, why should it be accounted strange when political associations did the same?

The real questions are how much money was spent on these entertainments, and from what sources it ultimately came. Unfortunately they cannot be answered until there is a thorough investigation of the records of the party Whips. The nature and disposal of party funds all through this period has up to now remained secret. For the earlier period Professor Gash uncovered some evidence that a Conservative central electioneering fund existed as far back as 1835, contributed to by prominent party adherents. He suggests that there may have been a routine subsidy of £500 per candidate.[3] The same sum is mentioned in letters to Disraeli in 1868.[4] In 1883 at the annual conference of the National Union, Lord Randolph Churchill launched into a forthright attack on the whole principle of secret finance: 'Whenever you have secret expenditure, you will have corrupt expenditure. The money that the Council [of the National Union] expends consists of doles from the Central Committee.'[5]

The Central Committee was dominated by the Conservative party Whip who had ultimate control over the funds. That the same method was followed by the Liberals was made clear by a curious incident in 1901[6] when allegations were made that

[1] See above, p. 199.   [2] *P.P. 1897*, xiii. 81–82.
[3] N. Gash, *Politics in the Age of Peel*, pp. 434–7.
[4] *Disraeli Papers*, xxiii. 3–4.
[5] *Minutes of the 1883 Annual Conference*, f. 9. This committee was abolished in 1884.
[6] *Spectator*, 23 Mar., 13–27 July–3 Aug. 1901; Add. MSS. 41215 'Campbell-Bannerman Papers), ff. 124–39.

Cecil Rhodes had offered Schnadhorst £5,000 for the party
funds in 1893 and that Schnadhorst had pocketed it. There was
a hurried correspondence between the leader of the party,
Campbell-Bannerman, the Chief Whip, Herbert Gladstone, his
predecessor, Arnold Morley (who was then in Venice), and the
Secretary of the National Liberal Federation, Hudson. Campbell-Bannerman was apprehensive lest the distinction between
the Whip's party fund and the exchequer of the National
Federation should be made known to the public.[1] Hudson was
completely ignorant of the matter—no record had been kept—
and Morley assured Campbell-Bannerman that (in spite of the
fact that Schnadhorst had been Honorary Secretary of the
L.C.A. as well as the N.L.F.) 'F.S. never knew anything about
either the amount or the destination of Party Funds, the control
of which I kept absolutely in my own hands'.[2] After Morley's
letter the leaders tacitly decided not to pursue the matter further
in the press. Thus it seems that in both parties the contributions
from supporters to the ordinary party activities were kept
separate from the Whips' funds for financing candidates, but
that is as much as can be said.[3]

The existence of non-parliamentary groups that ran their
own election propaganda also raises a question. The Brewers'
Association was generally known to have spent £100,000 on
propaganda in 1892.[4] The Loyal and Patriotic Union, the Irish
Unionist Alliance, various agrarian groups, even Ritualists and
Anti-Vivisectionists conducted their own propaganda in favour
of candidates favourable to their policies.[5] Some claimed that this
propaganda ought to be included in the expenses of the candidates, but the Act of 1883 did not cover such contingencies.
Undoubtedly, since there were more moneyed pressure groups
on the Unionist side than the Liberal there was some grumbling
about 'discrimination'. At meetings of the National Federation
the matter was often raised, and at their 23rd annual conference

[1] Add. MSS. 41215, f. 135. Campbell-Bannerman to Herbert Gladstone (secret)
19 Oct. 1901.
[2] Ibid., f. 139.
[3] Cf. H. J. Hanham, *Elections and Party Management*, pp. 375–83.
[4] *The Times*, 9 June 1892.
[5] Unfortunately J. D. Stewart's pioneer work, *British Pressure Groups* (Oxford,
1958), does not carry the study of the electioneering activities of pressure groups
back to the nineteenth century.

in 1901 both Lloyd George and Campbell-Bannerman made vehement speeches against 'the power of the purse', the latter agreeing that while anti-corruption legislation 'possibly prevented to a great extent the meaner and more partial methods of bribery and corruption [it] had left the larger, more audacious, more unblushing and more corrupting influences still in full operation'.[1]

For their part the Conservatives were able to claim that the sweeping promises of the 'unauthorized programme' of 1885 and the 'Newcastle Programme' of 1891 constituted bribery by promise. There was something to be said for the argument that promises of social benefits were tantamount to old-fashioned hand-outs, adapted to the conditions of the mass electorate.[2] But on the same view considerations of personal advantage could be read into most of the electoral behaviour even of the disinterested upper classes in the first half of the century, and at the end too, since Imperialism was not only an ideal but a money-making expedient.[3]

John Stuart Mill said of the ordinary citizen that 'once in a thousand times, as in the case of peace or war, or of taking off taxes, the thought may cross him that he shall save a few pounds or shillings in his year's expenditure if the side he votes for wins'.[4] But this claim, that the citizen even under open voting normally votes according to ideas of right or wrong rather than from selfish motives may be more justly pleaded once the element of personal corruption is eliminated. On balance, that is the conclusion that must stem from the survey of electoral conditions between 1883 and the end of the century. Even if other methods were available for spending money in politics, the actual cost of electioneering was reduced by three-quarters, which was a great advantage to the poorer candidates.

Average Cost Per Vote Polled

1880:[5]   United Kingdom   18s. 9d.

---

[1] *23rd Annual Report of National Liberal Federation* (13–16 May 1901), pp. 99, 126.
[2] See above, p. 183.
[3] J. A. Thomas, *The House of Commons. 1837–1901* (Cardiff, 1939), pp. 20–22, has shown that the number of M.P.s with imperial interests rose sharply in the last quarter of the century.
[4] Cf. G. Wallas, *Human Nature in Politics* (London, 1948, 4th ed.), p. 215.
[5] See Chap. V.

1885:[1]	England and Wales	4s. 6d.
	Scotland	5s. 8d.
	Ireland	2s. 9d.
	United Kingdom	4s. 5d.

Maximum allowed by the Act in England and Wales, £854,650
English and Welsh total actual expenses, £835,458

1886:[2]	England and Wales	4s. 1d.
	Scotland	4s. 7d.
	Ireland	2s. 5d.
	Maximum allowed (E. & W.)	£711,075
	English and Welsh total	£515,683

1892:[3]	England and Wales	4s. 2d.
	Scotland	4s. 8d.
	Ireland	2s. 9d.
	Maximum allowed (E. & W.)	£864,190
	English and Welsh total	£796,588

1895:[4]	England and Wales	3s. 10d.
	Scotland	4s. 7¾d.
	Ireland	3s. 1½d.
	Maximum allowed (E. & W.)	£797,492
	English and Welsh total	£638,953

Secondly, with all the reservations mentioned above, the drop[5] in the number of petitions presented, in spite of increased opportunities of petitioning, and their changed character, raise a presumption of a higher moral outlook. Direct bribery had become so rare that its discovery at Worcester in 1906 caused a considerable shock to public self-esteem. Treating, though more difficult to detect, was being gradually eradicated through judicial stringency.[6] Ostrogorski might complain that the judges were too indulgent, but in the view of a newspaper in the reformist tradition the decisions showed that some at least of the judges read the law with a careful eye to every comma,[7] and another

---

[1] *P.P. 1886*, lii. 483.   [2] Ibid. 563–7.

[3] *P.P. 1893–4*, lxx. 801–3.

[4] *P.P. 1896*, lxvii. 403–5. The higher Scottish averages are due to proportionately higher expenditure on agents, clerks, and messengers.

[5] While there is no tangible evidence that during this period any petitions were actually compromised there is a disquieting allusion in a letter from Campbell-Bannerman to Herbert Gladstone to the effect that an alleged breach of the law by the Tory member for Orkney and Shetland 'may be useful to you as a pawn for forcing the withdrawal of other petitions'. But this is an isolated reference. Add. MSS. 41216, f. 35 (9 Nov. 1900).

[6] The gallons of ale and tons of beef given before 1883 were a far cry from the pork-pie, cup of coffee, and sandwich given to election helpers at Barrow-in-Furness. See above, pp. 15, 189.

[7] *Pall Mall Gazette*, 25 Jan. 1896.

Liberal paper complained that the Act of 1883 was most unfair to the candidates and ought to be repealed.[1]

Riots and disturbances had occurred with monotonous regularity before 1883, afterwards the individual heckler became a feature of electioneering. Public drunkenness was almost a thing of the past; and likewise organized intimidation.

Constituency comparisons are not easy to make because the electoral geography of England and Wales was radically altered by the Redistribution Act of 1885. Nevertheless, of all the constituencies appearing in the election courts between 1868 and 1880 only four[2] were involved between 1883 and 1900. Out of twenty-nine petitions tried, six were from county divisions and only two of these were English counties.

The opinion that by the end of the century only the forms of corruption had changed was therefore untenable, however much politicians might go through the motions of pretending that all was still as it had been.

If, to quote Ostrogorski again,[3] the nationalization of parties erected political agitation into a system, that was only to be expected when the electorate had become too large to be controlled by personal electioneering, and if the caucus system did for politics what the Salvation Army did for religion—meaning that it forced it to rely upon enthusiasm, it was enthusiasm of a disciplined and orderly kind.[4]

[1] *Daily News*, 25 Jan. 1896. Both of these papers had supported the Act in 1883. See above, Chap. VI.

[2] Lichfield, Norwich, Southampton, and Worcester.

[3] Ostrogorski, *Democracy and the Organization of Political Parties*, i. 588. Ostrogorski does not stress sufficiently the ease with which the party associations were able to recruit voluntary help to keep within the expense limits of the 1883 Act.

[4] H. J. Hanham, *Elections and Party Management*, pp. 281–3, claims that there was a much more 'prosaic' reason for the improvement in electioneering standards after 1883—the disfranchisement of 30 out of 64 corrupt constituencies. That was certainly a help, although it does not account for the steep decline in the *proportion* of petitions to contests. Mr. Hanham is inclined to over-estimate the evidence of corrupt practices in the constituencies appearing in the courts after 1885 and he does not pay sufficient attention to the efforts of the electioneering professionals on both sides to make the Act of 1883 a success.

CHAPTER VIII

1900–1911

THE previous chapter has shown that by the end of the
nineteenth century electioneering methods had been reformed to an extent that would have been deemed impossible even twenty years earlier. The same process continued,
though at a slower rate, in the first decade of the twentieth
century.[1]

I

The 'Khaki Election' of 1900 deserves special mention since
it was the first general election since 1880 in which the Government systematically tried to prove the Opposition party unfit to
succeed by appealing to patriotic fervour, and as a result personal charges and counter-charges were a prominent feature of
the campaign.

Had the Government merely chosen the most propitious time
for an election the Liberals would have had little grounds for
complaint. What did, however, introduce the note of bitter
resentment and acrimony into the campaign was the exploiting
by the Unionists of the Clark-Labouchere letters, in order to
prove that some Opposition members were intriguing with the
Boers. The inevitable corollary to this argument was the slogan:
'A vote for the Radicals is a vote for the Boers', which appeared
under many forms during the campaign. Balfour made a speech
and Chamberlain sent a telegram expressing these very senti-
ments, and the rank and file followed suit. A poster used everywhere at Oldham by the supporters of Winston Churchill
warned the electors in enormous black type that 'Every Vote
Given to the Radicals means 2 Pats on the Back for Kruger and
2 Smacks in the Face for our Country'; a poster used at Stow-
market, Suffolk, said that 'Every Vote given for Mr. Horobin

---

[1] Twentieth-century elections are too complicated to cover adequately in a
small space and too recent to require extensive treatment here. A few features that
are relevant to this study are brought out in these pages.

[the Liberal candidate] is a Boer bullet fired at our fellow-
countrymen'; and in the Leeds constituency of Gerald Balfour
the clearest statement of all appeared: 'Our brave soldiers in
South Africa expect that every voter this day will do his duty.
Vote for Balfour. Remember! To Vote for a Liberal is a vote
for the Boers.'[1]

The Liberal leaders were somewhat taken aback by these
tactics, and worried by dissensions within the party over the war
and the whole question of Imperialism they were on the de-
fensive throughout the election. It was Labouchere who continued the struggle on enemy ground by boldly alleging that
the Chamberlain family had a vested interest in the war,[2] and
Liberal back-benchers followed this up by an all-out attack on
Chamberlain.

The attitude of the press to this general deterioration in
electioneering standards is interesting. What *Truth* called
scornfully 'the Chamberlain press'[3] reacted more or less identi-
cally. Even the most responsible papers supporting the Government turned a blind eye to the attempt to blacken the entire
Liberal party in the eyes of the electorate and concentrated only
on the dead-set against Chamberlain. The *Spectator* ran a special
article on the 'atrocious attacks' on Chamberlain which it
deplored 'from the wider national point of view'.[4]

The Times[5] complained that 'personal vituperation' was
obscuring the issues, and reproved Harcourt for denying
Chamberlain any credit for the South African victories; it kept
silent about the Unionist contribution to this obscurity.

[1] These three posters were afterwards reproduced in facsimile by Augustine
Birrell, *The General Election: How the Tories Won, Why the Liberals Lost* (Liberal
Publication Department, 1900). Birrell notes that the Balfour one (which was
photographed on the hoardings at Leeds) 'was afterwards impossible to procure'.
Towards the end of the campaign there was some evidence that the Unionist
leaders felt that they had gone too far, and attempts were made to explain away
these speeches (ibid., p. 23).
   The 'dear old flag' and the military connexions (sometimes obscure) of Unionist
candidates were prominently displayed on election platforms, posters, and addresses.
[2] Cf. *Truth*, 4–18 Oct. 1900.
[3] Of the halfpenny dailies the *Daily Express* and *Daily Mail* were pro-Unionist,
the *Echo* and *Star* pro-Liberal. The *Echo* (founded in 1868) was the oldest of the
mass circulation papers, the *Mail* was founded in 1896 and the *Express* in 1900,
shortly before the election.
[4] *Spectator*, 29 Sept., 6 Oct. 1900.
[5] *The Times*, 26 Sept. 1900.

When it was all over the independent *Economist*,[1] made an attempt to assess the peculiar features of the Khaki Election and its probable place in history. It discovered a resemblance between the abuse hurled at the opponents of the Crimean War and the treatment of the anti-Imperialist Liberals. Calmly stating that free criticism was of the very essence of free institutions *The Economist* asked if any rational being could seriously assert that the 1,374,000 who voted Liberal (as against 1,586,000 Unionists) could be called traitors.[2] It predicted that 'everybody will be ashamed of that nonsense in a few months' time'.

Thus the Unionist party perpetrated on a national scale what would, since 1895, in an individual constituency have caused a petition—the publication of false statements calculated to injure the opponents' chances of securing election. That this contributed to a general debasing of campaign standards might be surmised from the manner in which the radicals replied to the Government charges by dragging in personal innuendoes against Chamberlain, and from the abundance of invective[3] that appeared not only in election addresses and speeches, but also in newspaper reports and even leading articles.

Although the results of the election gave the Unionist Government a new lease of life and threatened the Liberals with further disruption, the methods used did not benefit the former in the long run. The Liberal dissensions were quickly healed, and their propaganda machine became geared to the requirements of the next election. During 1904 and 1905 the Liberal Publication Department waited impatiently for Balfour's downfall, staging demonstrations and piling up pamphlets. Balfour misread the signs. When he resigned at the beginning of December 1905 he expected the Liberals to be unable to continue. Instead Campbell-Bannerman immediately secured a dissolution.

---

[1] *The Economist*, 13 Oct. 1900.

[2] 'The most extreme opponents of the war have opposed it because it would injure the true interests of England . . . their patriotism is at least entitled to as much credence as that of the Jameson raiders or the rowdies of the music-halls' (ibid.).

[3] An extreme case of personal abuse (unconnected with the war issue) may be found in the campaign speeches of Major F. C. Rasch, Unionist member for Chelmsford, who made a series of insulting references to his Liberal opponent, H. C. S. Henry (a Jew), e.g. 'They had seen almost the last of the Semitic invasion, and they would soon see an end to this great fuss about a bit of pork'. Cf. *Essex County Chronicle*, 12 Oct. 1900. Rasch retained his seat by a majority of nearly three to one.

The Liberals knew that the tide was turning in their favour and campaigned with great zest.[1] The Chinese slavery and war supplies scandals were almost, but not quite, as well exploited by them as the Clark letters had been in 1900 by the Unionists. To give one example, it is impossible not to detect a motive of tit for tat in John Morley's election slogan: 'Every Vote given against the Government is a vote given for a tax on food.'[2] Disorders at election meetings, though not of sufficient gravity to warrant election petitions, nevertheless occurred on a considerable scale. Balfour, at the opening of his campaign in his own constituency, was subjected to 'a constant fire of senseless interruptions and disorderly noises'.[3] Chamberlain was unable to finish a speech at Derby. At a meeting addressed by George Wyndham in Dover a free fight broke out in the hall and the Unionist candidate at Peterborough was pushed out of his carriage and rolled in the mud. The Unionist leaders were the chief but not the only targets. The Prime Minister, who deplored these incidents, had an unruly meeting at Shrewsbury and Lloyd George was refused a hearing at Leamington.

The outbreaks of rowdyism seemed spontaneous and were not claimed to have been organized by political opponents.[4] They were probably a symptom of the increasing interest in politics stimulated by the popular press with its profuse photographs and advertisements.[5] Another reason was the old practice of spreading the contests over a fortnight; the flood of Liberal gains in the early results undoubtedly affected the constituencies that polled later, as they had in 1880.

The final result which gave the Liberals a margin of more than 200 over the combined force of Unionists and Liberal-Unionists certainly shook the supporters of the former Government.[6] With rare simplicity *The Times* wrote: 'We did not

---

[1] Cf. R. Jenkins, *Mr. Balfour's Poodle* (London, 1955), pp. 4–8.

[2] Cf. *Daily News*, 9 Jan. 1906.   [3] *The Times*, 6 Jan. 1906.

[4] Except that Lloyd George claimed that 'Birmingham roughs' had been sent to break up his Leamington meeting at Chamberlain's instigation. Chamberlain denied the charge. Cf. *Daily Telegraph*, 13 Jan. 1906.

[5] At the end of the campaign a Preston Public Health official complained that as a result of parents taking children to election meetings and keeping them out long after their bedtime the infantile death-rate had reached in the previous week the highest level in the town's history. Cf. *Daily Telegraph*, 26 Jan. 1906.

[6] And the Liberals too. Neither the leaders nor the party newspapers expected it. Cf. Spender, *Life of Sir Henry Campbell-Bannerman*, ii. 218; *Daily News*, 13 Jan. 1906.

expect, nor we believe did anyone, that its [the late Government's] dismissal from power would come in a manner so peremptory and decisive.' As in 1880, but to a much greater extent, the Liberal gains snowballed over the fortnight of polling. The 'swing of the pendulum', the havoc wreaked among the Unionists by the Tariff Reform controversy, and the personal rivalry of Balfour and Chamberlain all contributed to the Liberal victory.[1] Nor did the Unionists secure much of an advantage from their preponderance in motor transport. An advertisement signed by eight titled ladies (headed by Consuelo, Duchess of Marlborough) had asked London Unionists to lend their cars 'for the conveyance of voters on polling day'[2] and Lord Montagu of Beaulieu claimed that no less than 400 candidates were dependent on this new aid to electioneering. The Unionists, being wealthier, had more cars but there again Liberal supporters made up in energy for lack of resources.[3] Surprisingly enough, the conveyance of voters by cars was not raised as a substantial charge in any election petition.

The other feature of the election was that the Labour Representation Committee, which was but one month old when the Khaki Election took place, put up 50 candidates of whom 29 were elected, making with the other Labour members 54 in all. *The Times* ran a special article on the danger to the Liberals that this result implied.[4]

The year 1910 with its two elections of very different character in spite of a similarity of issues forms a unique episode in British electoral history.[5] The constitutional crisis that provoked

B. E. C. Dugdale, *Arthur James Balfour* (London, 1936), i. 429, wrote: 'Few on either side expected that the Unionists would be given a new run of power. No one on either side expected that the great Party which had ruled, with one brief interval, for twenty years, would be returned a leaderless remnant of 157.'

[1] *The Times*, 27 Jan. 1906. Three days before *The Times* had half-heartedly essayed an explanation: '(The result) is a protest against dilettantism in politics. . . . It expresses the weariness of the people not only with the late Government but with the House of Commons itself.'

[2] *Daily Telegraph*, 9 Jan. 1906.

[3] For example, the 'Free Church Motor-Car', which, plastered with slogans, toured the entire West country. Cf. *Daily News*, 9 Jan. 1906.

[4] *The Times*, 19 Jan. 1906. The article was replete with quotations from Blatchford and *The Clarion*.

[5] Roy Jenkins, *Mr. Balfour's Poodle*, despite its flippant title, is a serious study of the inner workings of the constitutional crisis and the elections of 1910. See especially pp. 53–57, 71–79, 128–31. The interval between the two elections was one of the shortest in British history.

the double election might be paralleled by the struggle between the two Houses in 1831–2. But this was virtually the only point of resemblance. In the struggle for the Great Reform Bill the two Houses were theoretically equal and to contemporaries the outcome was by no means assured. In 1910 one House fired by reactionary fervour placed itself in a false position from which a successful appeal to the people was the only possible way out, although the appeal was most likely to go against it. This was the *raison d'être* of the first election; whereas the second election was simply held to confirm a situation that the first had largely settled, the victory of the majority in the House of Commons. In addition, the canvassing of issues previously unknown to the British constitution both in theory and practice, the question of a referendum and the intervention of peers in the election campaign, made a further difference from 1832.

The peers indeed dominated the January campaign. Lords Lansdowne, Curzon, Cromer, and Dunraven rushed to take their case to the people though in 1880 Beaconsfield, Salisbury, and Cranbrook would not have dared.[1] Unionist peers went as far as they could by speaking on public platforms until the date of moving the writ. Their success was varied: several were shouted down as effectively as was an eminent press-lord during the 1945 election—especially the Irish Unionists, Lords Dunraven and Ashbourne.[2] But although there were bitter speeches on both sides, and many important speakers were interrupted, both the rowdyism and the personal animosity of the elections immediately previous were lacking.

The 'march of science' was evident not only in a more extensive use of motor-transport than in 1906—the party leaders made more speeches and covered a greater area than ever before—but in more elaborate publicity methods. There was an

[1] The distinguished constitutional lawyer, Professor A. V. Dicey (*The Times*, 7 Dec. 1910) and the *Spectator* urged the Unionists to promise a referendum on the Parliament Bill, if and when they got back to power. It was a useful campaign weapon at first, but many Unionists were uneasy when Balfour accepted an ironical Liberal challenge to hold a referendum on tariff reform. Cf. Jenkins, *Mr. Balfour's Poodle*, pp. 128–31; *Spectator*, 10–17 Dec. 1910. The question of a referendum was raised only in the second election campaign.

[2] *The Times*, 8 Jan. 1910, having praised the high qualities of the Lords by comparison with the Commons, went on to denounce the treatment they got as 'not fair play', saying that it 'disgusts all decent Englishmen'. They charged Asquith with 'tacit acquiescence amounting in effect to complicity'.

unprecedented number of posters, not as trenchant in their message as in former elections, but better produced.[1]

In the January election only 75 constituencies were uncontested, in the December election the number had risen to 159. The speeches and issues were much the same, although Home Rule played a larger part.[2] The only new issues were the referendum and an attack by Balfour on John Redmond and three of his followers for collecting 40,000 dollars during a tour of the United States and Canada in the recess and allegedly using it as an election fund. Lloyd George defended Redmond vigorously, but the legality of the matter was not subsequently tested in the election courts. Eventually the Government increased their majority by two seats in a poll which showed a drop of 16 per cent.—a result that no side found satisfactory.[3]

Although all parties found their funds depleted as a result of the two elections in 1910 the hardest hit was the struggling Labour Party which had been precluded by the Osborne judgement of 1909 from financing their candidates by means of a compulsory levy.[4] Half their members were deprived of the £200 a year which the party had been paying for them,[5] and in the first election their strength was reduced to forty, although they gained two seats in the second. In both contests Labour candidates angrily complained of the Osborne judgement, and in constituencies where they did not stand the party advised

[1] The 'Bread eaten by Protected German Workmen' (*Free Trade Journal*) is a good example. Posters were used not only by the parties but by pressure groups, e.g. the Tariff Reform League, the Free Trade Union, the British Constitution Association. Whether this lavish expenditure was within the election law or not was never established, since the question was not raised in the election courts.

[2] In the *Fortnightly Review* (Jan. 1911) Sir Sidney Low wrote that 'The general election was the most apathetic within living memory'. Cf. Jenkins, *Mr. Balfour's Poodle*, p. 128.

[3] For a detailed study of the election results in Jan. see S. Rosenbaum, 'The General Election of January 1910, and the Bearing of the Results on Some Problems of Representation', *Journal of the Royal Statistical Society*, lxxiii (May 1910), 473–511.

[4] The Amalgamated Society of Railway Servants was unfortunate enough to be the loser in the two lawsuits of this period which impeded the Labour movement— the Taff Vale judgement of 1901 (awarding damages of £23,000 against it on account of a strike) and the Osborne judgement (the decision of the House of Lords on the application by a member of the Union for an injunction prohibiting the political levy on the ground that it was not a legitimate union activity under the Trade Union Act of 1871). Cf. F. Bealey and H. Pelling, *Labour and Politics 1900–1906* (London, 1958), pp. 55 ff.

[5] J. H. S. Reid, *The Origins of the British Labour Party* (Minneapolis, 1955), p. 167.

their supporters to vote Liberal, since that would be the best chance of getting the Osborne judgement reversed. It does not appear, however, that the decision of the House of Lords was uniformly obeyed.

2

The petitions tried between 1900 and 1918 were, with one exception, of the same character as those of the previous fifteen years.

Five petitions were tried in 1900 of which three succeeded. In Maidstone John Barker (Liberal) was unseated for bribery by an agent. The judges were satisfied that a number of the lower classes expected a 'reward' for their votes. But the number of cases proved (25) and the rewards, ranging from 5s. to 10s., were so small that it could be presumed that those hopes were largely unfulfilled. A charge of general bribery arising from the inflated electioneering language of the candidate and his agent was proved groundless.[1] Another successful case came from Monmouth Boroughs where the return of the Unionist, Dr. Rutherfoord Harris, was impugned on grounds of illegal practices. His agent had paid one man for work which was not included in the official return[2] and, more important, Harris had attacked his opponent in the *Western Mail* on grounds which were novel in 1900, though quite common in 1906, namely that he had employed coolie labour in South Africa at a very low wage. Mr. Justice Kennedy and Mr. Justice Darling decided that the second charge was a false statement under the Act of 1895. Darling suspected that illegal practices might have extensively prevailed and wished that they could examine the case further.[3]

The three petitions that did not succeed came from Pembroke and Haverfordwest, Islington, and Cockermouth. The Islington petition was lodged entirely on technical grounds—whether returning officers were entitled to issue ballots after 8 o'clock to people who had entered the polling station before

[1] *P.P. 1901*, lix. 19–112. Barker had been promising the farmers of Maidstone studs of horses, grapes by the ton, and strawberries at 30s. a pound.

[2] Moreover he tried to circumvent the law by pretending that the voter's son (a non-voter) had done the work. Cf. *P.P. 1902*, lxxxii. 419–32.

[3] Dickens (Harris's counsel) gave up the case after the evidence on the employment charge had been heard. The judges had no power to recommend a Royal Commission on the ground that *illegal* practices were extensive.

that time. The judges decided that officers were not entitled to issue ballots after closing time,[1] but that a person who had *received* his ballot before 8 was entitled to mark it. Only fourteen voters were affected, not enough to upset the result.

The grounds of the Pembroke petition were also technical—whether the names of some of the voters for Lieut.-Gen. Laurie (Unionist) were entitled to be on the register.[2] The Court decided after the precedent of *Stowe* v. *Jolliffe* (1874)[3] that the register was conclusive evidence of a title to vote, and Laurie's counsel then withdrew a recriminatory case involving a supper party held by the Liberal Association, accepting the excuse that the party was arranged before the dissolution and that each guest paid a small charge.

The most interesting petition tried in 1901 was brought against John S. Randles at Cockermouth, partly because of a tea-party paid for out of the funds of the Liberal-Unionist Association but also on account of an abusive speech by Randles' agent about his veteran opponent Sir Wilfrid Lawson. Lawson had an income, he said, of £15,000 a year but did not give 1,500 pence to the district. He had had a chance to do something for 25 years, but he had done nothing except to help the Boers. Mr. Justice Darling, who delivered the judgement (with which Mr. Justice Channell agreed) decided that these statements were an 'intemperate, very foolish expression of opinion and nothing more'. Having analysed each part of the statement, Darling came as near as any election judge could to delivering a purely political opinion, by inferring that since Lawson had voted against sending supplies he had made it more difficult to conquer the Boers and was thereby helping them. Darling went on to say that the Act of 1895, the ground of the charge, was directed against criticism of a personal character, not of political action.[4]

[1] Cf. the Elections (Hours of Poll) Act, 1885 (48 Vict. c. 10). *P.P. 1902*, lxxxii. 409–15.
[2] It concerned some 'ancient righters'—county freeholders with tenements in the borough whose right to vote at borough elections had been reserved by the Act of 1884. In 1900 some of them had decided to vote in county elections in future, but the register had been drawn up before their decision could be implemented. *P.P. 1902*, lxxxii. 397–403.
[3] See above, p. 95, n. 3.
[4] Darling also displayed the sense of humour for which he was to be famous in the next two decades. Commenting on another of the abusive statements by

The three cases heard in 1906 attracted a good deal of publicity. First came the petition from a borough with an unsavoury
electoral history—Great Yarmouth.[1] Since 1895 it had been
represented by a wealthy baronet with estates in Ireland, Sir
John Colomb, who prided himself on his general benevolence
and approachability.[2] Wishing to retire in 1905, because of ill
health, Colomb introduced to the Conservative Hundred a
business acquaintance, Arthur Fell, a solicitor with ample
private means, and he was quickly adopted as the prospective
candidate in July 1904.

Fell's only previous acquaintance with Yarmouth had come
through yachting on the Broads, so he was anxious to make
himself popular. His wife decided in February 1905 to hold an
'At Home', ostensibly for the purpose of bringing Colomb and
his numerous friends together. But it was held in the Town Hall,
since their house was too small for the crowd they expected, and
nearly 800 people attended and were plied with tea, bread and
butter, and, on average, half a tot of whisky apiece. Between
then and the election Fell attended a number of meetings and
invariably had 'a drink with the Chairman'. On election day,
one Baker (whose father had been a Liberal candidate at a
municipal election and who had never been known before to
support the Unionists) got possession of a car and went round
asking voters to come to the poll and in at least fifteen cases
offered them small sums of money.[3]

In assessing the evidence the judges disagreed, the only
occasion of its kind during these ten years. The younger judge,
Mr. Justice Channell, held that the bribery alone was enough to
unseat Fell, since although Baker was not directly employed as
an agent yet he had the authority of the chairman of the candi-

Randles' agent that 'there was not a greater fool in the House of Commons' (than
Lawson), he said that the only way to disprove it would be 'to suggest who are the
other people who could possibly be bigger fools' (*P.P. 1901*, lix. 4). The judges
decided that the tea-party charge failed since it was arranged before the election
campaign—like the Pembroke tea-party. Nevertheless, they suspected that treating
was not absent from the campaign (ibid. 5–9).

[1] See above, p. 28.

[2] Colomb told the court that: 'My policy has always been as member for a constituency (he had sat for Bow and Bromley 1886–92) not to flourish party flags, but
I feel I represent all classes and all parties.' *P.P. 1906*, xcv. 189. The judges were also
told that he was so popular that even porters would go up to him, shake his hand, and
say: 'Good old Sir John; glad to see you' (ibid. 175).

[3] *P.P. 1906*, xcv. 5–24 (Judgement); 32–253 (Minutes of Evidence).

date's Vehicles Committee to take the carriage and bring voters to the poll.[1] However, Mr. Justice Grantham disagreed strongly. Ignoring Baker's own admission that he gave money to the people whom he drove, Grantham refused to believe that a man so recently a Liberal would bribe for the Conservatives. He also denied that Baker could be an agent. Most surprising of all, Grantham criticized the precedents of Elgin, Norwich, and Walsall which had determined that the expenses of meetings, &c., incurred from the date at which the candidature was announced must be included in the official return. They would make, he said, the maximum expense levels 'entirely illusory', and he agreed with Fell's submission that the legislature intended to draw a distinction between the candidature and the conduct and management of the election. In 1883, Grantham said, the practice of nursing constituencies had not begun and could not have been in the minds of the legislators.[2] Apropos of his own electioneering expenses he said: 'I will not refer to what my own were, or it might astonish you.'[3]

Since the two judges disagreed the election was not affected. The judgement was delivered early in May and was quickly followed by a series of angry letters to the press. C. R. Buxton in a letter to the *Spectator* summarized the Yarmouth judgement as 'the severest blow that has been directed for many years against purity of elections', and hoped that it 'may open the eyes of the public to the mockery which our Judges have made of the Corrupt Practices Act'.[4] Other correspondents agreed that the matter must not stop there. On 19 June Swift McNeill, one of the stormy petrels of the Irish Parliamentary Party, tabled a motion of censure in the House of Commons on Mr. Justice Grantham, the second time such a procedure was invoked against

[1] Channell also considered that the expenses of the 'At Home' ought to be included in the election return, even if it had not constituted treating, which was not certain.

[2] Although Mr. Justice Grantham had sat in the Commons as a Conservative when the Bill of 1883 was going through his memory seems to have been faulty. Nursing the constituencies was quite well known before 1883 and was mentioned in the debates of 1881–3. The distinction between the conduct of the election and the candidature was one which would indeed make the expense maxima of 1883 illusory: what Grantham meant by that epithet was that no one could be expected to fight an election without first ingratiating himself with the constituency, and that these preliminary activities ought not to be considered as election expenses.

[3] *P.P. 1906*, xcv. 21.

[4] *Spectator*, 19 May 1906. See also 26 May, *The Times, passim.*

an election judge. The sequel was interesting. The motion was
debated on 6 July. Apart from the proposer and seconder the
opinion of the House was clearly against it. The Attorney-
General, followed by Campbell-Bannerman and Balfour,
pointed out that the statutory procedure for removing a judge
could only be invoked in cases of misconduct or corruption, and
of these Mr. Justice Grantham was clearly not guilty. Therefore since there was no other possible penalty a vote of censure
was futile. He advised that the motion be withdrawn and Swift
McNeill complied.[1] While the motion was pending Grantham,
together with Mr. Justice Lawrence, had to try another petition
at Bodmin, where Agar-Robartes's return was challenged on
account of a garden party given by his parents, but organized by
his agent. Grantham agreed with Lawrence that the party involved corrupt treating, and unseated Agar-Robartes, although
the treating involved was less serious than at Yarmouth.[2]

The last 1906 petition came from Worcester, a city with an
electorate of nearly 8,500, which since 1885 had been represented by the Hon. George Higginson Allsopp, a member of the
brewing family. Like the member for Yarmouth Allsopp decided
in 1905 to retire. In November of that year the Conservative
party boss of the city, Alderman Francis Caldicott, invited one
of his fellow councillors, G. H. Williamson, to stand, and within
one month the Conservative 'Two Hundred' had ratified his
candidature. Then, just as at Yarmouth, meetings were held in
public houses, with drinks all round, during the month between
Williamson's acceptance and the election. All might have gone
well had the Liberals not decided to use a novel means to test
the morality of their opponents. They sent a private inquiry
agent who joined the Conservative Club and the National Conservative League, which had been censured in 1892,[3] and produced most of the evidence for the petition, which was lodged

[1] See 4 Hans. (6 July 1906), 369–414. A motion of censure on Mr. Justice Keogh
was also unsuccessful in 1872.
[2] The Spectator (23 June 1906) noted the inconsistency with some amusement:
'A petition is a serious matter. Mr. Justice Grantham at Yarmouth was garrulous
and jocose: at Bodmin he was garrulous and lachrymose; and we do not know which
form is the more painful.' Although the Spectator had deplored the motion of censure
when it was defeated, they wrote (14 July 1906) that Mr. Justice Grantham as
senior puisne judge 'will no doubt soon seek the rest which he has amply earned'.
The Bodmin petition evidence and judgement were not published.
[3] For the Worcester petition of 1892 see above, p. 198.

immediately after Williamson had defeated the Liberal candidate, H. D. Harben, by 129 votes out of a poll of 7,633.[1]

The evidence showed that an unspecified sum was furtively distributed in small bribes by the secretary of the Conservative Club[2] at the instance of Caldicott—one of the methods used was to leave money in a public convenience. On the fifth day of the trial Williamson's counsel, Dickens, admitted that he could not deny the accusations—ten cases of bribery had already been proved—and abandoned the case. The election judges agreed that they had not got to the end of the bribery, and reported to the House that corrupt practices had extensively prevailed.

The last Royal Commission to inquire into a British election sat at Worcester from 13 August to 13 October and produced their report on 22 November 1906. They established that a corruptible class, the extent of which they estimated at 500, or one-sixteenth of the electorate, still existed in the borough, willing to sell their votes for a small sum (generally not exceeding 10s.) or a drink, and not willing to vote otherwise. The venal voters were mostly concentrated in two wards, and were drawn from the poorest class in the city. Although the petition of 1892 had been dismissed on the ground that most of the charges seemed incredible, one witness, a very frank member of the National Conservative League, asserted that from his childhood he had known no election to be won at Worcester except through bribery. Some of those charged with bribery calmly admitted that for upwards of thirty years they had been accustomed to rewards for their votes.

The Commissioners concluded that both before and after 1892 corrupt practices had systematically prevailed at elections in Worcester City. They scheduled 96 people for bribery and treating and 2 for illegal practices, 31 of these including Caldicott and Thornborrow were refused certificates of indemnity and were liable to prosecution; Williamson was not scheduled.

The Attorney-General immediately issued prosecutions for bribery against six of those scheduled, including Caldicott and Thornborrow. The resourceful Alderman anticipated him by

[1] For the petition trial the judges were Mr. Justice Lawrence and Mr. Justice Walton see *P.P. 1906*, xcv. 5–23 (Judgement), 32–253 (Minutes of Evidence); for the Royal Commission see ibid. 477–84 (Report), 489–995 (Minutes of Evidence).

[2] G. H. Thornborrow. On the day after Caldicott handed him £100 he was found drunk on the streets.

appealing to Worcester Assizes against the judgement of the
Royal Commission chiefly on the ground that he had not been
found guilty by the election judges. Mr. Justice Bigham heard
this action—the first of its kind since 1870.[1] Caldicott conducted
his own case, denying that he had given bribes at any time
during the election, although he admitted giving money to two
perfect strangers. The Commissioners were not represented and
Mr. Justice Bigham, who had no experience of election trials,
believed Caldicott's story and ordered that the part of the report
of the Royal Commissioners that referred to Caldicott's com-
mitting corrupt practices be set aside, but that their verdict on
illegal practices be allowed to stand.[2]

The result of this singular appeal (which was never envisaged
by the authors of the Acts of 1854, 1868, and 1883) was that the
prosecutions were effectively forestalled and a precedent set
which might have made future Royal Commissions a good deal
less effective than they had been. Fortunately the opportunity
for invoking it never arose.

Three of the 1911 petitions came from England and three
from Ireland. Both groups curiously exhibited some traces of
old-fashioned electioneering habits. The case at East Nottingham concerned a generous Unionist member, Captain J. A.
Morrison, who during a hard winter had given charity to large
numbers of people irrespective of their political creed, although
the applications were to a great extent handled by his agent.[3]
The judges reviewed the history of similar cases in the past,[4] and
concluded that the agent intended the natural consequences of
his acts, increased popularity for the Unionists, but that it was

---

[1] In 1870 the Bridgwater Commissioners refused to some bribers, including
Henry Lovibond, certificates of indemnity against criminal proceedings which
(under 26 and 27 Vict., c. 29) they were entitled to give to all witnesses who had
made 'a true disclosure to the best of their knowledge'. Lovibond then applied
successfully to the Queen's Bench Division for a writ of mandamus compelling
the Commissioners to grant a certificate (*Lovibond* v. *Price*). Similar proceedings were taken in Norwich. Although the criminal proceedings were effectively
stopped there was no question of impugning the Commissioners' findings.

[2] Williamson had given Caldicott £100 for the election which was never accounted for to the official agent.

[3] *P.P. 1911*, lxi. 468–82. The judges pointed out that some of the witnesses for the
petitioners had been paid for their statements: that in itself was not wrong, but the
statements were ludicrous exaggerations. *The Times* called this 'an audacious
conspiracy' (23 May 1911).

[4] Especially the cases of Windsor, St. George's in the East, Plymouth, and Boston.

not the governing motive, and on that account they dismissed the petition.

At East Dorset and Hartlepool the issue was whether two different kinds of old-fashioned undue influence had been committed. In East Dorset[1] the Guest family had considerable estates and for generations influenced their tenants accordingly. In 1904, however, they changed from Conservative to Liberal, and in 1908 Captain Ivor Guest, who had been unsuccessful in three elections, came to an arrangement with the sitting Conservative member for East Dorset that at the general election he should stand for an Edinburgh constituency and leave the way free for Guest's return. Guest was duly adopted as Liberal candidate. During the campaign some sinister things happened: allotment holders were given notice, a workman was dismissed,[2] and an estate agent stood with a notebook outside the polling booth. The expenses were far above the scheduled maximum;[3] Lady Wimborne had a fleet of Daimlers for canvassing and numerous pamphlets and newspaper articles were published to rebut some scurrilous attacks on the Guest family. The judges found grounds for suspicion in all these activities but gave Guest the benefit of the doubt.

At Hartlepool the Liberal member, Sir Christopher Furness, was unseated because his agent, with his knowledge, had created an atmosphere of intimidation in the borough by hiring and feeding a band of miners for 'demonstrations'.[4]

Two of the Irish petitions (both after the second election of 1910) showed that in the county elections at least the lessons of the 1883 Act had not yet been learnt. In East Cork[5] the Chief Whip of the Irish Parliamentary Party, Captain Donelan, was opposed by William O'Brien, the leader of a nationalist splinter group, the United Irish League.[6] In spite of three M.P.s running

---

[1] Cf. *P.P. 1910*, lxxiii. 454–67. This was the only English county petition after the election of Jan. 1910.

[2] The excuse given was that the workman (who had been employed for twenty-five years) was unable to do a good day's work. The *Spectator* commented: 'One can only regret that twenty-five years of extreme patience should have been followed by an act of alarming precipitation' (21 May 1910).

[3] The maximum was £350, the expenses £2,694.

[4] The proceedings of this petition (like those of the Bodmin petition in 1906) were not printed.

[5] *P.P. 1911*, lxii. 3–28 (Judgement); 29–304 (Minutes of Evidence).

[6] For the continued dissensions in the Irish party after Parnell's death see F. S. L. Lyons, *The Irish Parliamentary Party, 1890–1910*, pp. 15–38.

the election for Donelan[1] many irregularities were committed—
extensive treating, sums paid out by other people as well as the
official election agent, accounts not kept properly,[2] and cars
fraudulently hired by the agents in the names of their owners.
The judges had no difficulty in unseating Donelan for illegal
practices, but they refused to believe the statement of one
authoritative witness that the reason why no election docu-
ments were produced was that they were destroyed, according
to the common custom.

In North Louth[3] another dissident, T. M. Healy, who had
sat for the constituency since 1892, was opposed by R. Hazleton,
a Redmondite—who found time to help Donelan in East Cork in
addition to running his own campaign. Healy was then going
through his worst phase of unpopularity. A meeting to be addressed by him in September, when there was no election in the
offing, was broken up by the Redmondites, and from his arrival
in the constituency for the campaign at the end of November
until polling day Healy had to have police protection and could
not address a single open-air meeting. Even his friends were
assaulted and their lives threatened. To add insult to injury, the
supporters of Hazleton circulated 20,000 copies of a libellous
pamphlet alleging that Healy's family were all place-hunters.
On polling day Hazleton had a majority of 488 over Healy out of
a poll of 4,556; in January Healy had won by 99 votes in a poll
of 4,786. The judges found that Hazleton's agents and supporters
were guilty of intimidation, treating, and, to a smaller extent,
bribery, false statements of fact, and illegal practices. The
election was thus annulled.

Among the nine English petitions after the December election,
the proceedings of which have not been printed, only two hold
much interest; the rest were technical. C. F. G. Masterman,
Under-Secretary at the Home Office, was unseated at West
Ham because of irregularities by his agent in keeping the election accounts—he had borrowed from the account for a client's
mortgage; and Sir Seymour King lost his seat on account of gifts
of coal and sweets in honour of his silver jubilee as member for

[1] Donelan got 3,171 votes, O'Brien, 1,834.

[2] More than £200 was spent over the agent's estimate of £700 (the legal maximum). The sum officially returned was £573.

[3] *P.P. 1911*, lxii. 306–34 (Judgement); 337–637 (Minutes of Evidence). John
Redmond led the main group of the Irish Parliamentary Party.

Hull, which occurred shortly before the election. That decision was very unpopular in the town and the judges were pelted with lumps of coal as they went to their train. These two decisions were as strict as any that had occurred in the previous twenty-five years. Before that they would have been inconceivable.[1]

A novel feature of the election campaigns of 1910, betting on the Stock Exchange, not only on the outcome of the election but on the risk of a petition, shows that to some of the public at any rate a candidate was envisaged as surrounded by hazards not the least of which was the many-headed electoral law.

3

Commenting on the petitions of 1910 *The Times* said that 'In certain towns with a vendible or irresponsible residuum' the tradition had grown up that 'at election times anything is permissible; that all breaches of election laws are venial'.[2] *The Times* believed that something more was needed than unseating a member or lecturing a constituency on its shortcomings, and suggested that the public prosecutor select two or three constituencies with bad records and start another round of prosecutions. The same feeling affected a number of members of both parties who between 1911 and 1913 tried to amend the electoral law through private members' Bills.

On 29 March 1911 a Bill by Crawshay Williams, supported by Allen Baker and Sir Henry Havelock Allen, to restrict charitable contributions of candidates to certain public and semi-public objects was given a first reading.[3] Its second reading was to be taken on 4 April, but was crowded out by the committee stage of the Parliament Bill.

Two questions were addressed to Asquith on 22 and 24 May to ascertain whether the Government intended to amend the Corrupt Practices Act so that the total expenditure for all purposes of a member within his constituency should, if exceeding a certain figure, be reckoned as part of his election expenses. The Prime Minister replied that the whole subject of election law 'is engaging the careful attention of the Government', and left it at that.[4]

[1] Cf. *The Times*, 12 Apr., 2, 20, 21 June 1911.
[2] *The Times*, 23 May 1911.   [3] 5 *Hans.* xxiii (29 Mar. 1911), 1338.
[4] 5 *Hans.* xxvi (22, 24 May 1911), 46, 258. The questioners were Robert Harcourt and Lees-Smith.

In the following session Crawshay Williams reintroduced his Bill,[1] but this time the second reading was superseded by a resolution moved by Asquith to give precedence to the Navy and Army estimates on that day. The last attempt to change the electoral law before 1918 was a private member's Bill introduced by Viscount Wolmer, supported by L. S. Amery, Lord Robert Cecil, and Lord Winterton.[2] It was intended to amend the Act of 1895 to cover any false statement by a candidate not only about the personality of his opponent but even about his policy. As evidence of this need Wolmer cited the recent campaign at Leicester where Ramsay MacDonald had said that not a single word in the Liberal manifesto was true: in his opinion under the influence of this 'eleventh hour lie' thousands of voters must have abstained. The only opposition to the Bill came from Sir Maurice Levy, who said that a very comprehensive Bill was needed to cope with the dozens of organizations that went around during elections 'for the purpose of preventing people really understanding the point at issue'.[3]

The question raised by these private members' Bills was one that had been frequently ventilated since the turn of the century. Then the Liberals had bitterly complained that in spite of all the legal sanctions the Conservatives were still able to exercise the power of the purse against them. In his address to the National Liberal Federation's annual meeting of 1901 Campbell-Bannerman[4] said that while the anti-corruption legislation had prevented the meaner methods of bribery it had left the 'larger, more audacious . . . and more corrupting influences still in full operation'. Lloyd George[5] at the same meeting described a Unionist member who 'had great possessions . . . subscribed liberally to every chapel, church and beanfeast, every cricket, hockey and other club; opened every bazaar, personally or by proxy and bought crazy quilts at crazier prices'.

Even allowing for Lloyd Georgian exaggeration this is a realistic picture of the social duties of a wealthy member of Parliament in the early years of this century. What he did not

---

[1] The Bill received a first reading on 22 July 1912; the second reading was fixed for 29 July.

[2] 5 Hans. liv (2 July 1913), 1895–8.   [3] Ibid. 1898.

[4] Report of the 23rd Annual Meeting of the National Liberal Federation (13–16 May 1901) (Liberal Publications Dept. London, 1902), p. 126. See above, p. 206.

[5] Ibid. 99.

say was that many members, even the wealthy ones, found these social pressures irksome and would have been heartily glad to be rid of them. As early as 1893 a member was complaining of the amount of money that he was expected to give in subscriptions to 'deserving causes'.[1]

Even after payment of members was introduced the average member of the Commons was probably paying out more money than his official salary. This trend mainly affected the members of the traditional parties; Labour members before they were paid out of public funds had to be supported by their Trade Unions—at least until the Osborne judgement.

Lloyd George was speaking of a wealthy and unintelligent member ingratiating himself with his constituents. What Campbell-Bannerman censured was the number of pressure groups, mainly Unionist, which especially since 1892 had spent large sums in publicizing their aims, and promoting the candidatures of people who agreed with them.[2] Campbell-Bannerman admitted that he could not suggest any remedy for this particular evil[3]—nor presumably for that mentioned by Lloyd George[4]—but he stressed that 'we ought to apply our minds to the discovery, if we can, of some means of stopping it'.

Some years later Graham Wallas made much the same point, that the fact that pressure groups could engage in electioneering propaganda (the Tariff Reform League and the Free Trade Union were the two best-known examples) which did not have to be included in the election returns, although many candidates might be providing the funds, circumvented the clauses of the 1883 Act restricting expenditure and prohibiting paid canvassers.[5] He went on: 'But it is acknowledged that unless the whole principle is to be abandoned, new legislation must take place; and Lord Robert Cecil talks of the probable necessity for a "stringent and far-reaching Corrupt Practices Act." '[6]

Wallas admitted that no remedy could be devised without 'new and hitherto unthought-of forms of interference with the liberty of political appeal',[7] and he was not prepared to think

[1] See Porritt, *The Unreformed House of Commons*, i. 164–5.
[2] See above, pp. 205–6.
[3] He admitted that it was not confined to one party.
[4] Lloyd George had spoken earlier in the discussion.
[5] G. Wallas, *Human Nature in Politics* (London, 1948, 4th edn.), pp. 211–13.
[6] Ibid., p. 213.   [7] Ibid., p. 213.

one out. The fact that neither Campbell-Bannerman, when he attained power, nor his successor made any attempt to frame a measure to widen the scope of the Act of 1883, and that Asquith showed such indifference to the private members' Bills of 1911–13, leads one to presume that they found it impossible to devise without curbing individual liberty drastically in other respects.[1]

Apart from this, the story from 1900 to 1918 is one of consolidating the traditions established between 1885 and 1900. Official expenses continued to drop until by December 1910 the average cost per vote in the United Kingdom was 3s. 8d.[2] The English petitions showed that the old-fashioned practices of bribery and treating were almost a thing of the past. While contests were becoming more numerous (the second election of 1910 was exceptional) petitions were becoming fewer and fewer. The discovery of bribery at Worcester had caused a great scandal, even though the total proportion susceptible to corrupt influences was not more than one-sixteenth of the electorate, and most of them had been voters before 1883. Landlord influence still lingered on in the counties where the rate of change was slower but even there it was as nothing compared to the old days.[3]

Corrupt electoral practices did not concern the Speaker's Conference that prepared the way for the Representation of the People Act 1918, yet this fact was nowhere noticed by the press. It was the measure of the success of the Act of 1883 that they had passed out of the public memory.

---

[1] J. D. Stewart, *British Pressure Groups*, p. 239, sums up the relationship between member and pressure groups as follows: 'An individual member of a legislature, unprotected by party discipline, is not likely to have much authority to resist the influence of pressure groups, although he may have the resources to do so. A political party, purely concerned to obtain power, lacks the resources to resist pressure groups even though it may have the authority to do so.'

[2] See App. IV.

[3] These remarks apply *a fortiori* to Scotland where no petition had been lodged since 1895. Ireland was in a different case. The petitions of 1910 showed that the old offences had not been eliminated—intimidation, if anything, was on the increase. At the election of 1918 the opposition to Sinn Fein was effectively quelled in many areas so that a quarter of the seats were uncontested, but in Ireland there was a tradition of opposition on nationalist grounds to British-made laws, irrespective of their merits.

CONCLUSIONS

THE time has now come to formulate the conclusions to which the mass of evidence that has been considered leads. It is clear enough that the period of constructive rethinking on electoral morality covered the fifteen years between 1868 and 1883, an era that was also productive of more reformist legislation in other fields than almost any comparable period in British history.[1] On examining the statements of politicians, especially in the House of Commons debates, during these fifteen years, two arguments occur again and again: the argument from principle, that corrupt practices were intrinsically wrong and making parliamentary institutions disreputable; and the argument from expediency, that with an expanding electorate the old practices ('customary tolls', and expenses of nursing the constituency, as well as plainly corrupt expenditure) were becoming an intolerable burden on all but the wealthiest candidates. The aggregate figure of electoral expenditure for 1880 astounded even those who themselves had spent more lavishly than before.

The desire to wipe out the tribe of electioneering parasites, the Walshes and Wreghitts, Hugheses and Lovibonds, proved to be a common goal transcending party differences; and that is the reason for the surprising degree of accord between the leaders of the two parties during the debates between 1880 and 1883.

The politicians were also affected by a natural sense of shame and frustration. At the time of passing, both the Acts of 1868 and 1872 were genuinely believed to be adequate to suppress corrupt practices, and the petition evidence after the general election of 1874 lulled both politicians and press into a false sense of complacency to which the revelations of 1880 came as a rude shock. Under such circumstances the draconian Act of 1883 was acceptable to most parliamentarians, since at least it meant disposing once for all of a troublesome subject. But this

---

[1] Including parliamentary representation, education (secondary and university), the civil service, the army, landlord-tenant relationships (in Ireland), and the Irish Church.

did not mean that the Act would necessarily be obeyed in the country—as *Blackwood's Magazine* said in 1883: 'the voice in Parliament is not the voice out of doors'.[1] The opposition to the bills of 1881–3 was based on the assumptions that a candidate *must* nurse his constituency; that a discreet amount of largesse was not only permissible but desirable; and that the proposed measures would penalize honest candidates anxious 'to do their duty by their constituents'. This was the argument of the propertied classes, the county landlords and the rich merchants seeking the favours of boroughs, perhaps far away from where they lived and worked. As has been seen, it had little weight in the House; the obstructive back-benchers were discouraged and ignored by their own leaders. But when they went back to their constituencies, was there not a chance of their continuing to carry on the old traditions with, of course, greater circumspection?

The lack of evidence from the counties (not a single petition was tried in an English county constituency between 1886 and 1910) must make any generalizations about them very tentative until further evidence comes to light. Nevertheless the Dorset petition of 1911 seems to show that landlord influence had not been entirely eliminated and treating, and perhaps bribery, could possibly go undetected. But even in the counties party competition was sufficiently keen to drive the old-fashioned practices underground—the traditionally Conservative county divisions were contested in 1906.

In the boroughs another influence worked on behalf of the Act of 1883. The new national party organizations which were playing an increasingly important role in elections reconciled themselves to the fact that the party agents could no longer avoid the consequences of their actions, and that no candidate would be safe if his agent did not familiarize himself with the intricacies of the electoral law. This was a completely new factor. The provisions of the Acts of 1854, 1868, and 1872, in so far as they concerned agents, could easily be circumvented; the Act of 1883 could not. The mass parties bowed to the inevitable and circulated to their local associations copies and abstracts of the Act; the poachers were turned into gamekeepers.[2]

---

[1] *Blackwood's Edinburgh Magazine*, cxxxiv (Dec. 1883), 728.
[2] H. G. Nicholas, *To the Hustings, Election Scenes from English Fiction* (London, 1956), xii.

The result was that in the first general election after 1883 the total official electoral expenditure was reduced by three-quarters. It must be added that on both sides the national party managers (Gorst and earlier Parkes) helped to bring about this result by advocating that paid agency be strictly regulated. They saw that the epoch of aristocratic, and even of middle class, influence was passing rapidly and that the new mass electorate, through increased education and a cheap press, would become politically free and independent in a sense that their predecessors would not have thought possible. In the 'admass' era the cost of electioneering on the old lines would be quite prohibitive and voluntary workers would have to be recruited. The party managers welcomed this change.

The next factor which made for the success of the Act of 1883 was the courts. From the very beginning the election judges set about building up a *corpus* of election law, the most important element in which was the Willes interpretation of agency—that a candidate should be responsible for the corrupt act of his duly accredited agent, even if he had forbidden him to do it. Before 1883 that was the greatest weapon the courts had against venal candidates. Admittedly the judges did not always agree on their interpretation of the Acts and there was always scope for differences in temperament, but from Mr. Justice Willes to Baron Bramwell and Sir Henry Hawkins there is a lucid and unbroken tradition of severity towards corrupt agents and candidates.[1]

The very reduced incidence and the altered character of petitions may be taken to indicate a reduction in the general prevalence of corrupt and illegal practices, since the petition trial has been throughout our period the main barometer of electoral morality. Moreover, after 1883 there were increased facilities for petitioning and the normally keen competition between the parties was sharpened by the disagreements over Home Rule, the Boer War, and the struggles over Tariff Reform and the House of Lords. As time went on and no attempt was made to augment their numbers, the old venal electorates were bound to be swamped by a voting public to which the common

---

[1] Even though Mr. Justice Willes and Baron Martin sometimes treated as trivial matters that the later judges would have regarded as grave. There was a distinct hardening in the attitude of the judges as time went on.

practices of Macclesfield and Sandwich would be as remote as the scot-and-lot voters and potwallopers. By 1906 when the last revelation of systematic electoral bribery was made by the Worcester Royal Commission, no voter under 30 could remember the pre-1883 era and the corruptible element in that constituency was estimated at one-sixteenth of the electorate. In those decades, however, the charge was made that large-scale promises of social benefits on the one hand and contributions to charity, and attractions such as tea-parties, concerts, &c., on the other were a subtle counterpart to the more open bribery and treating of the past.

The argument that individual bribery was succeeded by bulk purchase can be met by the counter-proposition that the social theory which eventually brought the welfare state into being was elaborated independently of electoral considerations, and was in no sense an attempt to fill the void left by the Act of 1883. Undoubtedly, the 'annual dinner and septennial bribe' had been regarded as a sort of social insurance by those lucky enough to be accustomed to them. It was not philanthropy but a desire of seats in the House that was the original motive; the 'duty to the constituency' argument was a later rationalization. Exactly the opposite is true of radical and socialist theory at the turn of the century. The extent to which voters' minds were genuinely influenced by promises of old-age pensions, national insurance, and the rest of the welfare-state shopwindow is a matter for social psychologists.

Since, however, the evidence is so vague and negative it is difficult to see what firm conclusions can be drawn apart from the inference that a bribe or a glass of beer confers an immediate personal advantage that a promise of future legislation does not, and in that difference may be discerned the element of moral weakness in the former. To attempt to divorce personal interest completely from political activity would be to strive after the unattainable.

The same argument holds in the case of the demands on a member of Parliament which increased publicity and easier transport made possible. Undoubtedly, a member who refused to patronize social functions—especially those with a charitable purpose—and who was niggardly about his subscriptions to deserving causes in his constituency, stood less chance of election than one who was the reverse.[1] Here again the relationships were more impersonal and the opportunity for corrupt motivation much less than in the earlier period. Furthermore, there was never any legal prohibition, and it would be impossible to devise one without curbing individual liberty drastically in other respects. After all, it was not the expenditure on a constituency between elections, but during campaigns, that determined whether petitions were successful or not. The Representation of the People Act of 1918 reduced the expense limits of the Act of 1883 still further at a time when the value of money was falling.

Much has been written about the connexion between material prosperity and increasing moral consciousness in the later Victorian period. It is indisputable that bribery in the middle of the century was regarded as a *malum prohibition* not a *malum in se*, and the same was true of the other corrupt electoral practices. The moral revulsion against these practices came at much the same time as the revulsion against drunkenness. Political consciousness also struggled forth: elections not only lost their corrupt aspects but also much of their colour and their festive character. The exercise of the franchise was at last regarded as a solemn duty, a right of citizenship but also a responsibility.

When all is said, however, it was the members of the House of Commons who from first to last set the moral tone, unprompted by outside pressure groups. At the cost of personal sacrifice to some of its members Parliament managed within one generation to sweep away traditions that were centuries old and were regarded by many as wellnigh ineradicable. It is an achievement of which any legislature might well be proud.

[1] As late as 1939 it was estimated that to be chosen as a Conservative candidate would involve an annual subscription between £250 and £1,000 to the constituency association, and at least half the election expenses—between £400 and £1,200. Cf. J. F. S. Ross, *Parliamentary Representation* (London, 1948, 2nd edn.), pp. 297–9.

APPENDIX I

Number of Petitions Succeeding on the Ground of Bribery, &c., 1832–1900

Parliament	Number of Petitions presented	Number successful
1832	23	6
1835	16	2
1837	47	4
1841	26	10
1847	24	14
1852	49	25
1857	19	5
1859	30	12
1865	61	13
1868	51	22
1874	22	10
1880	28	16
1885	8	3
1886	3	0
1892	12	5
1895	7	1

APPENDIX II

Total Number of Contests at General Elections 1868–1910

Year	Number of constituencies	Number of contests
1868	420	279
1874	416	299
1880	416	348
1885	643	606
1886	,,	424
1892	,,	558
1895	,,	458
1900	,,	398
1906	,,	529
1910 (I)	,,	568
1910 (II)	,,	484

APPENDIX III

Extracts from the Evidence of Walter Bagehot before the Royal Commission at Bridgwater

(13 October 1869)

42,078 (Mr. Anstey.) Did you undertake to pay the money?—No, I did not undertake to pay it. I do not know whether they might have gathered that.

42,079. Did not it occur to you that it was retrospective bribery they were asking you to commit?—No, I never heard there was such a thing. I never knew it until reading the Beverley Commission the other day. I am not alleging this as an excuse, but I never knew there was any such crime. I never knew the paying money under such circumstances when bribery had taken place was a criminal offence at all, till the other day.

42,080. Did it not strike you to be, whatever the law was, as complete an offence against the moral code as if you had previously authorized it?—I do not say it was right; that is quite another thing, but I thought you were asking me as to the law.

42,081. Did you not think it a violation of that pledge which you gave so admirably in the words you have read in your speech?—I do not think I did. I know I did not want to pay the money then. It was very reluctantly I ever consented to it.

42,082 (Mr. Price.) Was great pressure put upon you to pay this money?—The determinate circumstance in my mind was this, that it would be said I did not pay it because I was beaten, but I should not (*sic*) have paid it otherwise. If I had come in, that would have been the general impression down here, I know, that I did not like to pay this money because I had failed, and, so far from making a good moral impression, I should only have made the impression that I was a mean person. A successful candidate, at any rate, can clear himself of that by giving up his seat, but a defeated candidate is left to be virtuous at other people's expense. That was the feeling in my mind. I am not by any means defending it.

(earlier)

42,075 (Mr. Anstey.) Did you express your disgust?—I think I did. I looked it, I know.

42,076. Did you remind Mr. Lovibond, or Mr. Barham, or any of them, of the distinct promise you had from them in London?—I had not much discussion. I do not remember whether I did or not, it was a very short discussion. I know I was disgusted then, and would not have much to say to them.

(*P.P. 1870*, xxx. 1110.)

APPENDIX IV

Average Cost of Elections (1900–1910)

	Average cost per vote
1900[1]	
England and Wales	4s. 3d.
Scotland	4s. 7d.
Ireland	4s.
U.K.	4s. 4d.
1906[2]	
England and Wales	4s. 1d.
Scotland	4s. 6d.
Ireland	3s. 8¾d.
U.K.	4s. 1¼d.
1910 (I)[3]	
England and Wales	3s. 10d.
Scotland	4s. 5d.
Ireland	2s. 11d.
U.K.	3s. 11d.
1910 (II)[4]	
England and Wales	3s. 8d.
Scotland	3s. 7d.
Ireland	3s. 3d.
U.K.	3s. 8d.

[1] *P.P. 1901*, lix. 227–9.
[2] *P.P. 1906*, xcvi. 106–11.
[3] *P.P. 1910*, lxxiii. 779–81.
[4] *P.P. 1911*, lxii. 748–9.

BIBLIOGRAPHY

THE main primary sources for the study of electoral corruption are to be found in the Parliamentary Debates, the reports of election petition trials, of Select Committees, and of Royal Commissions, and the newspapers. Judgements on petition trials between 1868 and 1918 are bound together (generally in one volume to an election year) and with them are published the minutes of evidence of the more important trials. In the case of a very few the judgements were not published. The entire proceedings on petitions are preserved in the Record Office of the House of Lords.

For election years the files of the principal daily newspapers have been examined and *The Times* file during years between elections. The more important weeklies and (occasionally) learned journals and local newspapers have also been consulted.

Manuscript material has still to be fully explored. The main collections consulted were the Gladstone and Campbell-Bannerman papers in the British Museum and the Disraeli papers at Hughenden.

As far as secondary works are concerned this list is not exhaustive. All books cited in the text have been included.

A. GOVERNMENT PUBLICATIONS

House of Commons, Accounts and Papers, Reports of Select Committees, Reports of Royal Commissions. Public General Acts.
Return of Members of Parliament, pt. II (1878).
History of Parliament 1439–1509 (London, 1938).
Interim Report of Committee on House of Commons. Personnel and Politics 1264–1832 (1932).
Hansard's *Parliamentary Debates*, 1st–5th series.

B. REFERENCE WORKS

Annual Register.
Constitutional Year Book (annually from 1885).
Dod's Parliamentary Companion.
J. E. GORST, *An Election Manual, containing the Parliamentary Elections Corrupt and Illegal Practices Act, 1883*, London, 1883.
Journals of the House of Commons.
F. H. McCALMONT, *The Parliamentary Poll Book*, London, 1879.
PARKER's *Election Agent and Returning Officer*, 5th edition, London, 1950.
Parliamentary History.
H. S. SMITH, *Register of Contested Elections.*
E. L. O'MALLEY and H. HARDCASTLE, *Reports of the Decisions of the Judges for the Trial of Election Petitions in England and Ireland*, London, 1870—.

C. NEWSPAPERS AND PERIODICALS (NATIONAL)

Blackwood's Edinburgh Magazine
Contemporary Review
Daily Chronicle
Daily Express
Daily Mail
Daily News
Daily Telegraph
The *Economist*
English Historical Review
Fortnightly Review
Fraser's Magazine
History
Journal of the Royal Statistical Society

Morning Post
The *Nineteenth Century*
Pall Mall Gazette
Saturday Review
The *Scotsman*
Spectator
The *Standard*
The *Statist*
The Times
Transactions of the Royal Historical Society
Truth
Westminster Review

D. SECONDARY WORKS

I. BIOGRAPHICAL

ASKWITH, LORD. *Lord James of Hereford*, London, 1930.

BALLANTINE, W. *Some Experiences of a Barrister's Life*, London, 1890. 2 vols.

BENN, SIR E. *Happier Days. Recollections and Reflections*, London, 1949.

BUCKLE, G. E. *The Letters of Queen Victoria*, 2nd series, London, 1926.

DUGDALE, B. E. C. *Arthur James Balfour*, London, 1936. 2 vols.

GARVIN, J. L. *The Life of Joseph Chamberlain*, London, 1932-4. 3 vols.

HARRIS, R. (ed.). *The Reminiscences of Sir Henry Hawkins*, London, 1904.

HODDER, E. *The Life and Work of the Seventh Earl of Shaftesbury*, London, 1886. 3 vols.

HOLLAND, B. *The Life of Spencer Compton, Eighth Duke of Devonshire*, London, 1911. 2 vols.

IRVINE, W. *Walter Bagehot*, London, 1939.

MARCHANT, SIR D. LE. *Memoir of John Charles Viscount Althorp, Third Earl Spencer*, London, 1876.

MONYPENNY, W. F., and BUCKLE, G. E. *The Life of Benjamin Disraeli, Earl of Beaconsfield*, London, 1910-20. 6 vols.

MORLEY, J. *The Life of William Ewart Gladstone*, London and New York, 1903. 3 vols.

MURRAY, A. C. *Master and Brother*, London, 1945.

NEWBOULD, T. P. *Pages from a Life of Strife*, London, 1910.

PACKE, M. ST. J. *The Life of John Stuart Mill*, London, 1954.

PLUMB, J. H. *Sir Robert Walpole. The Making of a Statesman*, London, 1956.

REID, S. J. *Life and Letters of the first Earl of Durham, 1792-1840*, London, 1906. 2 vols.

SPENDER, J. A. *Sir Robert Hudson. A Memoir*, London, 1930.

—— *The Life of Sir Henry Campbell-Bannerman, G.C.B.*, London, 1923. 2 vols.

SPENDER, J. A., and ASQUITH, C. *The Life of Herbert Henry Asquith, Lord Oxford and Asquith*, London, 1932. 2 vols.

STEPHENS, L. *Life of Henry Fawcett*, London, 1886.

STEVAS, N. ST. J. *Walter Bagehot*, London, 1959.

SYKES, C. *Four Studies in Loyalty*, London, 1946.

TREVELYAN, G. M. *Lord Grey of the Reform Bill*, London, 1929. 2nd edn.

—— *Life of John Bright*, London, 1913.

WEMYSS REID, T. *The Life of the Rt. Hon. W. E. Forster*, London, 1889. 2 vols.

II. GENERAL AND HISTORICAL

ALBERY, W. *A Parliamentary History of the Ancient Borough of Horsham 1295–1885*, London, 1927.

BEALEY, F. and Pelling, H. *Labour and Politics 1900–1906*, London, 1958.

BEVINGTON, M. M. *The Saturday Review 1855–1858*, New York, 1941.

BUTLER, J. R. M. *The Passing of the Great Reform Bill*, London, 1914.

O'BRIEN, C. CRUISE. *Parnell and his Party 1880–1890*, Oxford, 1957.

DAVIES, G. *The Early Stuarts 1603–1660*, Oxford, 1937.

DAVIS, H. W. C. *The Age of Grey and Peel*, Oxford, 1929.

GASH, N. *Politics in the Age of Peel*, London, 1953.

GORST, H. E., *The Fourth Party*, London, 1906.

GREGO, J. *A History of Parliamentary Elections*, London, 1890.

HANHAM, H. J. *Elections and Party Management*, London, 1959.

HILL, R. H. *Toryism and the People, 1832–1846*, London, 1929.

HYLAND, S. *Curiosities from Parliament*, London, 1955.

JENKINS, R. *Mr. Balfour's Poodle*, London, 1955.

KEITH, A. B. *The Constitution of England from Queen Victoria to George VI*, London, 1940, 2 vols.

LYONS, F. S. L. *The Irish Parliamentary Party 1890–1910*, London, 1951.

MCKENZIE, R. T. *British Political Parties*, London, 1955.

MORRIS, H. L. *Parliamentary Franchise Reform in England from 1885 to 1918*, New York, 1921.

NAMIER, L. B. *The Structure of Politics at the Accession of George III*, London, 1929. 2 vols. 2nd edn., 1957.

NEALE, J. E. *Elizabeth I and her Parliaments 1584–1601*, London, 1957.

—— *The Elizabethan House of Commons*, London, 1949.

NICHOLAS, H. G. *To the Hustings. Election Scenes from English Fiction*, London, 1956.

OSTROGORSKI, M. *Democracy and the Organization of Political Parties*, London, 1902. 2 vols.

PARK, J. H. *The English Reform Bill of 1867*, New York, 1920.

PORRITT, E. and A. *The Unreformed House of Commons*, Cambridge, 1903. 2 vols.

REID, J. H. S. *The Origins of the British Labour Party*, Minneapolis, 1955.

SAUNDERS, W. *The New Parliament, 1880*, London, 1880.

SEYMOUR, C. *Electoral Reform in England and Wales*, New Haven, 1912.

STEWART, J. D. *British Pressure Groups*, Oxford, 1958.

THOMAS, J. A. *The House of Commons 1837–1901*, Cardiff, 1939.

VEITCH, G. *The Genesis of Parliamentary Reform*, London, 1925.

WALLAS, G. *Human Nature and Politics*, London, 1908. 4th edn. 1948.

WALPOLE, S. *The Electorate and the Legislature*, London, 1881.

WHYTE, J. H. *The Independent Irish Party 1850–9*. Oxford, 1958.

WOODWARD, E. L. *The Age of Reform 1815–1870*, Oxford, 1938.

Index

Boston borough, 102, 105 and n., 108 n., 133, 135 and n., 147, 150-1, 155 and n., 222 n.
Bouverie, E. P., 37 and n., 40-41.
Bovill, Sir William, C.J., 191 n.
Bow and Bromley, 218 n.
Bradford borough, 55-56, 60.
Bradford Review, 56 n.
Bradlaugh, Charles, 169.
Bramwell, Lord (Sir George W.), 98-100, 106-7, 191, 231.
Brand, H. R., 100-1.
Brassey, Henry, 152.
Brecon boroughs, 61 n.
Brett, William, 35 n.
—, Mr. Justice, 191 n.
Bribery, oldest offence, 2; increases after 1832, 15; defined, 24; in 1869, 63; absent in Scotland, 64; heavier penalties proposed, 74; after 1872, 86, 155-8; penalties in 1883, 174; declines after 1883, 187, 207, 228-32; *see also* corrupt practices, treating, petitions.
Bridgwater, 51, 53-55, 70 n., 86, 236-7.
Bridport, 21 n.
Bright, John, 27 and n., 31, 38, 42, 46 n., 59, 67 n., 72, 75, 102, 109 n., 120, 123 and n., 159 n., 171 n., 184.
Brinckman, Captain T. H., 148.
Bristol, 46, 61, 86.
British Lion, the, 44, 121 n.
Broadhurst, Henry, 168 n., 172.
Brocklehurst, J. C., 140.
—, John, 140-1.
Brogden, Alexander, 28 n., 55 n.
Brougham, Lord, 25.
Bruce, H. A., 28 n., 59, 81.
—, Mr. Justice, 199, 204.
Bruen, Henry, 127 n.
Buckle, G. E., 123 n.; *see also* Monypenny, W. F.
Buckrose, 186 n., 193-4.
Bullard, Henry, 187-8.
Bulwer, Sir Henry, 50.
Burdett, Sir Francis, 13.
Burke, T. H., 168.
Burman, Mr., 94-95.
Burroughs, Montagu, 146.
Burt, Thomas, 163 n.
Butler, Rt. Rev. George (Bishop of Limerick), 60 n., 62-63.
Butler-Johnstone, Henry, 148.
—, H. A., 148-50.
Buttifant, Josiah, 103-4.
Buxton, C. R., 219.
—, S. C., 150.

Caldicott, Alderman F., 220-2.
Callan, Philip, 166 n.

Calne, 15.
Cambridge borough, 28 n., 50 n., 61 n., 92 n.
Cameron, Dr. Charles, 115-16.
Campbell, Sir George, 116 n.
Campbell-Bannerman, Sir Henry, 122, 205-7, 211-12, 220, 226-8.
Canning, George, 120.
Canterbury, 25 n., 28 n., 133, 135, 147-50, 155.
'Captains of the Book', 141.
Cardiganshire, 62.
Cardwell, Edward, 1st Viscount, 75, 145.
Carlton Club, 17, 136, 146-7.
Cartwright, Major C., 25.
Cashel borough, 55 and n., 130.
Castlereagh, Viscount, later 2nd Marquess of Londonderry, 120.
——, later 6th Marquess of Londonderry, 130-2.
Caucus, 45, 129, 165, 183, 188 n.; *see also* Liberal Hundreds, Liberal Central Association, National Liberal Federation.
Cave, Mr. Justice, 187-8.
Cave, the, 32 n.
Cavendish, Lord Frederick, 168.
Cecil, Lord Robert, 198, 226-7.
Central News, 124.
Chadwick, David, 140-1.
—, W. H. (the Chartist), 186.
Chamberlain, Joseph, 45 and n., 110 and n., 129, 159 n., 171 n., 183-5, 210, 212-13.
Chamberlayne, Thankerville, 196 and n.
Chandos Clause, 14.
Channell, Mr. Justice, 217-19.
Chelmsford, Lord, 36.
Chester, 124 n., 133, 135-9, 155, 171 n.
Childers, H. C. E., 85-86.
Chippenham, 10.
Chippinge, 13; *see also* Weyman, Stanley.
Chitty, J. W., 146.
Church Defence Institution, 121.
Churchill, Lord Randolph, 134.
—, Sir Winston, 209.
Churchward, J. G., 33 n.
Cirencester, 194 n., 201 and n.
Clare East, 194 n., 196 n., 201 n.
Clarion, the, 213 n.
Clark–Labouchere letters, 209; *see also* Labouchere, Henry.
Clay's Act (1851), 17 n.
Clayton, N. G., 195.
Clitheroe, 28 n.
Clive, George, 35 n.
Cochrane, Admiral, later Earl of Dundonald, 13.
Cockburn, Sir Alexander, Lord Chief Justice, 19, 36-37, 42.

PRINTED IN GREAT BRITAIN
AT THE UNIVERSITY PRESS, OXFORD
BY VIVIAN RIDLER
PRINTER TO THE UNIVERSITY